Endpeace

JON CLEARY

Endpeace

HarperCollins*Publishers*

HarperCollins*Publishers*
77-85 Fulham Palace Road,
Hammersmith, London W6 8JB

Published by HarperCollins*Publishers* 1996
1 3 5 7 9 8 6 4 2

Copyright © Jon Cleary 1996

The Author asserts the moral right to
be identified as the author of this work

A catalogue record for this book
is available from the British Library

ISBN 0 00 225464 6

Set in Linotron Times by
Rowland Phototypesetting Ltd,
Bury St Edmunds, Suffolk

Printed and bound in Great Britain by
Caledonian International
Book Manufacturing Ltd, Glasgow

For

Natascia and Vanessa
Benjamin and Isabel
* family *

Endpeace

Chapter One

Malone felt distinctly uncomfortable at this big table in this big house, but no one would have known it; he had the relaxed air of a veteran police officer on the take. Of the eighteen people at dinner ten were family; the Huxwood family in itself was enough to intimidate any outsider. Added to them were the State Premier and his wife; a business tycoon and his wife; and the guests of honour, the British cabinet minister and his wife. Plus Malone himself and, the light at the far end of the table, his wife Lisa.

The cabinet minister's wife, a large, good-looking woman who had once played goalkeeper or front row for Roedean, whatever that was and she hadn't bothered to explain, was seated next to Malone. 'My husband has never forgiven you for what you did to him all those years ago.' She had a large voice which turned heads all the way down the table in her direction; it was said that she was the only woman in Britain who had been able to stop Baroness Thatcher when the latter was in full flow. 'Isn't that so, Ivor?'

Before Ivor could reply, Lady Huxwood looked at Malone; up till now she had virtually ignored him. 'You arrested Mr Supple?'

'No,' said Supple hastily, before another scandal could be added to the long list of British cabinet indiscretions. 'My wife exaggerates, Scobie. I only felt like that till I retired from cricket.'

'Twelve years,' said his wife. 'A long time to be unforgiving.'

'Not in this country,' said the Premier, who had the scars in his back to prove it.

At the far end of the table, seated next to Lisa, Derek Huxwood was grinning evilly. 'Twenty-two years ago,' he explained to the other guests, 'Ivor was one of the stars of the English Test team when they came out here on tour. In the match against New South Wales Scobie clean-bowled him for a duck first ball in each innings. The one and only time in his life that Ivor ever got a pair.'

Phillipa Huxwood favoured Malone with another look. 'Now I understand why Derek invited you, Mr Malone. I had no idea who you were.'

Derek's mother was in her seventies and from infancy had been treading on other people's feelings. Bone-thin, her once-patrician looks had deteriorated into gauntness, but there were hints, like the odd leaves on a dying tree, of the beauty she had once been. Short-sighted but too vain to wear glasses and unable to tolerate contact lenses, she leaned close to everyone she spoke to, so that her unwitting insults had an extra impact. She was now examining Malone closely and he returned her gaze. He had been examined and insulted by the best of lawyers and criminals.

'Are you still cricketing? You look much too old for that.'

'I retired years ago. I'm a police officer, a detective-inspector in Homicide.'

Nigel Huxwood, seated halfway down the table, put his head forward, said in his English voice, 'Homicide, really? In the UK I played detectives in several films, half a dozen times on television. Producers thought I had that unflappable look. I'm just as flappable in real life as the rest of us. Except Derek, of course,' he said and looked sideways across the table at his brother, a theatrical look that convinced Malone that Nigel must have been a bad actor. Or a bad detective.

At the head of the table Sir Harry, all famous distinction and charm, smiled at Lisa. 'What's it like being married to a policeman, Mrs Malone?'

Lisa had been asked that question so many times, but she paused now as if hearing it for the first time. 'Boring. And worrying. But it's what my husband wants to do . . .' She smiled down the table at Malone, telling him, *Let's go home before I commit homicide on this crowd.* They could read each other's eyes where others saw only blank stares. 'Does Lady Huxwood enjoy your being a newspaper publisher?'

'I've never asked her,' he said, still smiling; he was a constantly good-humoured man, or gave the impression of being one. He raised his voice, repeating the question to his distant wife.

'Of course!' She sounded indignant at being asked. 'All wives should enjoy what their husbands do. I'm no damned feminist!' She glared around the table, daring any feminist to speak up; but there were no takers. 'What about you, Enid? Do you enjoy being the Premier's wife?'

Mrs Bigelow jumped, surprised that her opinion might count; she was a tiny blonde with a lovely smile that she seemed afraid to display. She smiled now, weakly: 'I'm just background. It's where I like to be.' Then her smile brightened as she turned it on her husband, but he just scowled.

'What about you, Beatrice? You enjoy politics, don't you?'

Beatrice Supple, whether she enjoyed politics or not, knew how to handle dragons like Lady Huxwood; Britain, or anyway England, had its share of them. 'Ivor and I agree to disagree. He belongs to the MCC, I campaign against it because it treats women as third-class citizens. He's R.C., I'm Anglican –'

'Is there any difference these days?' said Derek.

The talk went on through the remaining courses. Malone, no stranger to a good meal under Lisa's care, was still impressed by what was put in front of him by the butler and the single waiter. There had been six courses and four wines before Lady Huxwood rose and announced, 'We ladies will have coffee in the drawing-room.'

Malone's look of astonishment must have been conspicuous, or perhaps Lisa was the only one who saw it. She smiled at him from faraway and disappeared with the ladies.

Then he was aware of Derek Huxwood standing above him. 'Don't mind my dear old mum, Scobie. She hasn't turned a page on a calendar since 1900. She's hoping the death of Queen Victoria is just a rumour.'

Malone, a man not given to team reunions, had caught only glimpses of Huxwood over the last twenty years. Huxwood was six years older than Malone, had been the State captain and Malone's mentor; he had been handsome and lissom and elegant to watch at bat. Now he had put on weight and the once-sharp and jovial eyes had dulled. The black mane of hair was now iron-grey and was cut short in what used to be called a crew-cut but was now, at least by the homophobes in the police service, called a queer-cut. The years had given Derek Huxwood no credit, he looked already on the far cusp of middle age. Only the mouth had not changed: there was still the whimsical smile that was only just short of a sneer.

3

'You want one of these?' He offered a box of cigars. 'I seem to remember you never smoked?'

'Still don't. Why did you invite me tonight, Derek?'

'Mischief.' He smiled, then shook his head. He lit his cigar, then went on, 'No, that's not true. I think I was looking for a memory of the good old days. Don't you feel like that occasionally? Lost youth, all that?'

Before Malone could answer, they were joined by the Premier. Bevan Bigelow was a short square man with a blond cowlick always falling down over one eye; it gave him a boyish look, which fooled some voters into thinking he might have more than the usual politician's quota of principles. Unfortunately his principles were as pliable as a licorice-stick in hot weather; he was all ears to all men and was known in the press gallery as Bev the Obvious. Three years before he had been chosen by the conservative Coalition government as its stop-gap leader and was still leader only because better men were still cutting each other's throats in their efforts to replace him. There was an election in six days' time and if the Coalition lost he was gone.

'I hear you've got trouble, Derek. Anything I can do to help?'

Huxwood half-shut one eye, but Malone was sure it was not due to the smoke from his cigar. 'No broadcasting, Bevan old chap. Okay?'

Bigelow appeared to recognize he had been perhaps too obvious. He looked at Malone as if the latter might be enemy: a newspaperman, for instance. But he knew that Malone was police: they could be just as bad. 'What do you know, Inspector?'

'Nothing,' said Malone and looked at Huxwood for enlightenment, but got none.

Then Ivor Supple came down to Malone's end of the table and drew him aside, pulling out a chair and sitting down so that they faced each other. 'I couldn't have been more pleased when I saw you here tonight, Scobie. I mean that.'

'Lost youth, all that?' Then he grinned. 'Derek has just been telling me that's why I was invited. It's all behind us, Ivor. My thirteen-year-old son tries to get me to talk about it, but, I dunno, it's like trying to catch smoke. What you're doing now must be more interesting?'

Supple shrugged. 'Maybe more interesting but not as pleasurable. Sometimes I doze off in the Commons and wonder why I ever got into politics. You're right about the lost youth and all that. In retrospect

4

all those seasons seem to have been one long golden summer. They like that for you?'

Malone nodded. 'They weren't, of course. Why are you out here now? Talking to them down in Canberra?'

'Only informally. My wife is here on business and I'm just tagging along. The baggage man.'

'I didn't know she was a businesswoman. Sorry, I shouldn't sound surprised —'

'Don't worry, old chap. Our generation didn't know what a businesswoman was. I didn't know what a woman politician was till I stood up against Boadicea Thatcher. She skittled me first ball, just like you did.'

Supple was tall and thin with an almost ingenuous smile. Malone was not sure what post he had in the new British cabinet, but he was certain that Supple would be popular with both voters and party members. He was equally certain that Supple would never be Prime Minister: nice guys who dozed off in the Commons dreaming of long-ago summers never made it to the top. Supple had been like that as a batsman: one minute thrashing the bowlers to all corners of the field, the next dreamily losing concentration and getting out to a ball that really hadn't challenged him.

'What does your wife do?'

Supple looked up as Derek Huxwood put his hand on his shoulder. 'I see you for a moment, Ivor? Excuse us, Scobie.'

It was polite, yet Malone abruptly felt shut out. His temper rose and for a moment he was tempted to go looking for Lisa and walk out. Then Supple's vacated chair was taken by a florid-faced man who had arrived at the dinner table just as the party sat down.

'I'm Ned Custer, one of the sons-in-law. Sheila's husband. You're the outsider, right?'

Where did this family learn all its insults? 'You could say that. I feel like a Jew at a Muslim picnic.'

Custer's laugh was full-bodied, genuine. He was not quite as tall as Malone and much thicker; what had once been muscle had softened into fat. Malone recognized him now: a corporation lawyer who had once been a prominent rugby forward. Twenty years ago he had led death-or-glory charges that had earned him the nickname Rhino. He had thinning hair that, perhaps influenced by his cheeks and scalp, looked pink; small, very bright blue eyes; and a wide hard mouth that didn't look as if it should emit such a jolly laugh. He appeared friendly, however, and Malone relaxed back in his chair, took a sip of the port that he had poured for himself.

'The Huxwoods have always been like that. I was an outsider right up till the day I married Sheila.' He seemed remarkably confidential for a lawyer, thought Malone; but maybe that was a policeman's suspicion. 'In a country as young as ours, they rank as Old Society. They didn't get here with the First Fleet, but the way they tell it, they were standing on the quay when the ships sailed.'

'You don't like them, do you?' Malone said it carelessly, as if it were a joke.

'I've never understood them, that's the truth. Not even after three years in the bosom . . . I'm Sheila's second husband . . . Ah, here's my friend Enrico. The other — what do you register as, Enrico? The de facto-in-law? The partner-in-law?'

Only then did Malone recognize that Custer was more than half-drunk.

Enrico Quental was a short, handsome man who, Malone immediately decided, was another outsider. When introduced to him earlier, he had assumed that Quental was the husband of Linden, the younger of the Huxwood daughters; whatever he was, he was quiet, withdrawn yet dignified. Malone could not remember hearing him utter a word during dinner. He had applied himself to what was placed before him with all the concentration of a food critic and Malone wondered if that was what he was. Sydney, Lisa had told him, now had more food critics than restaurants.

'Partner is the word, Ned. It covers a multitude of sins.' He had a slight accent, but his English sounded excellent. He smiled at Malone. 'Are you here in an official capacity, Inspector?'

'I hope not. I'm in Homicide.'

'Oh, there's murder all the time around here,' said Custer, downing his port in one gulp and reaching for the decanter. 'Verbal homicide. Am I right, Enrico?'

Malone wondered why a police officer, from any squad, should be expected here at the Huxwoods'. But there were currents in this big house swirling beneath the surface; he was suddenly aware of them as if his feet were being swept from beneath him.

6

Then Derek Huxwood reappeared and Malone had an abrupt image: *he's riding herd on me*. 'Time we went in to join the ladies, chaps.'

'A little soon, isn't it?' Custer held up his newly-filled glass. 'I'm still to starboard of the port.'

'Save it for next time, Ned. Tell the Old Man, Enrico, that we're going in. He's likely to sit there all night talking to Bev. He thinks politicians are interesting.'

'Can I be trusted to deliver the message?' But Quental smiled as he moved away towards Sir Harry.

Derek took Malone's arm as they moved towards the door of the dining-room. 'In-laws,' he said. 'They can be a problem.'

Malone's tongue, always straining at its leash, loosened now by four glasses of wine and the glass of port, was blunt: 'Am I a problem, Derek? I've got the feeling you made a mistake inviting us tonight.'

Derek squeezed the elbow. 'Yes, I did. That's not meant to be personal. I seem to have made a lot of mistakes lately.'

He glanced sideways at Malone and the latter wondered at the pain in the once-bright eyes.

2

'We had a dinner party last week at Parliament House,' said Enid Bigelow. 'Only when we sat down did I realize all the ladies were members of Alliance Francais. So we spoke French all evening. It was fun.'

'Oh *merde*,' said Lady Huxwood, who thought obscenities excusable if in a foreign language. 'Not for the husbands, I'll bet. Australian men must be the worst linguists in the world, after the Eskimos. Do police officers these days have to have a second language, Mrs Malone? All this multiculturism.'

'Only foul language,' said Lisa. 'Especially when dealing with the young. I've tried to teach my husband Dutch, I'm Dutch-born, but he doesn't have the ear for it.'

'Do you speak any other languages?' Linden seemed the friendliest of the women present; or at least the most relaxed.

'French and German. And a little Indonesian.' Lisa was surprised at herself; it was as if she was trying to establish her identity amongst

7

these women. Yet she could not have cared less what they thought of her. 'I worked on the diplomatic circuit for four years before I met my husband. And I had two years at finishing school in Switzerland.' She was tempted to say something in French, but it would be a cheap score on the poor Premier's wife. 'But the languages I learned there are really not of much value to my children. They're learning Japanese and Indonesian.'

All the women in the big drawing-room looked at the woman who had been to finishing school in Switzerland, then on the diplomatic circuit and had finished up marrying *a policeman.*

'You appear to have had an interesting life,' said the Premier's wife, and looked as if she wished desperately to know what an interesting life was like.

'We all have our own lives to live,' said the Huxwood younger daughter, then had the grace to smile. 'God, how smug that sounds!'

'Indeed it does,' said her mother.

The two Huxwood daughters were almost totally unlike, except that both had their mother's large myopic eyes. Sheila, the elder, had her mother's boniness without the beauty; she wore glasses with large fashion frames that actually made her look attractive. Linden, on the other hand, was comfortably fleshy and, Lisa guessed, wore contact lenses. Both were dark-haired, Sheila's in a Double Bay modified beehive, Linden's in a French bob with bangs. Both were expensively dressed in simple dinner dresses and both wore simple diamond pendants and rings that winked lasciviously at anyone who found value in jewellery. Lisa, feeling ashamed that she should even care, was glad she had worn the gold necklace she had inherited from her grandmother. She had always preferred gold to diamonds, though Scobie, bless his stingy heart, had never bought her either.

She had noticed that the other women guests had been as quiet as herself; Lady Huxwood did nothing to put anyone at her ease. The Premier's wife sat next to Lisa; we're the two wallflowers, thought Lisa.

Beatrice Supple sat beside Lady Huxwood, and the tycoon's wife had not sat down at all, hovering on the fringes like a lady-in-waiting.

'Sit down, Gloria, for heaven's sake!' said Lady Huxwood.

Gloria surprised Lisa by saying, 'My bloody girdle's killing me. Have I got time to take it off before the men come in?'

8

'Go for your life,' said Linden, giggling. 'Get a wriggle on.'

Gloria stepped behind Lisa's chair, grunted and gasped, heaved a sigh of relief and her girdle dropped to the floor. As if they had all been constrained by the same girdle, all the women suddenly seemed to relax. Then the men came into the room, bringing with them their air of self-importance. Or am I, Lisa wondered, becoming paranoid about this house?

Gloria Bentsen, who had now sat down, moved aside on her couch for Sir Harry to sit beside her. He did so, taking her hand, stroking it and smiling, not at her nor her husband but at his wife. Lady Huxwood smiled back, but Lisa couldn't tell whether she was indulging his mild flirtation or not.

Malone came and stood behind Lisa, leaned down and said softly, 'I hope you've got a bad headache.'

She reached up, took his hand and said just as softly, 'Splitting. But we can't leave just yet.'

Nigel Huxwood drew up a chair alongside Lisa. He was the handsomest of the family, with finely chiselled features; the only blemish was a weak mouth but that was disguised by the dark moustache above it and the beautifully capped teeth that were exposed when he smiled. He looked up at Malone. 'Go and chat to my sister, Scobie, while I try to charm your lovely wife.'

Not wanting to throw up on the big Persian carpet, Malone crossed the room and squeezed into the French two-seater beside Sheila. 'I've been sent to charm you,' he said and, hearing himself, wanted to throw up even more.

'Nigel is always doing that. It's never let *me* charm *you*. Brothers can be bastards.'

Gallantry did not come easily to Malone; from what he had read, Irish knights had been a bit slow on the chivalry bit. But he tried: 'Righto, let's reverse it. I'm not really good at the charm show.'

'Is that because you're a policeman?'

'That may be part of it.'

'Is the other part because you're out of your depth in this house?'

Malone had met snobbery before, but never arrogance like this. 'Not out of my depth. Just a different sort of breeding.'

She leaned away from him, to get him into better focus it seemed. Then she smiled, a very toothy smile but suddenly surprisingly

9

friendly. '*Touché*, Mr Malone. I didn't mean that the way it sounded, y'know. La Malmaison has sunk more people than you could guess at, over the years. I don't know whether it's the house or we Huxwoods.'

'I think it might be the Huxwoods.' He would never be asked again, so what the hell?

'Is that a police opinion or a personal one?' She didn't sound offended.

'Cops are not supposed to have opinions. We just gather evidence and leave the opinions to the jury.'

'Have you gathered much evidence this evening?'

'Conflicting.' He retreated, because all at once she sounded as if she might be likeable: 'Conflicting evidence never gets you anywhere in a court of law.'

'I must remember that,' she said, as if to herself; then she looked up as the tycoon came and stood beside them. 'Charlie darling, pull up a chair. You've met Inspector Malone?'

Malone was not sure exactly what a tycoon was: how rich, how powerful one had to be. There had been a barrage of tycoons in the past decade, most of whom had been shot down like so many balloons. But the newspapers, including the Huxwoods' own *Chronicle* and their *Financial Weekly*, called Charles Bentsen a tycoon. He had emigrated from Sweden at eighteen, one of the few Swedes heading Down Under; his name then had been Bengtssen. He had started as a labourer on a building site and within twenty years owned a corporation. He had built office buildings, shopping malls, roads and bridges: he also built a personal fortune that every year got him into the *Financial Weekly*'s Rich List. Like all the nation's New Rich, he had been subjected to the suspicion that no one had made his money honestly in the Eighties, but nothing had ever been proved against him. He possessed only one home, his art collection had been bought out of his own funds and not those of his shareholders, and his charitable works were not legendary only because he did not broadcast them. His wife Gloria had been his secretary and no one had a bad word to say about her. Malone knew very little of this, since he read neither the gossip columns nor the *Financial Weekly*, but he was prepared to take Bentsen at face value.

He was a big man, still with a labourer's shoulders; now forty years out of Göteborg, he still looked typically Scandinavian, except for the

10

Australian sun cancers. He had a wide-boned face, thick blond hair in which the grey was camouflaged, bright blue eyes; but the mouth looked cruel, or anyway uncompromising. Malone was sure that Bentsen had not made his fortune by patting people on the back.

'I've never met Mr Malone, but I've heard a great deal about him.' Then he looked at Malone. 'Assistant Commissioner Zanuch is a friend of mine.'

He would be, thought Malone: AC Zanuch spent his free time climbing amongst the social alps. 'It's nice of him to mention me.'

'I gather you get mentioned a lot, Inspector. You seem to specialize in cases that get a lot of attention.'

Malone tried to keep the sharpness out of his voice. 'I don't specialize, Mr Bentsen. Murder happens, we in Homicide have to investigate it.'

'Just like those bumper stickers, Shit Happens?'

'Usually a little more tragic than that. And sometimes messier.'

'Don't fence with him, Charlie,' said Sheila Custer. 'He has already put me in my place.' She put her hand on Malone's. 'Only joking, Mr Malone.'

Malone gave her a smile, but he continued to look at Bentsen. Crumbs, he thought, why is everyone in this house so bloody aggressive? What's scratching at them?

Bentsen said, 'I read murder mysteries, they're my relaxation. The old-fashioned sort, not the ones written by muscle-flexing authors.'

'I get enough of it during the course of a week. I can't remember when I last read a murder mystery − reading our running sheets is about as close as I get. Do you read books about business leaders?'

'Only those that fail,' said Bentsen and looked around him as if one or two fallen heroes might be here in the room.

On the other side of the room Lisa was resisting, without effort, the charm of Nigel Huxwood. In another location she might have good-humouredly responded to him; but not in this house. While pretending to listen to him, she had been taking in her surroundings. There were treasures in this room with which she would liked to have surrounded herself: the two Renoirs on opposite walls, the Rupert Bunny portrait of two women who might have been earlier Huxwoods. The chairs and couches and small tables were antiques, though the upholstery had been renewed; the drapes were French silk. The room

11

reeked of wealth well spent and, against the grain of her nature, she suddenly felt envious. This house was working on her in a way that made her angry.

She looked up almost with relief, any distraction was welcome, as the two female in-laws, who had been missing since dinner, came back into the drawing-room. They bore down on Lisa and Nigel, drawing up chairs to sit side by side like twins who always did everything together. Yet in looks they could not have been more dissimilar.

Brenda Huxwood was an almost archetypal Irish beauty; the only thing that stopped her face from being perfect was that her upper lip was too Irish, just a little too long. She had been an actress, but her talent had never matched her looks and British producers had always shied away from promoting an actress on beauty alone. She was Nigel's third wife and, if Lisa had asked her, would have said she was determined to be his last. She had started life with no money but always with an eye to attaining some; now she had grasped it she had no intention of losing it; her credit was that she loved Nigel, despite his faults. The brogue in her voice was only faint, like a touch of make-up to enhance the general appeal, though it could thicken into a soup of anger as others in the room knew.

Cordelia Huxwood, on the other hand, had had to borrow her looks: from hairdressers, beauty salons, aerobics classes. Her mouse-brown hair was tinted, her pale blue eyes somehow made to seem larger than they actually were, her figure, inclined to plumpness, slimmed down by only-God-and-gym-instructors-knew how many hours on exercise machines. The package was artificial, yet sincerity shone out of her so that one instantly liked her. She was inclined to blame herself for too much that might go wrong, to wear hairshirts, but since they were usually by Valentino or Hermés she got little sympathy, especially from her mother-in-law.

'Where have you two been?' said Nigel.

'Talking business,' said Brenda and made it sound as if she and Cordelia had been composing a poem. Everything with her, Lisa decided, was for effect.

'We in-laws needed to get a few things straightened out,' said Cordelia.

Lisa was never sure whether she had been born with a sharp eye, had acquired it as a diplomat's secretary or had learned it from Scobie:

whichever, she did not miss Nigel's warning glance. 'You must tell me about it. Later.'

'Oh, we'll do that,' said his wife. 'Voices will be heard.'

'They may even be strident,' said Cordelia. 'But we mustn't puzzle Mrs Malone with family problems. Do you have children?'

'Three. Eighteen, fifteen and thirteen. Two girls and a boy. So far, thank God, giving us no problems.'

'Lucky you,' said Cordelia. 'I hope it stays that way. How's Mother Dragon?' she said to Nigel.

'Starting to yawn openly.'

'She always does. She has a patent on the open yawn.'

Lisa couldn't help herself: she giggled. Both Cordelia and Brenda looked at her and smiled widely, as if pleased that an outsider had seen a family joke. But neither said anything and Nigel, covering hastily, turned the conversation off at right angles.

Malone, abruptly left out of a sudden conversation between Sheila and Bentsen, excused himself and headed for the door. Sir Harry, after a final pat of Gloria Bentsen, this time on her attractive knee, rose and followed him. 'Going, Mr Malone?'

'Soon, Sir Harry. But first I'd like to use the bathroom.'

'There's a lavatory off the library.' The old-fashioned word brought a grin to Malone's lips. His mother was the only other person he knew who talked of the lavatory instead of the toilet or the loo. 'This way.'

The library was a big room with the high ceiling that the rest of the ground floor of the house seemed to possess. It was the sort of room Malone saw in films and, secretly, yearned for; for some reason he had never confessed the yearning to anyone, even Lisa. In a room like this he would gather together all the books he had let slip by him, would wrap himself in the education that Lisa had and he had missed, would listen to the music that his heart would understand but that his ear had yet to interpret. He wondered if Sir Harry, with all his advantages, would understand his yearning.

A leather-covered door was let into a wall of books; Sir Harry gestured at it and Malone went in, under a complete set of Winston Churchill, for a piss. When he came out Sir Harry was standing at the tall bow-window that looked out on to the tiny bay and beyond that to the harbour. The only lighting in the dark brown room came from a brass lamp on the wide leather-topped desk. When Sir Harry turned back to face Malone, he looked suddenly much older in the yellow glow. The lines in his face had become gullies, the eyes had no gleam in them.

'A good piss is one of life's little pleasures.' Even his smile looked ghastly. Then he sat down at the desk, there was more light on his face and he suddenly appeared less frail. 'Were you and my son Derek ever close, Mr Malone?'

'Scobie . . . No, not really. We got on well, but there was the age difference. In sport six years is quite a gap. He'd been playing for five or six years before I got into the State team. We weren't real professionals back then, none of us earned the money they do these days.'

'I don't think Derek ever gave a thought to what he earned as a cricketer.'

'He could afford not to.'

The old man accepted the rebuke. 'Sorry. So you and he were not close?'

'Not as bosom friends, no. He was my — well, I guess my mentor.'

Sir Harry nodded. 'He was always good at that. Mentoring, or whatever the verb is. Except with his siblings.'

That was another old-fashioned word that, unlike lavatory, had come back into fashion. Malone, having no siblings, could think of nothing to say and, as he often did in interrogations, stood and waited. The old man seemed not to notice his silence; he went on, 'What's your heritage, Scobie?'

The question made Malone pause; he could not remember ever having been asked it before. 'Not much, I'm afraid. I've never bothered to trace the family further back than my grandparents. And even that far back I'm in the dark on a lot of things.' Including my own mother's early life; or anyway her early love. 'I'm Irish descent, the name tells you that. I guess all I've really inherited, if I knew about it, is a lot of pain and trouble. That's Ireland, isn't it?'

'It doesn't seem to have affected you. On the surface.'

'Maybe it's because I don't think too much about it. Maybe I should.'

Sir Harry shook his head. 'If you don't have to, don't. Heritage, I'm beginning to think, is like history — it's bunk. Henry Ford, one of history's worst philosophers, said that. But perhaps, who knows, he

14

had a point.' He had an occasional stiff way of putting his thoughts into words, as if he were writing an editorial. Then he smiled and stood up. 'I'd like you to come again, Scobie. I don't get to talk enough to –' Then he smiled again, without embarrassment. 'I was going to say the common folk. Does that offend you?'

'I'm a republican, Sir Harry. We're all common folk.'

'You must debate some time with my wife. She's a monarchist through and through. At Runnymede she would have been on side with King John. You've heard of Magna Carta?'

There it was again, the arrogance: unwitting, perhaps in Sir Harry's case, but endemic. 'They were still teaching English history when I was at school. I had to study it in a plain brown wrapper, so my father wouldn't throw a fit. He hates the Brits.'

'Perhaps you should bring him here to debate with my wife.'

'Are you a monarchist, Sir Harry?' All at once Malone was interested in the older man, wanted to put him in front of the video recorder in one of the interrogation rooms at Homicide. Take him apart, perhaps take a hundred and fifty years of Huxwoods apart. This family, this man, had wielded influence that had toppled governments, that had sent young men to a war they didn't believe in, that had, in various ways, influenced the running of the force in which Malone himself served.

'Mr Malone, I fear that all my beliefs, whatever they were, have somehow turned to water.' Then abruptly it seemed that he had revealed enough of himself: 'Shall we rejoin the others?'

They went out into the wide tessellated hallway. A curving staircase went up to the first floor, its polished walnut banister following it like a python heading for the upper galleries of a rain-forest. Four of the family stood in the hallway: Derek, Nigel, Sheila and Linden. Halfway up the staircase Lady Huxwood had paused, stood with one hand on the banister and stared down at her children. Malone, the outsider, unconnected to whatever demons were stirring in the family, was struck with a sudden image: he had seen it all before on some late night movie, *The Magnificent Ambersons* or *The Little Foxes*, Bette Davis or some other over-the-top actress pouring venom from a great height.

'You deserve nothing, none of you! I should have aborted the lot of you!'

15

Then she went on up the stairs, paused on the gallery that ran round the upper level of the hallway and looked back down into the pit. Malone waited for another spit of spite, was surprised when she looked directly at him and snapped, 'Goodnight, Mr Malone. I'm sure you won't come again.'

Then she was gone. There was absolute silence and stillness for a long moment, then the four siblings let out a collective sigh. Sir Harry touched Malone's arm, said, 'Forgive us, Mr Malone,' and went on up the stairs, moving stiffly and not looking back at his sons and daughters.

Malone had known embarrassment, but nothing like this. He looked for an exit, some way he could skirt the four Huxwoods and be ignored by them. Then Lisa appeared, seemingly out of nowhere, coat over her dinner dress. If she had heard what had just been said in the hallway, she gave no sign of it.

She held out her hand to Derek. 'Thank you, Derek. A most entertaining evening.'

Nigel and his sisters slipped away, not even looking at the Malones, just disappearing into the shadows of the house. Derek shook hands with Lisa, did the same with Malone, then escorted them towards the heavy front door.

'I'm glad you thought it was entertaining.' He was smiling, that whimsical grin just short of a sneer. 'Like *Macbeth* or *King Lear*. You should see us when we're in top form. Our paper's cartoonists could get a month's run out of us.'

3

Driving home Lisa said, 'Don't *ever* accept an invitation to that house again, understand? *Never*!'

'There's no chance of that. What happened while I was out with Sir Harry?'

'I don't know. All of a sudden the four of them were down one end of the room with Lady Huxwood, arguing in whispers. The rest of us were at the other end, trying to look as if we hadn't been left there like – what's that expression you use?'

'Like shags on a rock?'

'That's it. We never go there again, understand?'

He knew how adamant she could be, but never about anything as unimportant as a dinner invitation. He had, however, noticed a gradual change in her over the past few months. Last year she had been operated on for cervical cancer; the operation had been successful and there had been no metastasis since. She had undergone chemotherapy and it had had a temporary effect: there had been the recurring bouts of vomiting and she had lost some of her lustrous blonde hair. The hair had grown back, as thick as ever, and she was once again healthily vibrant; but her patience had thinned, she had less time for inconsequentialities. It was as if she had looked at the clock and decided it was closer to midnight than she had thought. She had not become self-centred, but she had begun to ration her time, her attention and her charity. He couldn't blame her: she had been fortunate to come out on the lucky side of a fifty-fifty chance.

'What drives them to be like that, for God's sake?' She was stirred, more than she should be. 'They have *everything*, there's nothing missing in their lives. Not the way ordinary people count things. And yet . . . Have you ever met such a bunch?'

'There's lots more around like them, I'm sure. We just never meet them. When we do, it's usually after a homicide and by then they've called a truce.'

'Lady Huxwood invites homicide. Anyhow, we never go there again. Watch the red light.'

'You're the one who's driving. You watch it.'

Chapter Two

1

For several years the Homicide Unit of the Major Crime Squad, South Region, had been housed in the Hat Factory, a one-time commercial building where the ambience had suggested that the Police Service was down on its luck, that the hat had had to be passed around before the rent could be raised. Recently Homicide, along with other units in the Major Crime Squad, had been moved to quarters that, for the first few weeks, had brought on delusions that money had been thrown at the Service which the State government had actually meant for more deserving causes such as casino construction or pork-barrelling in marginal electorates.

Strawberry Hills was the enticing name of the new location, though no strawberry had ever been grown there nor had it ever been really enticing. It had begun as clay-topped sandhills held together by black-butts, bloodwoods, angophoras and banksias, but those trees had soon disappeared as the men with axes arrived and development raised its ugly shacks. 'Environment', in its modern meaning, had just been adopted in England, but so far word, or *the* word, had not reached the colony. For years there was a slow battle between the sandhills and the houses built on them, but that did not stop a developer from naming his estate after the sylvan Strawberry Hill in England where Horace Walpole, in between writing letters to addressees still to be chosen, had built a villa that would never have got above foundation level if it had been built on the colony's sandhills. Time passed and gradually Strawberry Hills, like the sandhills, virtually disappeared off maps. The city reached out and swamped it. A vast mail exchange was built where once tenement houses had stood, but though Australia Post could sort a million letters an hour it couldn't sort out the industrial troubles in the exchange. Eventually the huge ugly structure was closed as a mail exchange, an impressive glass facade was added, as if to mask what a problem place it had been. Six huge Canary Islands date palms stood sentinel in the forecourt, looking as out of place as Nubian palace guards would have been. The winos across the street in Prince Alfred park suffered the DTs for a week or two, but became accustomed to the new vista and soon settled back into the comfort of the bottle.

Australia Post moved its administrative staff back in and then looked around for tenants who would be less of a problem than its unions had been. Whether it was conscious of the irony or not, it chose the Major Crime Squad. Level Four in the refurbished building was almost too rich in its space and comfort for the Squad's members, but it is difficult to be stoical against luxury. One of the pleasures for those in Homicide on night duty was to put their feet up on their brand-new desks, lean back and, on the unit's television set, watch re-runs of *Hill Street Blues* and *NYPD Blue* and pity the poor bastards who had to work in such conditions.

The morning after the Huxwood dinner Malone over-slept, but, a creature of certain habits, he still went for his five-kilometre walk before breakfast. It was nine-thirty before he reached Homicide and let himself in through the security door. Russ Clements was waiting for him, looking worried.

'You sick or something? I rang Lisa ten minutes ago –'

'I'm okay. I knew there was nothing in the synopsis –'

'There is now. Four murders in our Region alone, two in North Region's. You and I are on our way out to Vaucluse –'

'I'm not going out on any job. That's for you –'

The big man shook his head. 'I think you'd better come on this one, Scobie.'

Malone frowned. 'Why?'

'Lisa told me where you were last night. Malmaison House. That's where we're going. Kate Arletti's out there waiting for us – I sent her out as soon as Rose Bay called in. It's their turf, theirs and Waverley's.'

'A homicide at Malmaison?' *Lady Huxwood invites homicide.* 'Who? Lady Huxwood?'

Clements looked at him curiously. 'What made you say that?'

'Lisa and I were talking about her on our way home . . . It was a

19

bugger of a night, you've got no idea. She's the – she was the Dragon Lady of all time.'

'She probably still is. It was the old man, Sir Harry, who was done in.'

Malone managed not to look surprised. No one knew better than he that murder always held surprises, not least to the victim. But *Sir Harry*? 'How?'

'I'm not sure yet. Rose Bay called in, said there was a homicide, but gave no details other than that it was Sir Harry who copped it. The place is probably already over-run with the media clowns.'

'What about the other murders?'

'I've organized those. I'll tell you about them on the way out to Vaucluse.'

Homicide had been re-organized late last year in another of the Service's constant changes. Modern life, Malone thought, had been taken over by planners; they were everywhere, termites in the wood-work of progress. Change for change's sake had become a battle cry: if it ain't broke, let's fix it before it does break. Malone was still the Inspector in charge of Homicide, but he was now called Co-ordinator and his job, supposedly, was now more desk-bound. Clements had been promoted to senior-sergeant and was now the Field Supervisor. Murder was still committed, evidence was still collected, the pattern never changed; only the paper-work. Malone knew that conservatism was creeping over him like a slow rash, but he didn't mind. The itch, actually, was a pleasure.

The two detectives drove in an unmarked car out to the farthest of the affluent eastern suburbs. Vaucluse lies within the shoulder of the ridge that runs out to end in South Head at the gateway to the harbour; it is a small area facing down the harbour like a dowager gladly distant from the hoi polloi. The suburb is named after a property once owned by a titled convict who was as thick in the head as the timber that grew down the slope from the ridge. He built a small stone house and surrounded it with a moat filled with soil shipped out from the Irish bogs – 'to keep out the snakes'. The area has had several notable eccentrics since then, but Sir Henry Brown Hayes had established the standard. The Wentworths, a family with its own quota of eccentrics, were the first to give the suburb its social tone, which it has never lost.

20

The first Huxwood arrived in 1838, bought five acres along the shore and built the first stage of what was to become La Malmaison. Huxwoods still owned the five acres, paying local taxes that exceeded the annual entertainment allowance of the entire local council. There were three houses on the estate, which had not been sub-divided: The Big House, Little House One and Little House Two. Tradesmen, coming to the estate for the first time, had been known to expect fairies at the bottom of the extensive gardens and were surprised to find the family appeared to be both sensible and heterosexual.

Huxwood Road had been named by the founder of the family, determined to have his name on the map; in the 1840s, when he had suffered his first delusion of grandeur, it had been no more than a dirt track. Some years ago, Sir Harry, at the urging of his wife, had attempted to have the council change the name, insisting the family was not interested in advertising or being on any map. But Huxwood Road was now *the* street in Vaucluse, if not in Sydney, and the residents, having paid fortunes for the address, were not going to find themselves at a location that nobody would recognize. One didn't pay thousands of dollars a year in taxes to live in Wattle Avenue or, God forbid, Coronation Street.

When Malone and Clements arrived, the street had gone down several hundred thousand dollars in rateable value, at least temporarily. It was chockablock with police cars, press and radio cars, TV vans and an assorted crowd of two or three hundred spectators, most of whom looked as if they had rushed here from nearby Neilsen Park beach. The street had not looked so low grade since the titled convict's day. The snakes had taken over the Garden of Eden, Irish bog soil notwithstanding.

'Christ Almighty,' said Clements. 'It looks like the finish to the City to Surf gallop.'

He nudged the car through the crowd, in through the wide gates of the estate and down the driveway to the front of the house. Several vehicles were parked there, including three police cars and a private ambulance. As Clements pulled up, another car came down the driveway behind them. Romy Clements got out.

'What're you doing here?' It had the directness of a husband-to-wife remark.

Romy gave Clements a brush-off smile, looked instead at Malone.

'I thought I'd have a look at how the other two per cent lives. I used rank and told Len Paul I'd do the job.' She was the Deputy-Director of the Institute of Forensic Medicine and ran the day-to-day routine of the city morgue; normally she would not respond to a call for a government medical officer in a homicide. 'Shall we go in?'

'I'll bet she fingers the curtains first,' Clements told Malone. 'Then she'll look at the kitchen. *Then* she'll look at the corpse.'

Malone was glad there was nobody close enough to hear the banter. Outsiders might not appreciate that no disrespect was intended, just that murder was part of the day's work. They went in through the open door, beneath a carved stone replica, like a coat-of-arms, of the Huxwood Press logo: an open book marked with a bookmark, inscribed *Only the Truth*. The wide hallway inside seemed crowded with people standing around looking lost. It reminded Malone of a theatre lobby and latecomers wondering if seats were still available.

Kate Arletti pushed her way into Malone's path. 'Morning, sir. The Rose Bay officers are here and between us we've got a few facts. Can we go into that room there?'

It was the library, where Sir Harry last night had said his beliefs had turned to water. The room now had none of last night's shadows; the summer sun streamed in through the big bay window. Out in the tiny bay a small yacht rocked daintily in the wake from a passing ferry. Then a launch hove into view, crowded with photographers trying to capture the house from the water. Two uniformed policemen appeared down on the shoreline and waved them away. With the policemen was an elderly gardener holding a spade like an axe. Malone nodded, condoning the gardener's threat of assault and battery.

'The body was discovered at seven o'clock this morning,' said Kate Arletti. 'The butler went up with his morning tea. What's the matter?'

'I shouldn't be grinning. But all this sounds like something out of Agatha Christie. Butler, morning tea . . . We don't get many crime scenes like this, Kate. How did he die?'

'A gunshot wound to the side of the head, left temple. It looks like death would have been instantaneous. Dr Clements will confirm that, I suppose.'

'How are the family?'

'Shattered, those I've met. All except the eldest son, Derek. He's got some men from the *Chronicle* out in the garden room, he's organizing how the homicide is to be reported. He strikes me as cold-blooded. Sorry, I shouldn't be making comments like that so early in the piece.'

She was small and blonde, a little untidy in her dress but crisp in everything she did. She was dressed in a tan skirt and a brown cotton shirt; somewhere there would be a jacket and Malone would bet she had already forgotten where she had left it. She was pretty in an unremarkable way, her face not disfigured but lent character by the scar down her left jawline. When she had been a uniformed cop a junkie had tried to carve her up with a razor and she had retaliated by breaking his nose with the butt of her gun. Six months ago, when Malone had first met her, she had been in uniform, neat and tidy as a poster figure. Since coming into Homicide, into plainclothes, her natural untidiness had emerged. All that was still neat about her was her work. With a sartorial wreck like Russ Clements setting an example, Malone had never had the heart to ask her to do up a button or roll up a loose sleeve.

'What about Lady Huxwood?'

She hesitated. 'Composed, I guess would be the word. She's pretty – formidable?'

'That's another good word. I was here for dinner last night, I'll tell you why some other time. They're a weird mob, Kate. Don't entertain any preconceived notions about them. Take 'em bit by bit, inch by inch.'

'It sounds as if you didn't enjoy last night?'

'I'm not going to enjoy this morning, either.'

They went out into the hallway, which was less crowded now. Clements came towards them, biting his lip, an old habit when his thoughts did not fit as they should. Whether it was because Romy had dressed him or he had known, subconsciously, that he would be coming to this elegant house, this morning he was not his usual rumpled self. He wore an olive-grey lightweight suit, a blue button-down shirt and a blue silk tie with club or regimental stripes; though he had not belonged to a club in fifteen years and never to a regiment. His broad face, just shy of being good-looking, had a harried look, an expression unusual for him.

'I've had only a glance at the family so far – that's enough. Listening to 'em . . .' He shook his head. 'Keep an eye on 'em, Kate. We're going upstairs.'

23

He and Malone climbed the curve of the stairs. Halfway up Malone paused and looked down: this was the spot where Lady Huxwood had told her children she should have aborted the lot of them. It was an elevation for delivering pronouncements; he wondered how many other insults and dismissals had been hurled from here. Then he went on after Clements, following him into a bedroom off the gallery.

It was a big room with old-fashioned furniture: a four-poster bed, a heavy wardrobe and a dressing-table that could have accommodated at least two people. A large television set, in an equally large cabinet, stood in one corner. On a table by the two tall windows was the only modern note, a computer.

Romy, in a white coat now, was drawing off a pair of rubber gloves. She gestured at the body on the bed and nodded to the two men from the funeral contractors. 'You can take him to the morgue now. Tell them I'll do the autopsy.' Then she crossed to join Malone and Clements by the windows. 'Time of death is always guesswork, but I'd say he'd been dead ten to twelve hours. I'll take some fluid from his eyes when I get back to the morgue, check the amount of potassium in it. That gives a bit more precision in the timing, but don't expect me to pinpoint it.'

'Any sign of a struggle?'

'None. He could have been asleep when he was shot, I don't know. There are powder-marks on a pillow, looks as if whoever killed him used it to muffle the shot.'

Malone walked over to the bed to take a last look at Sir Harry before the contractors zipped him up in the body bag. The democracy of death had done nothing for Sir Harry's arrogance; a last spasm of pain looked more like an expression of distaste at the world he had just left. Malone nodded to one of the men and the zip closed over Sir Harry Huxwood, like a blue pencil through one of the many editorials he had written.

'There's this —' Romy pulled on one of the rubber gloves, took a small scrap of paper from the pocket of her white coat. 'Looks like he had a cadaveric spasm. It happens — the muscles tighten like a vice. It's usually the hand that spasms, but sometimes the whole body does, though that's pretty rare.'

Malone held the piece of paper with the pair of hair-tweezers he always carried. Clements said, 'It's a torn scrap, looks like it's been

24

torn off the corner of a letter or a memo. Good quality paper. Evidently whoever did him in tried to take the whole paper, but he wouldn't let go. If they shot him in the dark, maybe they didn't know it was torn till they got outside.'

'Why would he be holding a letter or a memo in the dark?' Malone held up the fragment. 'There's one word on it in red pencil. No – N–O, exclamation mark. Got your French letter?'

Clements produced one of the small plastic envelopes he always had in his pockets, grinning at Romy as he did so. He slipped the scrap of paper into the envelope. 'I've never used these as condoms, in case you're wondering.'

'I shouldn't be surprised at anything he did before we met,' she told Malone, taking off her white coat and folding it neatly. 'I'll see Ballistics gets the bullet when I've done the autopsy.'

'How's business? Can you do him this morning?'

'They told me before I came out here there'd been six homicides last night, plus four dead in accidents. He may have to take his turn.'

'He hasn't been used to that. Put him at the head of the list.'

'Inspector –' All at once she was not Mrs Clements but the Deputy-Director of the Institute of Forensic Medicine. Her squarely beautiful face became squarer as she set her jaw; her dark eyes lost their gleam, seemed to become even darker. It was what Clements called her Teutonic look. 'Nobody jumps the queue in our morgue. I'll get to him when I get to him.'

Malone was glad the funeral contractors had already gone with the body; he did not like being ticked off in public. Clements looked embarrassed for him, but said nothing.

'Romy, I'm not pandering to Sir Harry because of who he is. Or was. But with all due respect to the other five murder victims, the media aren't going to be interested in them. They're going to be on my back about *this* one. And so will my boss and the AC Crime and the Commissioner and the Premier and, for all I know, maybe God Himself.'

'Tough titty, as you vulgarians say. I'll do him when I do him. That all?' She had packed her small bag, stood like a wife walking out on two husbands.

Malone recognized he was not going to get anywhere with her. He nodded at the door to an adjoining room. 'Whose room is that?'

'Lady Huxwood's. I was told she wasn't to be disturbed.' Romy was still cool. 'I'll see you at home, Russ. Pick up the meat.'

Then she was gone and Clements said, 'Don't you know you don't push a German around? You went about that in the wrong way, mate.'

'Righto, you work on her, if you're so bloody subtle.'

'It's not that I'm subtle. I'm married to her. You learn a few things. I thought you would have known that. The Dutch are as stubborn as the Germans, aren't they?'

'One thing I've learned, never bring up ethnic differences in a marriage. That's a good way of starting World War Three . . . All right, see what you can do with her. I don't want to be carrying the can for the next week. Let's go down and talk to the family.'

Down in the hallway one of the Rose Bay detectives, a middle-aged man named Akers, was waiting for them. He was a senior-constable and had the resigned look of a man who realized he might, just might, make sergeant before he retired. His hair was already grey and his plump face was pink with blood vessels close to the surface.

'Some of the family are here, Scobie, some have gone home. You'll want to talk to them?'

'I'll talk to those that are here.' Malone looked up and around the high hallway. 'What's the set-up here? How many rooms?'

'Fourteen in this house, not including the bathrooms but including three rooms for the staff. There's a wing out the back for them, beside the garages. The butler and cook are husband and wife, name's Krilich, they're Yugoslavs. Outside there's what they call Little House One and Little House Two –' He made a face. 'I think Enid Blyton or Beatrix Potter must of stayed here once.'

'You're well read, Jim.'

Akers grinned, relaxing; up till now he had been a bit stiff. Local Ds never did like Major Crime Squad men appearing on their turf. 'My wife's a schoolteacher . . . Derek, the eldest son, and his family live in Little House One – it has eight rooms, I believe. Little House Two has six rooms and Sheila, the elder daughter, and her husband live there – they have a child, but she lives out.'

'What about Nigel and his wife? And Linden and her husband?'

Akers looked surprised that Malone was so well acquainted, but he made no comment. 'Nigel, the actor –' He uttered 'the actor' as he might have said 'the poofter'; the theatrical profession obviously got no rating with him. 'He and his wife, she's an actor too, I hear. Or was. They have a flat at Point Piper. He has two kids, a boy and a girl – he's been married twice before. The kids are from different mothers. The younger sister – Linden, did you say? – she and her husband – actually, he's her *de facto* – they live out in the country, somewhere south of Bowral. They have no kids, though she's been married before. They stayed here last night. In the *Big* House,' he said and just managed not to simper.

'Nice rundown, Jim. You been here before?'

'About two years ago. There was an attempted break and enter, but they were disturbed and got away.'

'Righto, let's go and talk to someone. Derek, the eldest, first.'

'He's in the garden room. Got three guys from the *Chronicle* with him. I'll leave him to you and Russ. I've gotta report to my boss at Waverley.'

'Tell him I'll check with him later.' It was the old territorial imperative, everybody protected his own little authority. 'He didn't put in an appearance?'

'Superintendent Lozelle leaves the silvertails to us. I think he finds the riff-raff easier to deal with. Don't quote me.'

Jim Akers, having had no rank for so long, had no respect for it. But he was not disrespectful of Malone and the latter let him get away with it. 'Maybe he's wiser than either of us. Give him my regards.'

Then he and Clements turned into the garden room, next door to the library. The entire wall that faced the harbour was one big bay window; the room was half-conservatory. Sections of the huge window were open, letting in some of the mild nor'easter, but the room was still warm. Derek and the three men with him were in their shirtsleeves. They stood as if lined up for a team photo, backed by a bank of palms in big brass-bound wooden tubs. There were no pictures decorating the walls, but flowers cried out for attention in a profusion of vases of all shapes and sizes. It was a room, Malone guessed, where the watering-can would be used more than tea or coffee-pot.

Derek stepped forward, raised his hand as if to shake Malone's, then thought better of it. He didn't smile when he said, 'So you're here officially after all, Scobie.'

Malone kept it official: none of the old cricket mates' act. 'That's how it is, Mr Huxwood. This is Detective-Sergeant Clements. Who are these gentlemen?'

Huxwood looked surprised, as if he had expected Malone to be less formal. Then: 'Oh yes. This is Mr Gates, our managing editor –' He seemed to emphasize the *Mr*. 'Mr Shoemaker, the *Chronicle*'s editor. And Mr Van Dieman, of –' He named one of the three top law firms in Sydney. 'We've been deciding how to handle the story of – of what's happened.'

'How are you going to handle it?'

'It's difficult. My own impulse – a member of the family, all that – my own impulse would be to bury – no, that's the wrong word –' Despite what Kate Arletti had said, Derek did sound flappable, something Malone had not expected. 'Put the story on one of the inside pages. But it's Page One stuff, let's face it. What the *Herald* and the *Australian* and the *Telegraph-Mirror*, especially *them*, will make of it, God only knows. And every other paper in the country.'

'Not to mention radio and TV.' Gates was a plump little man with soft brown, almost womanly eyes, a neat moustache above a neat mouth and an harassed air that did not appear to be habitual. Malone had no idea what a managing editor did, but Mr Gates was not managing too well at the moment. 'Christ knows what rumours they'll spout. I can hear them now . . .'

Shoemaker couldn't hear them; or if he could, he gave no sign. He was a tall, wide man with black kinked hair; he had fierce black eyebrows and a bulldozer jaw. Malone could imagine his scaring the pants off cadet reporters, boy and girl alike; but whatever his approach, it must have pleased the Huxwoods. He had been editor for ten years, a long time in modern Australian newspapers. 'We'll run the story straight, as if it was some other proprietor, not our own, who'd been murdered. Will you be in charge of the investigation, Inspector? Can I come to you for progress reports?'

'I'll let you know,' said Malone. 'For now it looks as if I'm in charge. But I could be out-ranked by lunchtime.'

Shoemaker grinned; or gave a grimace that might have been a grin. 'I follow. It could be like our Olympic challenge, everyone jumping into the act. Well, I'd better be getting back to the Haymarket.' Huxwood Press, its offices and printing press, was in an uptown area of the city, had been there for a hundred and fifty years. 'Give my sympathy to the family, Derek. I'll come back this afternoon, be more formal.'

'I'll come with you,' said Gates and was gone out the door ahead of Shoemaker.

'What does Mr Gates do?' said Clements, who liked everyone labelled. 'Managing editor?'

Derek looked at Van Dieman before he replied. 'It's a title we borrowed from the Americans and changed it a little. He sort of manages the editorial side.'

This, Malone realized, was office politics and he didn't want to get into that, not now.

'Do you mind if Alan stays?' Derek gestured at Van Dieman. 'Or will that look as if I'm preparing some sort of defence?'

'Do you expect to be on the defensive?' said Malone.

'No.' Derek sat down on a cushioned cane lounge, waved to the other three men to take seats. 'But it *is* murder. Christ!' He abruptly put a hand over his eyes, was silent a long moment. The others waited; then he withdrew his hand and blinked. But Malone could see no tears. 'No one deserves to go out like that.'

'We want no sensationalism,' said Van Dieman.

Resentment shot up in Malone like a missile; but it was Clements who said, 'The Police Service doesn't go in for sensationalism, Mr Van Dieman. It's the media does that.'

'That's what I mean,' said the lawyer, but he sounded a little too hasty to convey that.

Though he was no more than forty, he was a grey man: grey-faced, grey-haired, grey-suited. The only spot of colour was his tie, but even that was plain purple rather than the strips of regurgitation that had been the fashion for the past couple of years. He had a soft voice, a grey voice, and a composure about him that hid his reputation. Malone had never met him, but knew that Van Dieman was considered the toughest corporation lawyer in town, if not the country.

Malone decided it was time to get down to cases. 'It's only a guess at the moment, but we think the murder occurred last night somewhere around midnight. Had the dinner party broken up by then?'

Derek nodded. 'I think so. My wife and I were over in our house by eleven-thirty. The others who weren't staying here had gone.'

'Leaving who here?'

'My sister Linden and her – her partner. They usually stay here when they come down from Sutton Forest. And Ivor and Beatrice Supple are staying here – or they were. We moved them out an hour ago, sent them into the Sheraton-on-the-Park. Sheila and her husband live over in the other house.'

'Little House Two?'

'You find that quaint? Or twee? Don't look like that when you mention the houses in front of my mother. She thought she was being sarcastic when she named them, but everyone took the names seriously. If you can take names like that seriously . . .' Derek seemed to be talking too much.

'How is your mother?'

'Pretty shattered. She and Dad –' He stopped, looked at Van Dieman as if for advice, then went on, 'It's hard to describe how close they were. People outside the family might have mistakenly thought they were always at odds with each other. They weren't –' He shook his head. 'All our lives it was them against us. The children.'

'Derek –' said Van Dieman warningly.

'Ah Christ, what's it matter now, Alan? It's all going to come out soon enough.'

There was silence in the big room but for the rustle of a sudden breeze amongst the potted palms. Out on the water someone in the photographers' launch shouted something at one of the policemen on the shore; the policeman, risking being photographed in the act, gave the someone the finger. Then Malone said, 'What's going to come out? You mind telling us?'

A palm frond was brushing Derek's shoulder; he raised a hand and absent-mindedly stroked it, as he might have a woman's comforting fingers. He didn't look at either of the detectives as he said, 'There are certain members of the family want to sell the Press. Lock, stock and barrel, as they say.'

Malone looked at Clements, the business expert; the latter was frowning, not quite believing what he had heard. 'Sell Huxwood Press? Everything?'

'Everything. The papers, the magazines, the radio and TV stations in the other States . . . Sounds crazy?'

'But why? Huxwood is, I dunno, an *empire*. Its share price is higher

30

than anyone else in its field, higher than News Corp. or Fairfax, your debt is nothing –'

Derek looked at Malone. 'He's a ring-in, isn't he? He's not with Homicide?'

Malone grinned. 'Russ just does homicide as part-time . . . Sorry, that's tasteless, considering. No, he's a punter. Used to be on the horses, now it's on the stock exchange. He's probably got shares in Huxwood.'

'I have,' said Clements. 'But I won't get a say, will I? Or any of the other public shareholders?'

'Afraid not,' said Derek Huxwood and made no attempt to sound less than privileged. He was part of the dynasty, for a moment he had the arrogance of his parents. 'The family owns sixty per cent, we have the controlling interest.'

'And who has the controlling interest in the family?'

Van Dieman said, 'Is any of this really relevant at this stage?'

'Yes,' said Malone flatly. 'Everything is relevant that will give us a lead on why Sir Harry was shot.'

'Jesus!' Derek snapped off a piece of the palm frond. 'You're saying one of *us* killed him?'

'We're not saying anything like that. Everyone working on a homicide has got his own way of doing it. Russ and I work from the outside inwards. It's called elimination. You tell us everything about this house, the *three* houses, about the family, and we'll do our own picking and choosing what to eliminate. So who has the controlling interest in Huxwood Press?'

Derek said nothing, looked at Van Dieman. It seemed that they had arrived rather late at the idea that this was a matter that was out of their hands, that could not be contained by a *Chronicle* editorial or a legal restraining order. The lawyer tapped his fingers on the arm of his chair, then he nodded:

'Okay, the family shares are parked in a holding company which has no other assets. The shares will always be voted in one line to maintain control.'

'So who decides how the holding company votes?' Clements seemed to have taken on a whole new image, sounded smoother. He is turning into a lawyer or a banker before my very eyes, thought Malone, amused at the thought but backing Clements all the way.

31

'Sir Harry has – had the shares which carried the whole of the voting power.'

'What about Lady Huxwood?'

'No, not in Sir Harry's lifetime.'

'But she does now?'

'We-ell –'

'Why are you hesitating?' Clements persisted.

Van Dieman took his time, as if he expected to fob off the question with a brusque answer or two. He said almost haughtily, 'I wasn't hesitating –'

'Okay, you were stalling, then. Keep going.'

Both Van Dieman and Derek Huxwood glanced at Malone: *who's the senior man here, you or him*? But Malone just returned their gaze: 'You'd better give us an answer, Mr Van Dieman. We cops always have more time than lawyers. That's why we charge less for it.'

Van Dieman flushed and Derek Huxwood turned his head away in disgust: 'Jesus!'

Malone relaxed his official (officious? he wondered) air for a moment. 'Take it easy, Derek. We're not here to kick the shit out of you, we're trying to find out who killed your father. If you and Mr Van Dieman will stop fartarsing about and get down to cases, we can be out of here and get on to talking to other members of the family. Sooner or later *someone* is going to tell us the truth, give us the dirt, if you like, and I think it might be better if we got it from you. Okay?'

Derek stared at him; then abruptly there was the old whimsical smile: 'If you'd been as shitty as this as a fast bowler, you'd have played for Australia. You never had the killer instinct.'

'I'm older and wiser, Derek. And shittier – sometimes . . . Let's hear what you were almost going to tell us, Mr Dieman.'

'*Van* Dieman,' said the lawyer, as if it were a legal point. 'No, now Sir Harry is dead, the voting power drops off and passes to all the shareholders. Lady Huxwood has no more voting power than any of the others.'

'How did that arrangement come about?' said Clements.

'My father insisted,' said Derek. 'He'd be regretting it now.'

'Why?' said Malone.

Derek and Van Dieman looked at each other; then the lawyer said, 'There is – shall we say – dissension – in the family. For some

32

time now some of the younger ones have been threatening to ask for a winding-up of the company and a distribution of the group shares.'

'So the younger ones could then combine their shares and have some real clout?' Clements sat back, was his old self: a rough-edged cynical detective with class prejudices. Just like my Old Man, thought Malone: Us and Them. 'That right? All the yuppies suddenly turning greedy?'

'I don't know that they'd appreciate being called yuppies. These young people are not upwardly mobile, they don't need to be. But yes, I suppose you could call them greedy?' He looked at Derek.

'Greedy as hell,' said Derek. 'Some of them.'

'Who are the grandchildren?' asked Malone.

Derek said, 'There are my three — Alexandra, Colin and Ross. There are Sarah and Michael, Nigel's two. And there's Camilla, she's Sheila's.'

'All of voting age?'

Derek nodded. 'I don't know that all of them would want to sell.'

Van Dieman contradicted him: 'I'm not so sure, Derek. If they all combine their shares, it could be a stand-off. And that, I'm afraid —' he looked at Malone, 'is what's happening. Or was happening up till — till last night.'

Malone said, 'Exactly what is your position in all this, Derek?'

'You mean, how do I feel about selling? I'm against it, dead against it.'

'How much — clout do you have?'

Derek shrugged. 'No more than my brother and sisters. I'm executive editor and publisher of the newspaper and I'm deputy-chairman of the whole group. But that means zilch when it comes to voting.'

'Your father was chairman?' Derek nodded. 'And the rest of the family?'

'Nigel and my sisters are directors on the group board.'

'The in-laws, too? And the grandchildren?'

'They just run — what do they call it in American football? — they run interference. You'd go a long way to meet a more interfering lot of buggers, including the kids.'

Malone was surprised at the amount of venom Derek showed; but he made no remark on it. 'Is there a buyer for the business?'

33

Derek looked at Van Dieman again, left it to him: 'Let's say there is strong interest.'

'Who?' Van Dieman said nothing and Malone snapped, 'Come on, you're fartarsing again! We're here because of a *murder*, not some bloody business deal! Who?'

'Metropolitan Newspapers,' said Derek. 'From London. That is why Ivor and Beatrice Supple are here. She's deputy-chairman — chairwoman, chairperson, whichever you like — she's here for Metropolitan. There are two lawyers and two bankers with her, they're at the Sheraton-on-the-Park. But that's not for publication,' he said, apparently in his status as executive editor and publisher.

'Pull your head in, Mr Huxwood,' said Malone officially and officiously; he was getting stiff-necked about these two sitting opposite him. 'I'm not in the habit of shooting off my mouth to the media.'

Derek backed down. 'Sorry.'

Then there was a knock at the garden room door and the butler, Krilich, looked in. He was a tall middle-aged man, dark-haired, heavy-browed and thick-shouldered; even last night Malone had thought he looked more like a builder's labourer than what he had imagined a butler should look like. This morning he was in shirtsleeves and a blue-and-black striped vest, but wore a tie, a black one.

'Assistant Commissioner Zanuch is here, Mr Huxwood.'

2

Assistant Commissioner Bill Zanuch did not look uncomfortable in this big house. The air of arrogance was there as always, the familiarity with top company as apparent. Malone had once described him, though not in his presence, as being so far up himself he had turned ego into a pretzel. In the latest of the Service's shuffling of senior ranks, he had been moved from AC Administration to AC Crime, a criminal act in itself in Malone's opinion. Zanuch was very much hands-on, to the point of throttling those under him. He and Malone in particular were not mates.

'Hello, Bill,' said Derek Huxwood, rising from the couch. 'You here to take charge?' He avoided looking at Malone as he said it.

'No, Derek. I'm here to offer condolences – from the Commissioner, too. I'm not here to take charge.'

No, thought Malone, he's not here to take charge: in the same way that General Schwarzkopf didn't take charge of the Gulf war, as Napoleon went to Moscow for the snow sports.

'Any leads, Inspector?'

'Not yet, sir.'

'Well, go ahead with whatever you were doing. I'll just sit in.' He sat down, arranged the crease in his trousers, undid the button of his double-breasted suit so there would be no strain on it, laid his police tie, silk of course, flat on his white shirt. He never wore anything that showed a label, he aspired to be too wellbred for that, yet somehow he gave the distinct impression that everywhere on him was a label, only the best, waiting to be displayed. 'I'm here to help.'

But Malone wasn't going to fall for that. 'Sergeant Clements and I are finished here for the moment, sir. We have to see others in the family.'

'Who?' said Huxwood, irritation plain. 'I can tell you everything you want to know –'

'It's just routine, Mr Huxwood,' said Malone, waiting to be interrupted by Zanuch. But the Assistant Commissioner said nothing and Malone went on, 'We like to interview everyone at the scene of the crime.'

'Scene of the crime! Christ –' Derek Huxwood looked at Zanuch as if expecting him to correct his junior officer. Then abruptly his broad shoulders slumped and he gestured futilely. 'Why the hell am I protesting? It's what we'll call it in the paper tomorrow – the scene of the crime . . . Go ahead, Scobie. Talk to the others. They're all somewhere, here or in the other houses.'

'Your mother?'

'She's upstairs in her room. Leave her – please?'

Malone hesitated, then nodded. He and Clements said goodbye to Van Dieman and Zanuch and left the garden room. Outside in the hallway they met Kate Arletti, looking even more untidy than ever. 'Having a hard time of it, Kate? You've lost another button off your shirt.'

She looked down in surprise. 'So I have! Sorry, sir . . . This family

35

is worse than any Italian family I've ever met. They can't make up their minds whether to grieve or to argue.'

'Where's the elder sister, Sheila? And her husband?'

'They've gone back to their own house.'

'Righto, you and Russ continue with the others. I'm going over to Little House Two. Russ, give me the envelope with that scrap of paper.'

He went out through large French doors on to a wide stone terrace that ran the entire breadth of the main house, crossed half an acre of lawn, went through an opening in a head-high privet hedge and came to Little House Two.

The main house had been built in the 1860s, a hodge-podge of English country house, Roman villa and Colonial homestead, as if the architect, uncertain of his surroundings, had gone on a drunken spree yet had somehow produced something that was not an eye-sore. The two smaller houses had been built a hundred years later and the style, with just minor modifications, copied. The three stood in line facing north across the tiny bay, resembling nothing more so than a slapdash Nash project that, like the convicts, had been transported and survived the change.

Ned Custer met Malone at the heavy oak front door. 'I saw you coming, I've been expecting you. Finished with that lot over there? Van Dieman there, putting his oar in? Best lawyer in town. Pity he knows it better than anyone else.'

'How's Mrs Custer?'

Custer was leading the way into a large comfortable room that looked out past a lawn and a jetty, where a yacht was moored, to the bay. He was dressed in lightweight blue trousers, a blue-and-white cotton jumper and espadrilles; but at least his face showed appropriate gloom. 'Not the best. We don't get on, the family, but Jesus wept — *murder*?'

'What makes you say that?'

'What?'

'You implied someone in the family committed the murder.'

Custer waved his hands in front of him, as if beating off smoke. 'No, no! Christ, I didn't mean anything like that — oh darling. Here's Scobie, come to interrogate us.'

Spoken like a true lawyer.

36

Sheila was more appropriately dressed; she was not in funeral black, but at least she didn't look as if she were ready for a yachting picnic. She was in dark blue linen, skirt and shirt, with dark blue casual shoes. Her glasses did not hide the fact that she had been weeping. Without make-up she looked older than she had last night.

'Sit down, sit down.' Custer bustled about, like a front-row forward looking for the ball that had come out on the wrong side of the scrum. 'Drink? Coffee?'

'Nothing, thanks.' Malone sat down in a comfortable chair, one of four in the room meant to relax their occupants; this was a room obviously meant for relaxation, the afternoon read, the pre-dinner drink. It was, Malone guessed, what the Custers called their family room, though the furnishings were much richer than he had seen in other family rooms. One narrow wall was taken up with an entertainment ensemble: television set with the largest screen Malone had ever seen, video recorder, tape-deck and shelves full of videos, tapes, CDs and even a stack of old LPs. Yet the room showed no wear and tear, it was a room for a phantom family. Sheila was already seated and Custer now dropped into a chair beside her, but neither of them looked comfortable. 'All we're after at this stage is what you may know of last night.'

'You mean the murder? Bugger-all. Harry had gone to bed when we left.'

'What time was that?'

'I never wear a watch,' Custer said and looked at his wife.

'Midnight,' she said. 'What time is my father supposed to have been —?' Her voice was unsteady, she didn't finish the sentence.

'Around midnight, give or take an hour.'

'So whoever killed him could have been in the house while we were there?'

Custer got up, poured himself a whisky, straight, no ice, no water or soda.

'If it was an intruder —'

'Of course it was a bloody intruder!' The drink splashed in Custer's hand as he sat down heavily.

'What's the security like over at the main house?'

'Adequate.' Custer sipped his whisky. 'That's about all you can say for any security in domestic circumstances — you'd know that as

37

well as I do.' Malone nodded. 'We employ two security firms to watch the estate – and each other. But there was a break-in a coupla years ago – they caught no one – so it could easily have happened again. Burglars not so long ago didn't carry guns or knives. But now . . .'

There had been several incidents in the past year of murder by intruders, householders shot or knifed, people worth not one-hundredth of the Huxwood wealth.

'Is there any way up to the first floor over there besides up the main staircase in the hallway?'

'Of course.' Sheila was beginning to regain some composure. 'There's a rear stairwell for the staff. And there's all that latticework on the east wall. We've wanted to pull it down, but Mother wouldn't allow it.'

'What's that there for?'

'The roses, of course. The climbing roses, the Chinese hybrids – don't you *know* what Malmaison is famous for?'

'I thought it was – *famous*, if you like, for the Huxwoods.'

'Nicely put, Scobie,' said Custer. 'I'd have said notorious.'

'La Malmaison was where Napoleon's Josephine lived. She was the one who really popularized rose-growing in Europe, she had roses brought in by the boat-load from all over, China, Turkey, everywhere. My great-great-grandfather, who built the original house, was a great admirer of Napoleon and Josephine. And he loved roses. I take it you're not a gardener?'

'I grow camellias and azaleas, they're easy. But no, I'm not a gardener. *Burke's Backyard* leaves me cold,' he said, naming one of television's top rating shows.

'And,' said Custer, looking halfway to being half-drunk again, on one glass of whisky, 'you're not a student of Sydney's history?'

'Not this side of town, no. Ask me about the arse-end of Sydney and I'll give you chapter and verse. Sorry,' he said to Sheila.

'Take it easy, Ned,' Sheila told her husband, then looked back at Malone. 'We were saying . . . Yes, it would be easy to get up to the first floor, where the bedrooms are. Someone going up the east wall might get scratched or pricked, but not if he wore gloves.'

Malone took the plastic envelope from his pocket, extracted the scrap of notepaper with his tweezers. He held it out: 'I can't let you touch this, not till it's been fingerprinted. It was found in your father's hand, as if it had been torn off a full sheet. Do you recognize the notepaper?'

Both the Custers leaned forward; then they glanced at each other before Sheila said, 'It's the family's – well, Malmaison's. My mother orders it every year through the company – it's special paper. She likes us all to use it, so we do. Boxes of it are delivered to us, Derek, Nigel, my sister and I, every Christmas.'

'Did you use it to write your father a note?'

'No.' She was taking off her glasses while she answered, so he didn't see her eyes at that instant. Then she was polishing the glasses, carefully, giving them her attention. 'I was not in the habit of writing my parents notes. After all, they're just over there –' She waved vaguely.

'We think this may have been more than just a note. There's a very strong *No* scrawled on it in red pencil.'

'That wouldn't be Harry,' said Custer, getting up to pour himself another drink. 'He wasn't the type for expressing himself strongly. He was always the mediator, he liked to take options. He was a bugger for that,' he said as if to himself.

'So it could've been anyone in the family who wrote it?'

'I suppose so,' said Sheila, reluctantly, it sounded.

'Don't forget the kids.' Custer came back to his chair. 'The grandkids. They're all literate, very literate. And numerate, too. All interested in –'

'That's not fair, Ned,' said Sheila, as if this had been a continuous argument. Then Malone remembered that her child was Custer's *step*-child. Maybe this sort of argument went on in many families. 'They're not all interested in money, not all of them.' Her tone said: *not mine.*

Malone had had this feeling once or twice before, the urge to get up and walk away from a case. Detectives are driven to solve a murder, as doctors are towards a cure. But sometimes a murder becomes obscured by the atmosphere that surrounds it; the detective becomes at risk to other dangers. One's own values had to be protected, there was a limit to objectivity.

'How many children do you have, Mrs Custer?'

'Just one, a girl.'

'She lives here?'

'No, Camilla has her own flat. She's at work today – she works at

2HP, she's learning the ropes. We – that is, Huxwood – own the station,' she explained.

'How can you do that? With the rules against cross-media ownership in the same State?'

'I wouldn't know,' said Sheila, but she did know.

Beside her Custer grinned. 'Don't ask. You know the old one, about friends in high places. The media barons in this country have got that sort of friendship down to a fine art.'

'Careful, Ned,' said his wife.

'You mentioned money,' said Malone, 'Would you sell Huxwood Press?'

Sheila squinted, put her glasses back on; Custer held up his glass, as if looking for an answer in the half-inch of whisky still in it. Then he said, 'We'd probably sell. Anything for fucking peace and quiet.'

'Who told you the Press is for sale?' said Sheila.

Malone stood up. 'We're not answering questions at this stage. Just asking them. I'll be in touch.'

He made his own way out of the house, crossed the lawn again and went round to the east wall of the main house. The roses were there, as Sheila had said; and the latticework up the wall. The gardener was also there, the long-handled shovel he had brandished down on the shore now driven into the earth, a pair of secateurs in his hand. He looked at Malone: 'Lady Huxwood wants fresh flowers in the house every day. You think I ought to, today?'

'I wouldn't. You're –?'

'Eh? Oh yeah.' He appeared to look closely at Malone for the first time. 'You're one of the Ds?'

Malone introduced himself.

'Oh sure, I've read about you a coupla times. You work for someone publishes a newspaper, you read it all the way through. Just in case you get a mention, even in the obituaries. It'll be interesting to see what the Old Man's obit says . . . I'm Dan Darling. Or Darling Dan, as the Old Lady calls me. A poor bloody joke, but most of her jokes are. She doesn't have much chop for the intelligence of the working class.'

He said it without emphasis, neither bitterly nor with affection. He was in his sixties, a grizzled bear of a man with the face and arms of someone who had spent the best part of his life in the sun and, by

40

some miracle, escaped the rat-like nibbling of sun cancers. He had eyes and mouth of strong opinions and Malone wondered how he got on with Lady Huxwood.

'The feller from Rose Bay has already been around here, looking for footprints, he said. There's nothing.'

'Nothing on the latticework?' The gardener shook his head. 'If it was an outsider, how d'you reckon he got upstairs?'

'Up the back stairs. That door's never locked. All the bloody security, costs a bloody fortune, and the back door's always left unlocked.'

'Why's that?'

Darling shrugged. 'Beats me. Ask the Yugoslavs, the butler and his missus.' There was a sudden bedlam of birds in a nearby tree; it went on for almost half a minute, then the birds were gone as suddenly as they had come. The gardener spat into the dry soil at his feet. 'Bloody foreigners.'

'Who?' Dan Darling sounded like Con Malone, the xenophobe from way back. Malone had grown up listening to his father complaining about 'bloody foreigners'.

'The birds. They're Indian mynahs. Taking over everything.'

Malone said off-handedly, 'Do the family fight like those birds?'

Darling squinted at him sideways, but still challengingly. 'You don't expect me to gossip about the family, do you? Christ, I'm family, too. So the Old Lady is always telling me.'

'How long have you been here?'

'Forty-two years. I was a printer's apprentice at the *Chronicle*, in my last year. I got my hand caught in the rollers –' He held up his left hand and for the first time Malone saw how maimed it was, an ugly stump-fingered fist. 'I never went back, I was scared shitless of the rollers. Sir John, Harry's father, he was the boss then. He gave me a job here as under-gardener and I fell into it like a pig into muck – I didn't know it, but that was what I wanted to be, a gardener in a garden like this.' He waved his good hand, the one holding the secateurs, around him. 'The paper's gardening expert, she comes out to see me whenever she's got a problem.'

'You do it all on your own?' Malone looked around: the gardens were more extensive than he had thought.

'No, I've got a young bloke works for me. Two of us are enough. I been here all them years, I've got everything under control.'

41

'Where's he?'

'Well, I dunno. He ain't come in this morning, ain't rung. I can't say it's not like him, he's only been here a coupla weeks. I dunno him that well.'

'What's his name?'

'Dwayne Harod. His dad's a Turk, he says, his mum's a Lebanese. He lives out in Marrickville with an uncle and aunt. Dwayne's an old Turkish name, I gather.' A crack of a grin, dry as an eroded creek bank.

'So I wonder why he didn't come in today, of all days?'

'He'd of heard about it on the radio. He's pretty quiet, maybe he just wanted to miss all the commotion. Maybe he ain't a stickybeak, like them out there.' He gestured towards the launchful of photographers, now retreating like other, earlier invaders who had been repelled by the natives. 'I wouldn't worry about Dwayne, you got enough on your plate. You think flowers would be outa place in the house today?' He snapped the secateurs, as if they were used every day and he hated the thought of interrupting the routine.

'Not today, Dan. I'll be in touch. They smell beautiful, though.'

As he walked round the corner of the east wall he heard a sound coming from an open window on the first floor. He wasn't sure whose room it was, but it was in the main bedroom wing. The sound was a low moaning, faintly ululating, a primitive murmur of grief, almost animal-like.

3

Assistant Commissioner Bill Zanuch moved around the Big House without hurrying, with the proprietorial air of an old friend or a bailiff. He had his hands clasped behind his back, a habit he had adopted since he had, several years ago, been assigned to accompany Prince Charles on another Royal visit to Australia. It had been a characteristic of the Duke of Edinburgh, the prince's father, and the prince himself had adopted it. Lately, however, Zanuch had noted from newsreels that the prince had moved his hands in front of him, where they nervously wove patterns in the air as if practising argument with his estranged wife. The Assistant Commissioner had none of the royal problems; he had not made a nervous gesture since kindergarten and even there the other infants had known who was Number One.

Socially he had never aimed higher than God; he always felt that he fitted in. Wherever he went in the city's social circles he was treated as an equal amongst equals, proving that flattery is no burden if one leaves others to carry it. He knew, just as the prince did, who would be king one day. Soon, maybe just a year or so down the track, he would be Commissioner. The thought did not make him giddy, since he had been tasting it ever since he had been promoted to sergeant, but he savoured it every day.

He stood outside the bedroom door listening to the low moaning coming from inside. He was not insensitive, but he knew Phillipa Huxwood would have to be interviewed and it was better that he do it rather than one of the five or six detectives still on the estate. After all, he could talk to her as an equal.

But first he moved along the hall to the next door, which was open. He had never been upstairs here, but this, he guessed, was Harry Huxwood's room. He went in, ducking under the Crime Scene tape across the doorway. Another tape was strung round the four-poster bed, like a decoration from some old wedding-night bed.

Then the door to the adjoining room opened and Phillipa Huxwood stood there. Her face was even gaunter than usual, her eyes were red from weeping; but her carriage was still stiff and straight, her voice as firm as ever: 'Do they have to put that ridiculous piece of ribbon on the bed?'

'I'm afraid so, Phillipa. How are you?'

She waved a hand, almost a dismissive why-do-you-ask? 'It's unbelievable, isn't it? I've been laying there –'

She used the Americanism. Up till her late teens she had lived a nomadic life with her archaeologist father and travel-writer mother; she still threw in local usage like postcards, as if to show she had been around. When she used a foreign phrase the accent was always immaculate, no matter what the language. Yet she wrote to reporters and anchor-people on the corporation's radio and television stations who said 'd-bree' for 'debris' and used other Americanisms. She was rigid in her inconsistency, as despots are.

'How are the others taking it?' She led him back into her own room,

43

seated herself in what he took to be her favourite chair by a window that looked down on the rose gardens.

'I've only seen Derek,' he said. He remained standing, aware of the disorder of her room, which surprised him; he had always thought of her as a meticulously neat person. But her bed was rumpled, the sheets twisted as if she had writhed in them in a frenzy. Her clothing, her dress and underwear, were thrown on the second chair in the room; the underwear, he thought, looked skimpy for a woman of her age. There was also a couch, an antique chaise-longue, but it was against a far wall; he could not seat himself there and talk to her across the width of the room.

'How is Derek? Shocked?'

'Of course.'

'When I saw Harry —' She closed her eyes, was silent for a moment, then she opened them. 'I'm alone now, Bill. What do I do?'

He knew she didn't want an answer. They were acquaintances, not friends, which is how it is in half of any large city's social circles. He had known nothing of the intended selling of the publishing empire till Derek had filled him in this morning. What he knew of this family, even though he had been coming here for years as a dinner or luncheon guest, had been gleaned from observation and not from confidences.

'How long have we known you?' Her mind, it seemed, was shooting off at tangents this morning.

'Twenty-five years.'

She looked at him in astonishment. 'You're joking!'

'No. I first came here twenty-five years ago on a police matter —'

'Ah.' She nodded, was silent a while. He thought she was going to say no more, then she went on. 'There was mystery then, too, wasn't there? This is a mystery, Bill. Or is it?' She glanced sideways at him, almost slyly.

He didn't take the bait, if there was any. 'Yes, I think it is, Phillipa. But we'll find whoever killed Harry. I promise you that.'

She nodded. 'Yes, I'd like that,' she said, as if he had promised her no more than a small gift. 'I'll miss him, Bill. We fought, oh, often we fought . . . But we loved each other. Those downstairs don't know what love is. Do you?'

But she didn't wait for his answer. He wondered if she talked to her children, *those downstairs*, as she was now to him. He knew how

44

people could sometimes confide in strangers thoughts they would never expose to those close to them. But why had she chosen him?

'I'll have to go down soon and face them all, I suppose. I'm the matriarch, they'll expect it. When we first built the other two houses, Derek and Cordelia and Ned and Sheila used to come here every evening, we'd dine *en famille*. It was Harry's idea. I've never liked the idea of matriarch –'

You could have fooled me.

'– but Harry saw himself as the patriarch. He always wanted to fill his father's shoes and there never was a patriarch like Old John. You met him?'

'Once.' Twenty-five years ago.

'He was Biblical, he and I never got on. The *en famille* idea lasted a year, no more. The nuclear family is a pain in the uterus.'

He loved social gossip; but this was not gossip. 'Phillipa, don't tire yourself –'

She gave him the sly look again. 'I'm talking too much, you mean? Why did you come up here if you didn't want to talk to me?'

He was wearing out his welcome, she would turn nasty in a moment; he had seen it once or twice over the years. 'Phillipa, did you hear the shot next door?'

She stared into space, the myopic eyes blank; then she blinked and looked back at him. 'I'd taken two sleeping pills, I was upset last night. I heard nothing, the roof could have fallen in . . .'

He began to move towards the door. 'Fair enough. We'll leave you alone now, you and the family.'

'But you'll be back?'

'Not me, but Inspector Malone and one or two of the other detectives.'

'I wish you would take charge. You can be circumspect.'

Now he knew why she was taking him into her confidence. She had said exactly that, *you can be circumspect*, twenty-five years ago.

Chapter Three

1

The air waves shivered with indignation and horror at the news of Sir Harry's murder. Nobody was safe if as important a figure as Sir Harry could be murdered in his own home, said another important figure, Premier Bevan Bigelow, unsafe in his own House. Editorials sang the praises of the dead man but had nothing to say in praise of law and order. Only the columnists, as plentiful on the ground in modern journalism as Indian mynahs and just as raucous, mentioned rumours of a possible sale of the Huxwood empire. The coming election was pushed to the edges of the front pages, to the relief of the voters.

'Law and order doesn't apply,' said Clements, 'when the throat-cutting is in the family. Don't they know that?'

'We don't know anyone in the family killed him,' said Malone.

'No, but I'd make book on it.'

They were at a morning conference the day after the discovery of the murder. All nineteen detectives from Homicide were there, plus Greg Random, Chief Superintendent in charge of the Major Crime Squad. Some of the detectives had been assigned to the three other murders that had occurred in South Region, but the main topic was the Huxwood homicide. Notabilities were not frequent visitors on the Sydney murder scene. True, it was only a press baron who had been done in: had it been a star jockey or footballer of the status of O. J. Simpson there would have been a special session of parliament, the Minister and Commissioner would have brought camp beds into their offices and the media contingent outside Homicide would have looked like a grand final crowd. Still, the pressure was bad enough as it was.

'I think,' said Random, sucking on his pipe which no one had ever seen him light, 'we'd better not start pointing the finger just yet. Let the newspapers do that, they have more experts than we do.'

'Righto,' said Malone. 'What've we got? Kate?'

'I've been right through the family, grandkids and all. God, what a bunch!' Her antipathy towards the Huxwood clan seemed to have increased since yesterday. 'There are six grandkids, three of them with minor records. Car-stealing –'

'Car-stealing?' said Andy Graham. 'With their money? They'd all own Porsches at least.'

Kate Arletti shrugged. 'Rebellion, I guess. They're a rebellious lot, most of them. Two of them have drug charges against them, possession of. None of them says he or she knows anything of what happened the night before last.'

'What about the rest of the family, the kids' parents?' asked Clements.

'They were mine.' Phil Truach coughed, a hint that the meeting had gone on long enough without his having had a smoke. He and Random were the only two grey-heads in the group: Random the senior by five years and a chief superintendent, Truach only recently promoted to sergeant. But rank had seemingly never worried Phil Truach and if he never hurried himself, there was no one in Homicide more thorough than he. 'Nobody heard nothing, nobody has a clue why the old man should've been shot. They've all got their backs to the wall, a blank wall.'

'Not entirely blank,' said Malone. 'Derek let his hair down a bit to me and so did the Number One son-in-law Ned Custer. The rumours of a sell-off of Huxwood Press are true and it's turning into a dog-fight in the family.'

'Who's for it and who's against it?' John Kagal was the handsomest and smartest dressed in the group. He was also the only detective with a university degree, a distinction he had once quietly flaunted but which he had now learned to hide. Elitism is tolerated and admired in the criminal classes, but in the rest of the native working class, including the police, it is looked upon as a criminal offence. Some day, as inevitably as crime would continue to be committed, Kagal would have Greg Random's rank, but he had learned, too, to hide his ambition. He had been given a lesson in police service culture: that seniority was as sanctified as motherhood. Wedded motherhood, that is.

'I don't know who's for or against it,' said Malone. 'Who checked the butler and his wife?'

47

'I did,' said Kagal. 'They're clean. They've been in Australia eighteen years, they're Australian citizens. They've worked for the Huxwoods for five years, got good reports.'

'I checked the gardener,' said Malone. 'That leaves only the under-gardener as a regular on the place. Plus the security guards who patrol each night.'

'I've checked them,' said Andy Graham, restless as ever on his chair. He was always ready to be up and away, usually like a bull at a gate. 'The first lot check on the hour through the night, the other lot on the half-hour. There'd be a gap of, say, twenty minutes between each check. Time for an outsider, if it was an outsider and knew the routine, to nip in and do the deed.'

'That leaves the under-gardener. He didn't come in yesterday. Why?'

'He's in today,' said Kate Arletti. 'I was out there early this morning, double-checking.' Her diligence equalled that of Andy Graham, though she managed to be more restrained than he. 'He had a virus or something yesterday, he said. He's okay today.'

I'll talk to him, Malone told himself. He didn't, however, tell that to Kate; he didn't believe in implying that a job was only well done when he did it himself. 'What's the report from Ballistics?'

'One bullet, a Thirty-two. If a pillow was used to muffle the shot, Clarrie Binyan thinks the gun could be a Browning, or something like it.'

'Any shell?'

'No sign of one. He collected it, looks like.' Clements closed his notebook. 'It doesn't look like a professional job, not if he didn't use a silencer.'

'Would an amateur collect the shell? Why would he go in for housekeeping like that?'

Clements shrugged. 'I dunno. I still think the answer's in the family.'

'Don't harp on that,' said Random. 'The family has a friend upstairs.'

Malone kept quiet, but Truach said, 'The Minister?'

'No, AC Zanuch.'

'Oh shit!'

'Exactly. And that's what'll hit the fan if we start talking about the family. I'll see you outside, Scobie.' He rose, unhurried as usual, nodded at the group in general and left.

Malone got up from behind the table where he had presided over the meeting, made an I-don't-know gesture at Clements and followed Random out of the room. The chief superintendent led the way down towards the lifts. He had put his pipe in a side pocket, as if he no longer needed a prop in a man-to-man conversation.

'Nobody wants this one, Scobie. Steve Lozelle, out at Waverley, it's in his command. They'll set up the incident room and do the donkey work. But he wants us to run it, subject to him being in nominal charge. Okay?'

Malone nodded, wondering why the usual jealousy of turf was being sacrificed in this case. Perhaps the Waverley commander already knew that AC Zanuch might interfere.

'There's another thing.' Random took his pipe out of his pocket, had it halfway to his mouth when he had second thoughts and put it away again. 'Have you seen the *Tele-Mirror* this morning? They say you were a dinner guest at the Huxwoods' night before last. They're playing it up as if you're that guy in *Burke's Law*, the cop with the stiff neck and the corset. My wife tells me Alan Jones had something about it on 2UE this morning, that you're a friend of the family —'

'Balls! I'd never met the family till two nights ago. I hadn't seen Derek Huxwood in years —' He explained the circumstances of the dinner invitation.

'Well —' Random took the pipe out of his pocket, tapped it in the palm of his hand. He looked almost nervous, something Malone had never seen before. 'It's too late now — that would only confirm what they're hinting, if we took you off it. Just watch it, that's all. Any hint of the family being suspected is out, okay? Bill Zanuch is leaning on me —'

'How close is he to them?'

'I don't know. But you know him — if he'd been alive at the time he'd have been at the Last Supper. Then he'd have gone to lunch with Pontius Pilate the next day.' He looked around him to make sure he wasn't overheard; then he let go his slow smile. 'Christ help us if ever he becomes Commissioner. We won't be able to arrest anyone without first checking with the social editors.'

49

Both men were silent a while, contemplating an awful future. Then the lift doors opened; the lift was empty. 'Ride down with me.' The doors closed, locking them in a small chamber where secrets could be exchanged. 'I don't know whether he knows anything, but he's protecting the Huxwoods. I don't like it any more than you and Russ do, but I've got to wear it. Zanuch's been specific. He wants none of what we had last year with the Cabramatta murder.' A prominent politician, campaigning against gang crimes in his electorate, had been shot in a western suburb where there was a large Asian community. 'From the first the media started pointing the finger at the Vietnamese, there wasn't a shred of evidence to support it—'

'We still haven't nabbed who did it.'

'Nonetheless, we had to keep denying it. Just watch it, Scobie.' They had reached the ground floor, the doors opened. 'Let me know everything, *everything*, that turns up. 'Luck.'

'Thanks,' said Malone drily and pressed the button to go back upstairs again.

Clements was waiting for him. 'What'd he have to say?'

'The usual. We tread carefully about the family.'

Clements bit his lip. 'What d'you think? One of them did it?'

Malone took his time. 'I dunno. An amateur wouldn't take the time to collect the cartridge shell. But you never know — TV shows you how to do everything, including commit murder . . . I'd like to see the family lined up all together. I still haven't met the grandkids. I gather they're all old enough to have pulled a trigger. I'm going out there, see if I can round up one or two of them. You want to come?'

Clements shook his big head. Since he had become the Unit Supervisor, had had to assume more paperwork, he appeared to have lost his once-habitual unhurried approach. The re-organization in Homicide had not worked quite the way the planners had planned it, but that has been the way of the world since ivory towers were first built and graphs took the place of commonsense.

'I've got too much to do here. You should be here, too,' he said almost critically. 'You're supposed to be the Co-ordinator.'

'I'm the most un-coordinated bastard you ever met,' said Malone, remembering his loose tongue.

He picked up his hat and left. Downstairs Kate Arletti was crossing the lobby towards the front doors. 'Where are you heading, Kate?'

'Out to Vaucluse, sir. I'm going to talk to that under-gardener, Harod or whatever his name is.'

'Cancel your transport. You can come with me.' He had a police car of his own, unmarked, but he did not like driving if he could persuade someone else to drive him. One of the advantages was that he never had a parking problem. 'You can drive.'

They left Strawberry Hills and drove towards the far eastern suburbs, the city changing gradually as they drove, housescapes merging into housescapes, *fresco secco* into *buon fresco*, till at last they reached Huxwood Road, still cordoned off by a police barrier with a uniformed officer there to allow only residents and tradesmen past the barrier. Yesterday morning's crowd had gone but Malone noticed that in several houses owners and their guests were having morning coffee on the front verandahs, some even out on their front lawns under large umbrellas. Curiosity was endemic, not just a disease amongst the lower classes.

Malone paused as he and Kate Arletti got out of the car. 'Kate, you heard what Chief Superintendent Random said – don't lean too heavily on the family. You're developing a thing about them.'

'Sorry, sir.' She looked neat this morning, but it was still early in the day. She was in a linen dress with a matching jacket; there didn't appear to be any buttons that could come undone or a sleeve unrolled. 'It's just – '

He didn't move. 'Go on, Kate. What's on your mind?'

She looked away from him, at no place in particular. She reminded him of all the young actors in movies and television these days who, every time they were asked a question by another actor, looked off-screen as if their next line was written on some blackboard there. But Kate Arletti had obviously been chewing over her lines for the past two days; she looked back at him, her jaw set:

'The *Chronicle* ruined my father, killed him. He was Italian, you know that, he was much older than my mother. As a young man he was a Fascist, Mussolini was his hero, but once he came to Australia he put all that behind him. He started his own business, he was a job printer. Then he decided, after he'd become a citizen, to run for local government, the local council, he never stopped being political-minded. The *Chronicle* was doing a series on local government, the

51

sort of people who ran for council aldermen. Alderpersons. Somehow they dug up Dad's past, they really dug the dirt on him. All of it was true, I'll admit, but it was past, dead and buried. They buried Dad with it, literally. He lost his business and then he committed suicide. I was ten years old, I was the one who found him –' She stopped and looked away again, put up a hand to wipe away tears.

'Kate –' He waited till she looked back at him. 'You're off this case. I'm sorry.'

She shook her head angrily, almost like a child being denied. 'No, sir! *Please*.'

'Kate, you're biassed –'

'All police are biassed, we can't help it –' Then she broke off, drew a heavy breath. 'Sorry, sir. I didn't mean you –'

Less than an hour ago, Greg Random had suggested he might be less than disinterested. But it was true: it was a rare cop who could deny bias once he was into a case. Sometimes it was no more than a counter to bafflement, the effort to find an answer, any answer.

She was more in control of herself now: 'This is my first big case, sir. I've made a mistake, but I think I can overcome it. Give me today. If you still think I'm biassed against the Huxwoods –'

'It wasn't the family who would have written that series.'

'It was. I looked them up when I was older, when I understood what had gone on. The series was written by Derek Huxwood. The editorial that summed them up was written by Sir Harry, that was the most unfair of the lot. It wasn't signed, but I found out who'd written it.'

There was silence between them. At the wide gates into the Huxwood estate Crime Scene tapes fluttered in the slight breeze, like the long tail of a child's kite lost amongst the shrubbery. A kookaburra in a nearby jacaranda laughed hollowly; mynahs, the foreigners, instantly swooped on it and chased it away. On the opposite side of the road a woman paused in the act of pouring coffee for two guests and looked across at the man and the girl beside the unmarked car, looked at them, Malone thought, as if they were trespassers.

He nodded at Kate Arletti. 'Righto, today's your test. But if I see any –'

'You won't, sir. I promise. Thanks.' She moved towards him and for a moment he thought she was going to kiss him. But she went by

him and ducked under the tapes. 'The under-gardener or the family —
who's first?'

'The under-gardener. Dwayne the Turk.'

Malone had never heard the term under-gardener before; he would
have called the man the assistant gardener, if he called him anything.
He could only surmise that it was an English term.

Dwayne Harod was short and slim and outgoing; hawk-faced but
handsome, dark-skinned and dark-haired and in his early twenties. He
was working amongst the roses when the two detectives approached
him having skirted the house and, so far, avoided any of the family.

'I couldn't believe it when I heard it on the radio yesterday morning.
It sorta floored me.' His accent was broad Australian; Anatolia was
somewhere back in the memory mist of childhood. 'I was pretty sick,
anyway, I got this virus that's been going around. Or maybe it's an
allergy, I dunno. That'd be a joke, eh? If I was allergic to flowers.'
He waved an arm; he was waist-deep in the last roses of summer.
Long-stemmed blooms, already cut, lay on a sheet of plastic. 'These
are for inside the house. Lady Huxwood wants them, same as usual.'

'We understand you've been here only two weeks, Dwayne. Is that
your real name?'

He had a charming smile. 'I give it to m'self when I was fifteen,
sixteen. My old man named me Kemal. He was a great admirer of
Kemal Ataturk. You heard of him?'

'Vaguely.' This seemed to be Old Dictators Week. Malone glanced
at Kate Arletti, whose father had admired a dictator, but she was
apparently ignorant of Kemal Ataturk. Malone only knew of the Father
of modern Turkey because he had once spent a month unsuccessfully
chasing two Turks who had killed a man in a botched bank robbery
and who had somehow escaped the nets at airports and vanished back
to Turkey. 'Does Kemal mean anything?'

There was an embarrassed smile. 'It means "perfect".'

'I don't blame you for changing it. Are you legally Dwayne
then?'

'Well, no. Legally, I'm still — perfect.' The smile this time was not
so embarrassed.

'Bully for you. How did you get this job? Have you been a gardener
before?'

'I answered the ad in the paper. There were eight of us come for it and they picked me. No, I never been a gardener before. I used to work in the canefields up in Queensland till I come down here.'

'How long have you been in Sydney?'

'A month. I live with my uncle and aunty out in Marrickville.' He was laying himself out like an open book, almost a little too eagerly. Malone had seen this before, when kids had been afraid of the cops, but Dwayne Harod gave the impression that he was afraid of no one. 'I was lucky to get this job so soon, considering.'

'Considering what?'

Harod looked puzzled, as if he didn't understand why Malone didn't know the state of the nation. 'The unemployed. The recessions's supposed to be over, but it ain't by a long chalk, not for guys with no education or training. That's why I'm grateful for Mr Derek giving me the job —'

'Mr Derek took you on?'

'Well, he was the one told me I had the job. But the Old Lady — I mean Lady Huxwood, I think she had a say in it —' He gave another smile, an old lady's favourite.

'Righto, Dwayne. Can we have your home address, just in case?'

'I have that,' said Kate Arletti.

Harod looked at her in surprise, then said, 'I might be moving from there soon, now I've got a job. Is that all you want?'

Malone told him that was all they wanted for the time being and he and Kate walked away, going round the northern corner and coming out on the wide lawn that ran down to the water's edge. There were no cruising cameramen today, the invasion had been put on hold.

'What d'you think, Kate?'

'He's pretty cheerful, isn't he?'

'That's what I thought. He said the news of the murder when he heard it on the radio floored him, but he seems to have picked up pretty quick. He's got over his virus, too.'

'He didn't mention the murder again. He also didn't mention Sir Harry once by name.'

Malone nodded. The girl was learning to develop a police ear, to hear what was unsaid as much as what was said. 'Don't cross him off our list, we'll get back to him. Now who's next?'

'If you want to see the grandkids, there's probably only one of them home — he's a uni student. All the others have jobs.'

'In the company?'

'Only three of them. The youngest, Ross, Derek's son, is doing economics at Sydney. He's one of the rebels, a real tearaway, I'm told.'

Malone sighed. 'I love tearaways. They're a real pain in the butt. Righto, let's see if he's home.'

Ross Huxwood was home, sunning himself on the terrace of Little House One with his mother Cordelia. He was a big lad, taller than Malone and bulkier, most of it muscle though there was a hint of beer fat round his middle; Malone had seen scores like him around the rugby clubs and the better watering holes, the elite of ockerism. He was blond and good-looking in a beefy way, his cheeks and jaw too heavy, his wide mouth sullen. But he had been taught to be polite: he stood up as Malone and Kate Arletti came up on to the terrace.

'Ah, the lady detective! Mum —'

Cordelia must have been dozing behind her dark glasses. Her head jerked and she sat up on the lounge where she had been stretched out. She was in a sleeveless yellow sun-dress and her son was in a tight pair of blue shorts. So far, it seemed, the mourning weeds were still in the wardrobe.

'Oh Scobie! Or do I have to call you Inspector? Do sit down. You too, Miss —?'

'Detective-Constable Arletti.' Kate's voice was chill.

Cordelia lowered her dark glasses to look at Kate over the top of them; but she said nothing. The two detectives sat down at a wrought-iron table under a blue umbrella. Ross, at his mother's command, went away to get coffee and Malone said, 'I think we'd better keep it on an official basis, Mrs Huxwood.'

Cordelia looked disappointed; Malone wondered now if that was her normal expression. 'Well, I suppose it's to be expected . . . Have you come up with anything? I don't know how the police work — how would I? — but have you made any progress?'

'Very little.' He paused before he went on, 'Except that we've heard there is a lot of tension in the family about the sell-off.'

'Where did you hear that?' she said sharply. 'Over there?' She nodded across the lawn towards the hedges that half-hid Little House Two.

He didn't answer that directly: *don't point the finger.* 'We've had

55

detectives here for the past twenty-four hours. Including Detective
Arletti. How many people have you interviewed, Kate?'

'At least a dozen, sir.'

'So you see, Mrs Huxwood, the word is around about the sell-off.'

She said nothing, waited while her son came back, followed by the
housekeeper with a tray. The housekeeper put the tray on the table
between Malone and Kate, ignored them and spoke over their heads
to Cordelia.

'Will that be all, senora?'

She had a strong voice, thick with accent. She was middle-aged,
big and square in build and face, dark-haired and with unflinching
eyes. And self-contained: very self-contained, thought Malone. He
and Kate Arletti might have been down at the water's edge for all the
notice she took of them.

'That will be all, Luisa. Thank you.'

Still without a glance at the two detectives, the housekeeper returned
to the house, her broad back dismissing them as of no account.

Malone looked at Kate. 'Did you interview her?'

'Yes. She doesn't like police.'

'Is she from the Big House?' Malone asked the Huxwoods.

'No.' Ross was seated again in the sun, dark glasses on. Both he
and his mother shone with sun-cream; streaks of light moved on him
like silver worms. 'She's ours. She's Spanish, she's been with us since
I was a kid.'

'You didn't get anything out of her?' Cordelia looked at Kate, a
hint of malice in her sweet voice.

'I got enough,' said Kate, tapping her notebook. 'She's in here.
Even if she doesn't like the police.'

'Who does?' said Ross, expressionless behind the shades.

'That's enough,' said Cordelia, but her voice was as expressionless
as his had been.

'You have something against cops?' said Malone.

The boy shrugged, the silver worms slid along his broad shoulders.

'Did you like your grandfather?'

A bean-ball, but the boy didn't flinch. 'No.'

'Did you dislike him enough to want him dead?'

'Stop this!' Cordelia snatched off her glasses, leant forward as if
she might strike Malone. Beside him Malone felt Kate Arletti tense

56

and he wondered what she would do if Cordelia actually attacked him.

Malone ignored the mother, kept his eyes on the son. 'Where were you the night before last, Ross?'

'He was here, at home,' said Cordelia.

But the boy proved to be the rebel Kate had said he was: 'No, I wasn't. Let's stick to the truth, Mum. I spent the night at my girl friend's.'

Cordelia turned her head away, looked for a moment as if she might get up and stalk away into the house. Malone said, 'Her name?'

'She's Rosie Gilligan.'

Malone looked blank, but Kate, it seemed, was *au fait* with a wider world. 'The fashion editor of the *Chronicle*?'

'Yeah,' said Ross and his mother turned back to give him a glare that was apparent even through the dark glasses.

'How do you get on with your cousins, Ross?'

The boy shrugged again. Malone wondered what he himself had been like at twenty, though he didn't think he could have been as ungracious and surly as this kid. But behaviour, like tastes, always looked different from another generation.

'And with your brother and sister?' Malone glanced at his notebook. 'Colin and Alexandra?'

'We're a happy family,' said Cordelia.

'I was talking to your son, Mrs Huxwood ... Do you ever get together, Ross, you and your brother and sister and your cousins and discuss the family fortune?'

Cordelia abruptly stood up; her greased arms shivered with light. 'No, shut up, Ross!' as her son went to make some reply; then she turned on Malone. 'That's enough, Mr Malone. You've gone too far –'

He interrupted her: 'Mrs Huxwood, I don't think you appreciate just how far we often have to go to solve a murder. Now you can get a lawyer, if you wish –' He took his time about getting to his feet; it was one small way of showing her that he, and not she, was in command here. 'I overheard you and your sister-in-law the other night saying that voices will be heard. They will be, Mrs Huxwood. Police voices asking questions that you may not like but that you'll be expected to answer. Thanks for the coffee.'

As the two detectives turned away, Ross Huxwood said, 'Shit.'

Malone turned back. 'You talking to me?'

The boy, still lolling back in his chair, stared up at him, the shades hiding his eyes. Then he shook his head. 'No. Sorry you heard that.'

'You could teach him some manners, Cordelia,' said Malone and led Kate across the lawn towards the Big House.

'Good on you, boss,' said Kate. 'I was just itching to clout him across the ears. When I was in uniform I broke the arm of a lout like him.'

'You're a real killer, aren't you?' he said, remembering the junkie's nose that had been broken by the butt of her gun. 'But I think young Ross would've been a bit big for you. Who's his girl friend? Rose whatever-her-name is?'

'Rosie Gilligan. She's the fashion editor of the *Chronicle*. They reckon she'll be another Ita Buttrose or a Nene King before too long,' she said, naming two of the country's most successful women editors. 'I'd have thought she was a bit long in the tooth for young Ross.'

'How old?'

'I'm only guessing, but she must be thirty.'

'How old are you, Kate?'

She grinned: she was very attractive, he decided, when she smiled. 'Twenty-four. But Rosie's not only *old* she's pretty soiled, too, so I hear. She's a real man-eater, she's called the Nutcracker Suite.' He raised his eyebrows and she made a mock duck of her head. 'Sorry.'

'You get around, Kate. So you think Ross is her toy-boy and his mum doesn't like it?'

'Something like that. Mums never want their boys to get involved with older women. Do you think Ross wants more money so's he can keep up with Rosie? She's pretty extravagant, so I'm told. Likes to lunch at all the best restaurants, Rockpool and Level 41, places like that, takes her holidays overseas – she wouldn't come cheap.'

'Kate, where do you get all your dirt?'

'I have a younger sister who's a model. She goes to all the fashion parties and all they do is gossip, she says. When she's with me, that's what we do.'

'Well, you and I have had a nice little gossip –' Then his pager beeped. 'Let's get back to the car.'

On the car phone he dialled Homicide and asked for Clements. 'What is it, Russ?'

'Another report in from Rose Bay. Two shots were fired last night

58

in Point Piper, at The Briarcliff. They hit a Mercedes, just missing the driver and his wife – they were unhurt, fortunately.'

'So?'

'Scobie, the Merc got in the line of fire – the shots were meant for the two people getting out of a Daimler, another guy and his wife.'

'Russ, right now I'm not interested in *attempted* murder –'

'You haven't caught on, have you? The Briarcliff, that's where Jack Aldwych Junior and his wife live. They were the couple getting out of the Daimler.'

2

'We didn't want any fuss,' said Jack Aldwych Senior. 'If that couple downstairs hadn't complained you wouldn't have heard anything about it.'

'Jack,' said Malone, 'that couple downstairs almost copped those shots in the head. They had a right to complain.'

The old criminal boss (retired, he insisted, not reformed) nodded reluctantly. 'I suppose so. But in the old days –'

'These aren't the old days, Jack. You agree with me?' He looked at Jack Junior.

The son sighed with exasperation. 'I don't think Dad realizes how much it shook me and Julie. Neither of us has ever been shot at before.'

'You haven't lived,' said his father.

'Mrs Chang, downstairs, passed out,' said Juliet Aldwych. 'So did her husband, almost.' She said it with the superiority of someone who had never fainted in her life, as if she were as accustomed to passing bullets as much as her father-in-law. 'One doesn't expect that sort of thing, not in Point Piper.'

The Briarcliff was a block of eight apartments, none of which could be bought for less than several million dollars. Six of the apartments were owned by Hong Kong Chinese, all unable to believe their luck in getting a waterfront home for less than half they would have paid for a place halfway up The Peak in Hong Kong. Point Piper, a manicured finger of land pointing out into the harbour, was one of the best addresses in Sydney. True, it had been named after a naval officer who was both a rake and a conman, and he had been followed by

59

others of the same inclination, none of them reducing the locality's value with their reputations. Sydney's eastern suburbs residents, so long as they have a water view, are prone to forgive their neighbours anything. Except, perhaps, seduction of their own wives and a looting of their assets.

Kate had dropped Malone off at the entrance to the apartments. Crime Scene tapes roped off a silver Mercedes, giving the impression that the car had somehow strayed in from the used car lots out along Parramatta Road. One of the Physical Evidence team, a redheaded slim young man, came across to Malone.

'Morning, sir. We've found the bullets – Thirty-twos, they look like. And a cartridge shell out there –' He nodded towards the quiet street. 'Looks like they were parked at the kerb there, waiting. We haven't found anything else.'

Then Clements had arrived from Strawberry Hills and the PE man went back to examining the Mercedes. 'What d'you reckon? Were they after Old Jack?'

'Let's ask him.'

And Jack Aldwych had told them: *we didn't want any fuss.*

'You sure they were meant for you?' Malone asked.

Jack Junior spread his hands. Both father and son were distinguished-looking men, tall and heavily built; the father's face, however, in repose had a hint of latent cruelty in it, like that in the faces of Italian *condottieri* or some of Genghis Khan's lieutenants. Jack Junior was not soft-looking, but, unlike his father, he had never had to kill a man or, as a small businessman, start life as a hold-up thug. He had had respectability thrust upon him by his mother and so far the mantle had not slipped. Well, not very far and then only once.

'You mean they might have been after Mr and Mrs Chang?' He shook his thickly-thatched head. 'When we bought this apartment, Dad had everyone else in the block checked.'

'I had Les Chung do it for me,' said Jack Senior, naming a one-time partner in crime, another of those now pushing open the door into respectability. 'There are no Triad bosses in here. They are all Hong Kong business people, some of 'em retired, some of 'em still in business back in Hong Kong. They're here because they dunno what's gunna happen in 1997, they're taking out insurance. You can't blame 'em, you never know what the Commos are gunna do.' Like all true-

60

blue criminal bosses, Aldwych was a true-blue conservative; socialism and communism were the heinous crimes. 'Whoever fired the shots was after Jack and Julie.'

Juliet shuddered, but it seemed more an act than a genuine shiver of fear. Malone had not seen her in two years, since she and Jack Junior had been involved peripherally in another case, but she did not appear to have changed in the slightest. Her dark hair was still cut in the same stylish bob, her skin was as flawless as ever and her voice was still throaty and, Malone thought, phony. He was surprised that she and Jack Junior were still together, but he had long ago given up trying to analyse relationships. Come priests, counsellors, lawyers, marriage was still an equation that ran right off the blackboard.

'Perhaps they thought you were in the car with us,' she said, then glanced at Malone and Clements. 'He stayed here last night instead of going home to Harbord. Jack and I went out to dinner, but Dad stayed home to watch TV.'

'*NYPD Blue*. Love those cop shows.' Aldwych grinned.

'Why would they be after you, Jack?' said Clements.

'They weren't,' said the old man flatly.

'So they were after you?' Clements looked at Jack Junior. 'Why?'

'I haven't the faintest idea.' But he couldn't hide the doubt in his dark brown eyes. Unlike his father, his eyes would always give him away: Shirl, his mother, had left him the wrong legacy.

'I think you do have an idea,' said Malone. 'Come on, out with it.'

The son glanced sideways at his father; there was a moment's silence, then Jack Senior said, 'Have you found out why Harry Huxwood was shot?'

'Not yet.' Malone kept the surprise out of his voice. 'You think last night had something to do with the Huxwood murder?'

'Better tell 'em, Jack,' said Aldwych.

Jack Junior took his time, looking down at his big hands as if they held an invisible file of notes. Then he looked up. 'We're in the bidding for Huxwood Press.'

Malone still held on to his surprise. 'I didn't know the selling-off was that public.'

'It isn't. Or it wasn't up till yesterday, when the other papers started to print what they'd only been guessing at. There are half a dozen starters, but the two favourites are Metropolitan Newspapers from London and ourselves.'

'Ourselves? Who exactly are *ourselves*? I don't know how much Huxwood Press is worth, but if it's anything like the bid for Fairfax and the *Herald* several years ago, you'd be talking – what?'

'Two billion,' said Clements, figures always at his tongue-tip. 'For complete control, the whole kit and boodle. Have you got that sort of money, Jack?' He looked at the elder Aldwych.

'No.' Nobody, not even the old man himself, knew how much he was worth. He was on the board of none of the companies that, through his son, he owned; but neither is God on the board of the Vatican. The knee was always bent to Aldwych, even in his absence.

'So you've got partners?' Malone left it to Clements, the business expert, to ask the questions.

'Yes.'

'We're not pulling out your teeth, Jack,' said Clements. 'Loosen up a bit. Who're your partners? They might be the next ones shot at. Next time the bullets may hit home.'

Again Juliet shuddered: Malone began to think she might well be afraid.

Jack Junior took over from his father. 'They are an overseas concern, I can't tell you their name, not yet. Our holding company has eight per cent of Huxwood stock and we're still buying.'

'The price went up this morning,' said Clements. 'Soon's the word got out Huxwood might be for sale, the sharks moved in. They probably haven't given a thought to the murder.'

'Capitalism,' said Aldwych senior, grinning again. 'Whoever said it had any time for sentiment?'

'Or sympathy,' said Malone.

'You're a Commo, Scobie.'

'Our overseas friends are ready to come in and buy up seven per cent – fact is, they're doing that now.'

'That still leaves you a helluva lot to buy if you want total control.'

'We don't want one hundred per cent control. We have someone local who'll throw in their share and that'll give us enough control, when we've made our bid.'

'Who's the local?'

Jack Junior shook his head. 'I can't tell you that, either. I've already told you too much.'

'No, you haven't,' said Malone. 'When we've got a murder on our hands and an attempted murder, you can never tell us too much. That right, Jack?' He looked at the old man.

'Scobie, I'd never tell the police how to work,' he said piously. He was dressed in a dark-blue checked shirt, dark-blue trousers and a purple-red alpaca cardigan; he looked like an old Renaissance cardinal on holiday, too old for minor sins but still capable of the major ones, like murder. 'But I'll be calling up some old friends, see that Jack and Julie don't have to worry.'

'Protection, you mean? Jack, don't start anything.'

'The other side, whoever they are, have already started it. Aren't you giving protection to the rest of the Huxwood family, the ones who want to sell?'

'We haven't sorted them all out yet. Do you know who they are?'

'Haven't a clue,' said Aldwych, stone-faced except for the amused glint in his still-bright eyes.

They were sitting out on the terrace of the apartment, shaded from the sun by a large umbrella. Malone looked out at the harbour as a sleek launch swung round in a swift curve, slicing the water into a long white shaving; a flock of gulls exploded upwards, mewing in protest. A boy and a girl in the speedboat waved to someone onshore, then sped away down the harbour.

'The Chang kids,' said Juliet.

'They don't seem too upset that Mum and Dad have been shot at,' said Clements.

'They're Orientals,' said Aldwych, amusement still glowing in his eyes. 'Maybe they're fatalists. Les Chung is always preaching to me about it.'

'I didn't think he'd need to preach, Jack, not to you. If ever I've seen a fatalist, you're one.'

Aldwych smiled. 'Nice of you to say so, Scobie. I'll tell Les.'

'Jack and I aren't fatalists,' said Juliet. She was from Roumania where crystal balls, despite or perhaps because of the gypsy population, are suspect.

'No, you're not,' said her father-in-law, 'and that's why you're gunna get protection.'

'When do you make your bid for Huxwood?' asked Clements. 'How much are you offering? They were eleven-fifty on yesterday's board, but they've gone up since then.'

'You follow the stock exchange?' said Jack Junior.

'I have two thousand Huxwood shares.'

Jack Junior did not seem all that impressed that a police sergeant should own twenty-three thousand dollars' worth of shares in one company. But Aldwych Senior, who had once bought cops as his son bought shares, raised an eyebrow.

'We're offering twelve-fifty,' said Jack Junior.

'That won't get you many takers.'

'Meaning you wouldn't sell at that price? Russ, you always start with a low bid – you do if you're sensible. We're not like some of those ratbags back in the Eighties.'

'I'd take a shot at him myself if he offered too much,' said his father, and Juliet shuddered again but was smiling as she did so.

Malone stood up. 'Any more trouble, Jack, and you get in touch with us, okay? And if you get a lead on who fired those shots . . .'

'You'll be the first to know, Scobie,' said Aldwych, but both men knew that wasn't the truth.

Juliet escorted the two detectives to the front door through an apart-ment where money had been spent lavishly. Back in Roumania she had been born to a heritage that had soon disappeared under Commu-nism, but the rich touch takes several generations to filter out of the blood and so far she hadn't lost a drop of it. Jack Junior was her second husband, richer than her first, and she had brought as her dowry all her inherited extravagance. Out in the entrance hall, standing on carpet that Malone could feel through his shoes like oozing cream, he said, 'Mrs Aldwych, if there's any hint of more trouble, let us know. Your father-in-law won't.'

'You don't think I'd dare go against him, do you?'

'Yes, I think you would.'

She smiled, opened the door that looked as if it could withstand a tank charge. 'Possibly. Where I came from, Inspector, second thoughts were always best.'

She gave each of them her hand, palm down, as if expecting them to kiss it. Malone managed to restrain himself: where he came from,

Erskineville, kissing hands was never given even a first thought. You would be suspected of perversion.

3

Out in the driveway Malone looked at the Mercedes, no longer surrounded by Crime Scene tapes. The PE team had gone and a middle-aged Chinese was about to get into the car.

'Mr Chang?' Malone introduced himself and Clements. 'When you drove in here last night, did you take any notice of a car standing out there at the kerb?'

'No, Inspector.' He had a lean pleasant face spoiled only by the pitted cheeks; smallpox had marked him when he was young, before he had had the money to pay for vaccination. He was conservatively dressed with the care that Malone had remarked in people who did not want to be noticed, the new rich who did not want their riches displayed. Yet they always somehow gave themselves away: the top-of-the-range car, the expensive apartment, the gold watch that proved they could afford all the time in the world. 'There *was* a car parked there – I think. But when I'd got over the shock –' He shook his head. 'It was gone.'

'You have no enemies, Mr Chang?'

'Oh no, no! My wife and I live very quietly, Inspector –' He did not appear offended by the question. He said innocently, 'Does Mr Aldwych have enemies?'

The bugger's having me on. 'I don't think so, Mr Chang. The Briarcliff, I'm sure, could be mistaken for a convent, everyone's so spotless.'

'You're having me on, Inspector.' The pitted cheeks creased in a smile.

'Never, Mr Chang.'

Taking the unmarked police car out of the driveway Clements said, 'Where to now? Back to the office?'

'While we're here on Point Piper, let's call on Nigel Huxwood and his missus. You've got their address?'

The Nigel Huxwoods lived not on the waterfront but up on the ridge of the point, in the penthouse of a ten-storey block. The two

65

detectives announced themselves over the intercom and when they stepped out of the lift Nigel was waiting for them at his apartment's open front door. As he had been two nights ago he was all charm; once again Malone wondered what sort of detective he had played on British screens. He couldn't remember ever seeing a charming cop on British screens, at least not on television. They were ex-alcoholics, misogynists or had a chip on their shoulders against all their colleagues.

'Come in, gentlemen, come in! Any progress? Coffee? Oh darling, here are the police again.' His wife had come into the room, followed by a boy and a girl who looked like twins, in their mid-twenties. 'Oh, my – our son and daughter, Michael and Sarah.'

Brenda Huxwood, in a yellow silk shirt and dark green slacks, gave the police a bright smile and seated herself on a couch behind a coffee table. The elder Huxwoods, either through unconscious theatrical habit or with deliberate intent, were spreading charm like jam. The junior Huxwoods, however, were glum and stiff, though Malone was glad to see that they did not appear to be cop-haters like their cousin Ross.

The girl said she would get the coffee and the boy sat down beside his stepmother. Nigel fell into a deep chair, relaxed and affable, almost as if he welcomed the detectives' arrival. Malone wondered what he did with his time, if he was bored.

'So there's no news? Is that good news, as they say?'

'Not for us, it isn't,' said Malone. *Crumbs, isn't someone in this family grieving?* 'We're still looking for a motive for your father's murder. Unless, of course, it all stems from the selling-off of Huxwood Press? We gather there are some members of the family who would like their share of the loot.'

'Loot?' said Brenda, charm suddenly gone. If she hadn't married money, eventually she might have played characters like her mother-in-law.

He had used the word deliberately, annoyed by Nigel's seeming insouciance. But (*don't lean on the family*): 'I'm sorry. We cops tend to talk in basics.'

Out of the corner of his eye he saw Nigel Huxwood grin. 'Nice line, Scobie.'

Michael, the son, was watching his father and his stepmother. He was slim and dark-haired, handsomer than his father and only saved

66

from being a pretty boy by the heavy Huxwood jaw. There was an air of repose about him that Malone had not found in the other Huxwoods; or perhaps it was an air of retreat, shutting himself off against whatever currents ran in this small family or the extended Huxwoods. He only looked at Malone when the latter spoke to him.

'Are you an heir, Michael?'

Brenda went to say something, but Nigel waved her silent. The boy gazed at Malone as if debating whether he should answer, then he nodded. 'Yes, my sister and I are heirs. All the grandchildren get equal shares. Roughly fifty million dollars each. The loot, as you call it.'

Then his sister came back into the big living room, put down a tray with cups and saucers, a coffee pot, a jug of milk and a plate of small pastries. Nigel at once reached for a pastry and began to eat it, gesturing to Malone and Clements to do the same. For him, it seemed, this meeting could not have been cosier.

'Are we talking money?' said Sarah, sitting down beside her brother, who moved up on the long couch to make room for her. She was as tall as he, also dark-haired, as good-looking but without the slightly heavy jaw. She did not have his composed air, there was more vitality to her, as if in her own circle she was accustomed to leading.

'We are,' said Brenda, pouring coffee. 'The subject seems to concern Inspector Malone.'

'We'll drop the subject, Mrs Huxwood, if you could suggest another reason why your father-in-law was murdered.'

The word 'murdered' seemed to jolt Sarah; her cup rattled in her saucer. Her brother put his hand on her bare knee; the pressure of his fingers seemed excessive for a comforting squeeze. When he took his hand away Malone saw the red marks left by his fingers.

Clements took over the bowling: 'Were you surprised at the murder?'

'Naturally,' said Brenda, in the most natural way.

Nigel had taken another pastry, was biting into it. He appeared to have taken a back seat, as if he had decided to be a spectator, though a hungry one. Like Brenda he was dressed brightly, in a red-and-blue checked shirt, French-blue cotton trousers and white boating shoes. Another Huxwood home where the funeral weeds had not yet been taken out of the closet.

'There was another near-murder last night.' Malone hoped that might jolt them; and it did.

Nigel put down the half-eaten pastry and leaned forward, flicking a crumb from the corner of his mouth. 'Who? You mean one connected to my father's murder?'

'We're considering the possibility. Have you heard of Landfall Holdings?'

Nigel nodded. 'Yes, they are in the bidding for Huxwood, they only let us know this week. Someone didn't try to kill Jack Aldwych? I used to read about him before I went overseas —'

'How do you know he's associated with Landfall?' said Clements. 'He's not on the board.'

'My father told me. He knew more corporation secrets than any man I know. Was it Jack Aldwych they were after?'

'The shots were fired at his son and his wife . . . I didn't think Jack Senior would be in the bidding. He's retired. From everything, he tells me.' Malone bit into a chocolate eclair, playing his own relaxed game. Licking his fingers, wiping cream from his lips, he looked as if he spent all his mornings at tea parties. But the party was no longer cosy, at least not on the part of the four Huxwoods. 'You know what he used to be? I thought you'd have missed out on his history, being away as long as you have been. From Australia, I mean.'

'How do you know how long my husband has been away?' said Brenda.

'I checked, Mrs Huxwood.' He hadn't; but lies are dangerous only in court. 'You know Jack Aldwych, the old one?'

'I know his daughter-in-law,' she said. 'We are on a couple of charity committees. For distressed actors.'

He managed to keep his tongue under control. She was an actor, but he'd bet she had never been distressed. Especially not now, with a starring part in the Huxwood money.

Nigel said, 'Isn't Jack Senior somehow related to the Police Minister?'

'Why, yes he is.' Malone affected surprise; but he knew Nigel wasn't taken in. 'His daughter-in-law's sister is married to Mr Sweden. If you follow the connection —'

'Oh, I do,' said Nigel. 'Connections are always useful, no matter how tenuous.'

Michael was still the most composed of the family, still lolling back as if discussing a picnic he had missed. 'There was nothing in the papers this morning, or on the radio about any shots at the Aldwyches.'

'Unless the *Chronicle* is going to run a piece on it?' Clements' mouth was half-full of pastry. 'We don't think it would do much for Huxwood Press if it got out that someone is prepared to do multiple murders to stop the sale of the Press. Do you?'

'Who told you the murderer is against the sale?' Sarah, suddenly tense, leaned forward.

'That was just a guess on Sergeant Clements' part,' said Malone. 'Do you mean your grandfather was shot because he *didn't* want to sell?'

'Nobody knew what the bloody hell he wanted!' Nigel got up quickly, stood a moment, then abruptly sat down again.

'So we've been told,' said Malone mildly.

'Oh? Who told you that?' But Malone just smiled and shook his head and Nigel went on, 'Well, whoever it was, he or she was right. I don't think any of us knew which way Dad would go on the sale.'

'Someone did,' said Malone. 'He – or she – must've guessed that your father was *for* the sale. That was why he – or she – took the shots at young Jack Aldwych, to frighten off the bidders.'

'There are other bidders?' said Clements, mouth clear now. 'We've heard there are.'

Nigel frowned, but it was his son who said, 'The London crowd? Mrs Supple? You mean she might be on the list?'

Malone dodged the question. 'What do you do, Michael?'

'I'm a merchant banker. With Kohn and Company.'

'Are Kohn and Company involved in all this?'

'Not at my level, no. At senior partners level, yes, they are advising.'

'You must find that interesting. Whether the senior partners are going to help you net fifty million dollars?' *Oh, am I leaning on the family!*

'That's a bit close to the bone, old chap,' said Nigel, but did not appear unduly upset.

'We get that way sometimes . . . Neither you nor your sister went to work today? What do you do, Sarah?'

'I'm in the classified ads department at the *Chronicle*, learning the ropes.'

'The rivers of gold,' said Clements.

Everyone looked impressed; even Malone. Sarah said, 'You seem to know a lot about newspapers, Sergeant.'

'Not much,' said Clements modestly. 'I just know what generates money.'

'I advised them to take today off,' said Brenda, the sun striking in through a window, turning the yellow silk to bright gold. 'As a gesture of mourning. The funeral is tomorrow.'

'The body's been released?' said Clements. 'It's usually not as quick as that in a murder.'

'My brother Derek pulled some strings,' said Nigel.

'They always come in handy, don't they?' said Malone, rising from his chair. 'The strings, the connections. Assistant Commissioner Zanuch?' He was treading on dangerous ground here.

'Possibly,' said Nigel, ravelling the strings. 'My brother seems to know everyone.'

Malone was ready to go. It was his belief that police interrogations should be like night club acts: always leave them wanting more. It often did not work with experienced crims, but the general public, brought in for questioning or questioned in their own home as now, always wondered what the unasked questions would have been. He would be back to ask those questions, including one or two about the scrap of notepaper in his pocket.

'You have a wonderful view. Can you see the *Chronicle* building from here?' He doubted it: nobody knew better than he the dips and ridges of Sydney.

'No.' Sarah stood up beside him. She pointed, not once but twice. He had remarked that she used her hands awkwardly, like a bad actor or a television reporter who had been directed to 'do something with your hands'. 'But it's there, we can *feel* it, even if we can't see it. The *Chronicle* is an institution, it's been on that site, not the same building, of course, for a hundred and fifty years.'

He looked at the distant city skyline, at the buildings whose architecture did not have the distinction of certain other cities but in their clean silhouettes complemented the clear light that bathed it. It was his city and in his heart he was sworn to defend it. Its history was not ancient, but it had its traditions and institutions. And the *Chronicle*, as Sarah had said, was one of them.

'You're one of those who don't want to sell, aren't you, Sarah?'

Though his back was towards them, he felt the alertness, even the tension, of the other three Huxwoods.

'Yes,' she said, her own back turned to her parents and her brother, not even glancing over her shoulder at them.

He wanted to say 'Good', but he had warned Kate Arletti against bias. He just nodded and hoped he looked non-committal.

Going down in the lift Clements said, 'This family has so much money! Why the hell do they want more?'

'Do you think one of them killed for it?'

'Yes. You and Greg Random said not to point the finger. But sooner or later one of the Huxwoods is gunna point the finger at another of them. I want to be there when he or she does it.'

'He or she?'

'Gender doesn't enter into it, not with fifty million bucks as your part of the kitty. You couldn't get a better prize for equal opportunity.'

'You're a cynic.'

'Yeah. It makes you feel good, doesn't it?'

4

The first John Huxwood had set up shop in the Haymarket in 1840: a job printery that also published a two-page newssheet which he called the *Sydney Chronicle*. He lived behind the shop six days a week, driving home by horse and buggy to spend Saturday night and Sunday with his wife and small family at Vaucluse. The shop was surrounded by pubs and brothels. Wool wagons would come in from the outlying districts and the brokers would meet the wagoners in the pubs to do their deals; they possibly also came across each other in the brothels, but the commodity there had nothing to do with the national wealth. The *Chronicle* was the first paper to run a list of wool, grain and hay prices. It didn't bother to run quotes on sex, since the price remained constant. The brothel madams and their pimps knew the value of a cartel.

The weekend nights in the Haymarket were often wild, but somehow the printery, in the midst of the fights and riots, was never wrecked. The occasional brick was thrown through the shop's windows, but

71

that was only a more solid version of a letter to the editor and not unusual in those days. The *Chronicle* printed what those who could read wanted to read: gossip. About the 'bunyip aristocracy', the free settlers who wanted to create a colonial equivalent of the class system they had left back in England; about the peccadilloes of unnamed (but recognized) officials; and about the Queen and her penny-pinching Consort. Later, Huxwoods conveniently forgot that their institution started life as a tabloid.

The number of pubs decreased, the brothels moved further east as the area around the Haymarket began to prosper. John Huxwood and then his eldest son Roger bought up the sites on which the pubs and brothels had stood and enlarged the premises of the *Chronicle*, which had now become a daily and was edging towards respectability and influence. Its soiled edges had been washed out, its liberalism watered down, its classified advertisements as important as its news pages. The Huxwoods now featured in the paper's own social columns. John Huxwood travelled home to England, went to Buckingham Palace, bent his knee and was knighted by the Queen, who had never read the *Chronicle* and wasn't quite sure why she was dubbing him Sir John. Another institution was being built: the Huxwoods themselves.

Huxwood Press expanded: other newspapers were bought and absorbed. In 1935 Sir John Huxwood, the first Sir John's grandson, built the present building, a thumb-to-the-nose at the Depression by the most quixotic of the Huxwoods. The Press moved to temporary premises and the finest example of Art Deco architecture in the city, ten storeys above ground and three below, went up in just ten months. The building unions, forever afterwards, thought of it as their biggest shame and wondered what sort of scabs must have been employed.

Osbert Beckett had researched all this when, five years ago, he had written a history of the *Chronicle* to mark its one hundred and fiftieth anniversary. In terms of service he was the senior employee, longer there than even some of the printers; he, too, was an institution. He had begun as a cadet on shipping rounds, done local government meetings, been a crime reporter, worked in the press gallery of both State and Federal parliaments, written editorials: he was that rarity today, an all-round newspaperman. He was sixty-two years of age, a small man with a jockey's face and a bookie's scepticism; but he had never been a turf writer, horse-racing being one field in which he preferred to remain ignorant. His one opinion on the game was that bookmakers were the supreme philosophers: they were constant in their reading of Man as a sucker.

Yesterday he had been at the eleven o'clock conference, the first of the three daily editorial meetings, when the decision had been made on how to cover the Huxwood murder. Usually Derek Huxwood, as executive editor, presided over the gathering of the editor, the managing editor, the four deputy editors, the chief-of-staff and the two associate editors, of whom he was one.

Gary Shoemaker, the editor, had taken the vacant chair, just beating Warren Gates to it. Gates had had wide experience as a journalist before being promoted to general manager; jealous of his journalistic reputation, he had insisted that he be called managing editor. He and Shoemaker were bitter rivals, but only he let it show. The other six men at the long oval table pretended not to notice the grown-ups' version of musical chairs.

The meeting was about to start when Donald Derx, the literary editor, put his head in the doorway. 'I was planning to run a page on Saturday about true crimes, I've got a dozen books on my desk. You think that might be in bad taste in the circumstances?'

Derx, a wispy little man who wore his glasses on his forehead, was another veteran, another cynic. He had once suggested running a campaign to have Elle Macpherson ('I never read anything I haven't written myself') as chairperson of the Literature Board, but the idea had been scotched.

'Oh, I wouldn't run it, Donald,' said Gates, jumping in ahead of Shoemaker. 'You're right, it'd be very bad taste.'

'Yes, I thought so, too,' said Derx and looked wryly round the table and disappeared.

'Okay, let's get down to cases,' said Shoemaker. 'Who do we put on the story? The murder?' He looked down the table at Beckett. 'How about you, Ossie? Like to try your hand at crime again?'

'I don't think so.' Beckett had grown lazy, something he admitted to himself but not to anyone else. 'I'll sub it, but I don't think I should take it away from Grace Ditcham.'

Grace Ditcham was the best all-round crime reporter in the State; she had all the best contacts on both sides of the line between police and criminals. Beckett had lured her away from the main opposition, the *Herald*, and he was determined to remain her protector. She would come to the Huxwood murder with a completely open mind, she was free of the jealousies and prejudices and loyalties that infected most of those who had worked for the *Chronicle* for a number of years. Including all those seated round this table this morning.

'How much do we give it?' said Gates.

'I'm not giving up any space,' said Errol Dibbs, the foreign news deputy editor. He guarded the rest of the world as if it were his empire; local news was incidental, not at all ever likely to be history.

'I suppose we should mention it.' That was Tony Bolte, the business deputy editor. 'It may cause a blip on the market.'

Beckett listened to the conversation as it roller-coastered round the table, his experienced ear picking out the innuendos as each man tried to guard his domain. With no domain to protect, he stirred the pot: 'The obit's written, it's on file. But are we going to have an editorial? Who'll write it?'

'That'd better be me,' said Gates quickly, pulling at his moustache. 'I've known him longest –'

'I'll do it,' said Shoemaker flatly, and that was that: Gates subsided.

In the end the *Chronicle* treated the murder of its publisher with restraint. Also in the end, Osbert Beckett wrote the editorial. Shoemaker came to him after the meeting and said, 'Os, you knew the Old Man better than any of us. He could be a bastard, but do right by him. If the paper's sold, at least let's give him a decent send-off.'

That had been yesterday. Beckett wrote the editorial, tried to be fair but was not sure that those in the know would not have read between the lines. He had a feeling of demolition.

Then he looked out through the open doorway of his cubbyhole of an office and saw Scobie Malone and recognized the demolition man.

5

Clements had dropped Malone outside the newspaper's offices. 'I'll talk to Rosie Gilligan on my own. Two of us might frighten her, we're not fashion material.'

'Watch out for her,' said Clements. 'She's a man-eater.'

He drove away before Malone could ask him where he got his

gossip. He went into the building, told the uniformed man on the reception desk who he was and whom he wanted to see. 'You investigating Sir Harry's murder? And you wanna see the *fashion* editor?'

'Are you an editor?' The man shook his head. 'I thought you might've been, from that question. Miss Gilligan, please.'

He rode up to the fourth floor, stepped out into the main newsroom and asked for Rosie Gilligan. Like most cops he had a suspicion of the media; in all his years in the service he had never been in a newspaper's newsroom. He walked down the vast room, past the journalists tapping away at their VDTs, phones cradled on their shoulders, some eating an early lunch; those that recognized him, old police reporters, waved to him, eyeing him warily. The boss was dead, murder had come home to the *Chronicle*. Had they missed something that reporters from other newspapers had dug up? Whom, as the reporters over fifty would have put it, was he coming to see? *Rose Gilligan*, for Crissake?

Malone felt the energy around him; newspapers pumped blood into the community, not always good blood. He wondered how much of the *Chronicle*'s own blood would be lost if and when the paper was sold.

Rosie Gilligan's office was a glass-walled closet in which one could not have swung a cat-o'-nine-tails: a description which, Lisa could have told him, had been applied to Miss Gilligan's pen. Two walls were decorated with press photos of herself with celebrities, both recognizable and unrecognizable; Malone wondered if she was one of those people who couldn't define themselves unless they were tagged with some celebrity. In a quick glance around he saw that he was surrounded by her smile, miles of it.

She rose to greet him, all smiles. 'Fred downstairs said you were on your way up –'

She was not beautiful but, with skilful make-up, she had managed to create the impression that she was. Her face was too square, her mouth too wide, her neck too short; but she had attractive lively eyes, a mane of reddish-brown hair that looked as if it had been cut to toss, and a figure that was perhaps a little too rounded but suggested an abundance of sensuality. Malone could imagine any young man like Ross Huxwood wanting to experience her in more ways than the

75

obvious. She would have a talent for educating young men.

She waved him to the single chair in front of her crowded desk, tossed her hair and sat down. 'Is this about Sir Harry's murder? Why me?'

'That's what Fred downstairs asked. I didn't tell him it was because of young Ross.'

'*Young* Ross? Is that a dig at me?' But she was still smiling.

'Don't let's get off on the wrong foot, Miss Gilligan. Your relationship with Ross is none of our concern.'

'Sorry. I thought you must've come from a little talk with his mum. She thinks I'm going to be the ruin of him.' She sat back in her chair. She was dressed in a white shirt and a green skirt; a green jacket hung on a hanger in a corner, obscuring half a dozen photos. Malone wondered if fashion editors always had to be better dressed than their subject. 'The romance, affair, fling, whatever you want to call it, is over, Inspector. I ended it two nights ago.'

'The night Sir Harry was murdered?'

Her smile widened; her teeth, he guessed, were capped, expensively so. 'You don't think there's any connection, do you? No, I shouldn't be facetious. Sir Harry was a nice guy, we'll miss him. An old guy but nice, especially to us girls on the staff.'

'How well did you know him?'

'I worked for him.' All at once she sounded guarded. 'I've been here at the *Chronicle* thirteen years. He was not one of those chairmen who stayed in the boardroom all the time. He knew us all.'

'Monday night – what time did you show Ross the door?'

She laughed; she had a good laugh, right from her belly. 'I like that. I showed him the door about, I dunno, about ten o'clock, I guess. We'd been out to dinner and we'd been arguing all night.'

'What about?'

'Come on, Mr Malone – I'm not going to tell you that. It was personal, between him and me.'

'Fair enough. So he didn't spend the night with you?'

She was sharp: 'He said he did?' She shook her head; the mane swung back and forth like a shampoo commercial. 'No, he was gone by ten o'clock. I haven't seen him since.'

'Did Ross ever talk about his grandfather?'

She shook her head again; this time the hair hardly moved. 'Is Ross a suspect or something? If he is, find your own evidence, Inspector.'

'If Sir Harry was such a nice old guy, I thought you might help find who killed him.'

She stared at him, then looked past him at someone in the doorway. Malone turned his head; a young girl stood there. Something told him she might have been standing there for some seconds before Rosie Gilligan had acknowledged her presence.

'Yes, Alex? Inspector Malone, this is Alexandra Huxwood, Mr Derek's daughter. My assistant.'

She was about twenty, Malone guessed. She had her mother's, rather than her father's, looks; she would never compete against the models of the fashion world. But under someone's tutelage (her mother's? Rosie's?) she had done her best to make the most of what she had. Her make-up was as skilfully applied as Rosie's, she wore a dark-blue mini-dress that showed off her good legs. All that spoiled her was a certain hardness of look, an unspoken aggressiveness. Malone had seen it before: in the faces of those who had had to take the silver spoon from their mouth and swap it for a wooden coffee stirrer. Life at the bottom could be difficult for some.

She nodded to Malone without smiling. 'Nice to meet you, Inspector. My father has mentioned you.'

'I'm afraid I'm going to be mentioned quite a lot for a while. Till we find out who murdered your grandfather.' He was bulldozing his way into this family, but so far the gentle, sympathetic approach had not got him far.

She didn't flinch or look hurt. 'You haven't got very far, have you? So Dad tells me.'

'It's early days yet. We've just solved one case that's taken us seven years. Detective work isn't like fashion – the seasons have nothing to do with it.' He smiled, but the chill from both women suggested winter fashions were just around the corner.

'What is it, Alex?' Rosie's tone suggested that her junior had taken up enough time.

'There's a fax from Karl Lagerfeld. Apparently you can have only one seat for their spring collection. In the back row.'

Malone abruptly felt like the net-cord judge in a tennis match; he was likely to be hit in the ear at any moment. The fashion editor and her assistant were not playing a friendly game.

'I'll talk to you later.' Rosie Gilligan waved a dismissive hand, gave her attention once more to Malone. 'What were we saying, Inspector?'

Malone had turned his back on Alexandra Huxwood, but he could feel her standing in the doorway for a few seconds; then she was gone. Rosie Gilligan said, 'I have my problems with young Alex. You always do with the boss's kids.'

'How many others have worked here?'

'They all have, in their school holidays, before they went on to other things. Where were we?'

'I was hoping you'd help me find who murdered Sir Harry.'

'So you were. Why me?' Then once again she looked past him. 'Come in, Ossie. You know Inspector Malone?'

'Old mates. G'day, Scobie, I saw you come in. You getting some fashion hints? I'm told pleated trousers are out this year. Or are they in?'

Malone had known Beckett in his days as a crime reporter, but he had lost track of him when he disappeared into the editorial upper reaches of the *Chronicle*.

'Hello, Ossie. Miss Gilligan and I have just been discussing a mutual acquaintance. I don't think she'd give me any hints on fashion.'

'Oh, I'd give you a hint,' she said. 'Wear an overcoat, buttoned up to the neck. You must be the squarest dresser since Kruschev.'

'She talks to me the same way,' Beckett grinned. 'They have no respect for anyone, fashion editors. You here about Sir Harry's murder?'

Malone nodded. 'You thinking about coming back on police rounds to write about it?'

'Nah, nah.' He had a flat voice, the vowels squeezed out. 'I'm now an associate editor, whatever that means. I'm supposed to edit what Rosie, amongst others, writes, but nobody ever takes any notice of me. You don't, do you, old girl? It was better back in the days of sub-editors – nobody argued with our blue pencils. You wanna come along to my cubbyhole?'

Malone looked around him. 'You work in a closet, too?'

'Huxwood Press has never believed in fringe benefits. Only at our boardroom level. Don't quote me.'

'Why do you all stay on, then? Miss Gilligan says she's been here thirteen years, you've been here since – when? The Boer War?'

Beckett looked at the fashion editor. 'Why have we stayed, Rosie?'

Again there was the toss of the mane as she took her time. She had been smiling at the two men, but now she sobered. 'Loyalty, I think. Loyalty to the principles of the paper. There's been no other paper in Sydney that's stuck to its liberal principles the way the *Chronicle* has.'

Malone hesitated, then said, 'It wasn't too liberal during the Vietnam War. It was all the way with LBJ.' He had escaped the draft because he had just joined the police force, but he could remember as a cadet having to fight with demonstrators, young men whom he had agreed with but who saw him as the enemy.

The fashion editor and the associate editor looked at each other, then Beckett said, 'We're not proud of that, those of us who were here at the time. Those editorials were written by Lady Phillipa, or were dictated by her. Sir Harry gave in to her, we never knew why. She was a hawk, always has been.'

'Sir Harry wasn't?'

'I'll tell you a story,' said Beckett, leaning against the wall; over his shoulder the Queen and Rosie Gilligan smiled at each other. 'In my early days I was a communist. Okay, a white-collar one, a parlour pink, if you like, but I belonged to the Party. We had a big crime story to cover, but I was laid up with a fractured ankle, I was hobbling around on a stick. Harry, he wasn't Sir Harry then, told me I'd still have to cover it, that he'd get me a car and a driver. Two hours later he took me down into the street and there was a brand-new Holden. In those days the waiting time for delivery of a Holden was something like twelve months. Harry opened the door, handed me in, leaned in and said, ''The Party couldn't do that for you, could it, Ossie?'' That was the only time he ever mentioned he knew I was a Commo. So long as I did my job, I was okay.'

Malone stood up, thanked Rosie Gilligan for her time. 'You won't mind if I come back? I'll wear my best rags.'

'I don't think there'd be much improvement. You're the sort of Aussie male makes me want to emigrate to Italy. Did you ever wear a safari suit?'

'No, but I've worn socks with my thongs.'

'I'm not surprised.'

79

Passing through the newsroom, all eyes on them with search-light intensity, Beckett said, 'You been talking to her about young Ross Huxwood?'

'You know about that?'

'Everybody does. He used to hang around her like a love-sick pup.'

'She says she's finished with him.'

'Good,' said Ossie Beckett and sounded prim.

His office was slightly bigger than Rosie Gilligan's but still a cubby-hole. He dropped into his chair behind a desk much less cluttered than the fashion editor's had been, leaned forward on his elbows and said, 'So who do you think shot the boss?'

'As you used to write, Ossie, we haven't a clue. From what little I've learned so far, there could be half a dozen or more killed him. You got any suspects?'

'I wish I could name one. Harry had his faults — Christ, did he! — but he was a good boss and, except for Vietnam, he kept the paper to its principles.'

'What about Derek?'

'The same. It hasn't always been easy, there were others in the family besides Lady Phillipa who wanted the paper to take a different line on certain things — the republic issue, for instance. But Harry and Derek stuck to their own line, the one most of us agreed with.'

'What were some of the old man's faults?'

Beckett sat back. The walls of his office were undecorated; he could have spent thirty-five years in the newspaper game without ever having met a celebrity or read a headline that appealed to him. Elbow on the arm of his chair, he cupped his pointed chin in a thin, long-fingered hand. He was reluctant to answer Malone's question, but he had always had respect for the police and knew the difficulties they had with witnesses who abruptly clammed up.

'He was a vacillator, Scobie. Not all his life, just these past coupla years. He used options like playing cards, he'd throw a dozen on the table, then get up and walk away.'

'Someone else told me much the same thing,' said Malone, remembering Ned Custer. 'What other faults did Harry have?'

Beckett was even more reluctant this time, then he shrugged. 'If I don't tell you, someone else will. He was a ladies' man, he couldn't resist them. He tried to be discreet about it, but some of us knew what he was like. We kept quiet, for Lady Phillipa's sake. And the paper's too, I guess.'

'Was Rosie one of his ladies?'

'You don't miss much, do you? Yes, about three or four years ago. I don't think it lasted long, about six months or so.'

'Did he play around with any other women on the staff?'

Beckett stroked his chin, then dropped his hand, sat up, tried to look busy by pulling some copy-sheets towards him. 'No, I think I've told you enough, Scobie. I was never a gossip-hound and I don't think I want to start now.'

'Ossie, you can't leave me hanging out on a line like this. This is *murder*, mate – Sir Harry's murder. Who else did he go out with on the staff?'

It was a long moment before Beckett said, 'No one but Rosie Gilligan, not lately. Twenty-five years ago there was a girl here named Pamela Arnburg, a real looker. She was the librarian. Some of us knew about her and Harry, but we kept quiet. We all liked Pam, she was quite a dish, a bit reserved but she got on well with everyone. Harry did his balls over her, it was more than just an affair. Then one day Pam just literally disappeared. She went home from here one night and never came back. No word to anyone, no resignation, nothing. After a week the police were called in –'

'By Harry?'

'No, he just retreated from the scene – we didn't see him around the office for, I dunno, a coupla months at least. No, Dirk Prosser, who was the editor then, he got in touch with Missing Persons. They came in, made enquiries, but got nowhere. Those of us who knew about Pam and Harry kept our mouths shut. The police were here a coupla days, then we heard no more from them. I was on police rounds then, but I didn't follow it up – I guess I didn't want it to come out about Harry and Pam. Harry Danforth was in charge, but he said to forget it, that the file had been closed.'

Harry Danforth, who would have been a sergeant when in charge of Missing Persons, had retired several years ago as a Chief Superintendent, a rank that even his mother, if she had been alive, would have conceded he had not achieved on merit. Even though he had not known Danforth in his Missing Persons days, Malone could imagine

81

his closing a file without argument. Danforth had never been known to go looking for work.

'You ever see Danforth?' Beckett asked.

'No.' He and Russ Clements were convinced that Danforth had murdered a man they were trying to protect, but they had had no proof and the Chief Superintendent had taken his superannuation and retired. The case had been a complicated one and in the end Malone had been glad to walk away from it. It had been another of the frayed threads in a cop's life, but he had long ago come to recognize that justice was a loom in which the warp and weft were always likely to come apart. 'He lives up on the Gold Coast, I think.'

'I don't think so. I bumped into him a month or so ago. His wife's an asthmatic, the Gold Coast didn't suit her. They're living somewhere up in the Blue Mountains. I never liked him.'

'Who did?' said Malone, pleased that he could be so restrained. He got to his feet. 'Thanks, Ossie. What you've told me doesn't go any further, okay?'

'I've kept my mouth shut for twenty-five years. A while longer won't hurt me.'

But Malone had a feeling that secrets were beginning to stir.

As he passed down the newsroom he saw Alexandra Huxwood standing at a desk on the far side of the room. He smiled at her, but got no smile in return. He was tempted to cross the big room and ask her how she would vote on the sale of Huxwood Press. But as he slowed his step, she turned and walked quickly down the room and disappeared through a doorway.

Chapter Four

~~~~~~~~~~~~~~~~~

1

'I was born here,' said Kate Arletti. 'Just up the road.'

In her six months in Homicide this was the first time she had come out with John Kagal as his partner. He was more reserved than anyone else in the Unit and she was never entirely sure of herself with him. In basic intelligence he was no better than the boss, Inspector Malone, but he was certainly better educated than anyone else, including herself. She knew that he lived in the eastern suburbs, but she had no idea where he had originally come from, whether he came of immigrant parents like herself, whether Kagal was the original family name or a corruption. Still, he was handsome, a beautiful dresser and a pleasure to be seen with. Much better than some of the uniformed cops she had patrolled with.

They were in Marrickville Road and Kagal looked up and down the long lines of shops on both sides of the street. His parents' name had been Kagalovic when they had arrived from Yugoslavia thirty-five years ago; they had started their new life in a shop much like these in Leichhardt, another inner suburb. There the names above the shops had been mainly Italian, with one or two Yugoslav and Greek names thrown in for seasoning. Here, as far as he could see, the names were mostly Greek and Lebanese, with the occasional Italian pizza bar or café tossed in as pepper.

He remarked on it and Kate said, 'No, wait till we move further up, past Illawarra Road. Up there practically all the names are Asian – Chinese and Vietnamese. The Greeks and the Lebanese *own* the shops, they've been here the longest, but the Vietnamese rent and run them.'

He smiled at her. 'Russ Clements' blood would boil.'

'Oh, he's not that bad.' But she knew that the blood that ran in

Clements' veins was Type O for Old Australian: laced with prejudice, thick with regrets for the passing of an Australia that she and John Kagal had never known. 'After all, he married a German.'

'Another breed of Saxon . . . Let's go and talk to Dwayne Harod's uncle and aunty.'

The Ankara delicatessen was next door to the Cypriot Bank; on its other side was the Saigon Discount House. A young Vietnamese stood under an amplifier which blared out a Guns 'n' Roses number; he gave them a broken-toothed smile and offered them *Elvis Lives!* T-shirts for a song, not necessarily one of The King's. Kagal, who wouldn't have worn a T-shirt unless it were personally autographed by Armani or Ralph Laurent, never by Elvis, shook his head and stood back to let Kate enter the delicatessen.

Jack Harod was a brawny man with a bald head and a fierce black moustache; he looked like a cartoonist's idea of a Turk. He also looked worried when the two detectives produced their badges and asked if they could see him in private for a few moments. He said something in Turkish to his wife, who looked equally worried, then led Kagal and Kate into a store-room at the back of the shop.

'Whatsa matter? We ain't in trouble?' He had a surprisingly high voice for such a bulky man; or perhaps fear had shredded it.

'No, we're not here to worry you, Mr Harod,' said Kagal. 'It's about your nephew Dwayne.'

'Oh, him. What's he been up to now?' His voice actually did drop a tone or two. He leaned back against a box of butter, his bald head between two cheesecloth-covered legs of ham. The store-room had a wealth of smells, a treasure-house for a hungry man. There were Turkish, Greek, Lebanese, even Vietnamese delicacies on the shelves, a United Nations for the stomach.

'Does Dwayne get up to much?' Kate had learned from Malone the art of switching the bowling: two questioners are more disturbing than one.

Harod looked at Kagal. 'She's a detective?'

'Yes. One of our best, Mr Harod.'

Harod ran his hand over his head, upset at what the world was coming to. He had a fundamentalist view of women's place in the scheme of things and was certainly not prepared for their having anything to do with law and order. He was glad he had no daughter,

84

if what he heard from other Muslim fathers was true. It was bad enough having a nephew like Dwayne . . . 'My nephew goes his own way.'

'Getting into trouble?'

'Sometimes. Some day he will get into serious trouble. Why you wanna know about him?'

'He works out at Vaucluse, right? For Lady Huxwood, as a gardener.'

'So he tells us.'

'He works there,' said Kate. 'He doesn't tell you about it when he comes home?'

'We never see him, hardly. He comes, he goes, our house is like a bus-stop for him.'

'You live above the shop here? He gave this address.'

'No, we live over at Dulwich Hill. He lives there – when he comes home.'

'Was he home yesterday? Sick with a virus?' said Kagal.

'He ain't been home a week, maybe more. He could be dead, all we know.'

'No, he's very much alive, Mr Harod. It's his employer who's dead, Sir Harry Huxwood.' There was no reaction from Harod and Kagal said, 'You heard about that?'

The Turk shook his head. 'No, I don't read the newspapers, I can't read English too good.'

'It was on radio and TV.'

'I never listen to radio, all that talkback, that terrible music. I watch TV, but I never see the news, I'm home too late from the shop. I watch SBS, sometimes they have Turkish films.'

The two detectives looked at each other, both of them hardly comprehending how, in today's world of too much communication, there were still people who missed out. There would always be, Kate thought, back roads that the information superhighway would miss. Mercifully perhaps: but she would never voice that thought.

'Did Dwayne work in the canefields up in Queensland?' she asked.

'He did something up there, I dunno what.' Jack Harod sounded as if he had no interest in his nephew. 'He never talked much, you know what young people are, their uncles and aunts ask questions, all we get –' He illustrated with a shrug.

85

The two young people nodded. Then Mrs Harod put her head round the door jamb, her face pinched with exasperation, said something in Turkish that made Harod shrug his shoulders again and gesture at the detectives.

'What did she say?' said Kagal.

'There's customers in the shop. It's nearly lunchtime, people want sandwiches. We finished? I don't like wasting time on my nephew. You talk to him, ask him about himself. I ain't interested.'

As she and Kagal followed Harod back into the shop, trying to leave on a friendly note, Kate said, 'How's business, Mr Harod?'

Harod dropped his voice, one eye on the half a dozen people waiting at the counter. 'Was better before them Asians come. They sell everything cheap.'

Kagal, who had a sense of history, wanted to ask him how he, a Turk, got on with the Greeks; but maybe old hatreds were buried under new prejudices. They thanked him for his time and stepped out into the crowded main street of Marrickville. Above their heads the amplifier was shaking with Meatloaf telling the world he'd do anything for love, but he wouldn't do that, whatever *that* was. Beneath the blast the Vietnamese gave them the gap-toothed smile again and waved his hand at the T-shirts. Two beer-bellied ockers, in shorts and dirty T-shirts that Elvis wouldn't have been seen dead in, stumbled out of an hotel and two women in *chadors* cringed aside and hurried on while the ockers said something after them that was lost in Meatloaf's love lyric.

'Do we go back to Vaucluse and talk to Dwayne?' said Kagal.

Something told Kate that he was asking her to make the decision, something she had not expected. 'You're the senior.'

He looked at a pretty Lebanese girl going by; then back at her. 'You remember Peta Smith, she was killed last winter? Shot in the back. I've regretted I never treated her better than I did. I was a male chauvinist, just like —' He almost said *the others*, but chopped the words off in time. 'If we're going to be partners, Kate, you have as much say as I do.'

'Thanks,' she said and warmed to him.

'While we're out here, do you want to go and look at the house where you were born?'

'No,' she said, remembering the house where her father had blown his brains out one Sunday morning while she and her mother had been at Mass. 'Let's go up and talk to the Marrickville cops, see if they can tell us anything more about Dwayne.'

'I'd thought of that,' he said.

I'm still the junior partner, she thought; but smiled at him nevertheless. He might improve with time.

2

Fingerprints came up with nothing on the torn scrap of paper that Sir Harry had clung to in his death grip. Physical Evidence reported that they, too, had come up with nothing. Sir Harry, it seemed, could have been killed by a ghost. Yet Malone, who had learned from long experience not to be disheartened by lack of evidence, had not lost confidence. He was uneasy, yes, but still confident. There was always evidence to be found *somewhere*.

'You think you're on the right track?' said Zanuch.

'There's no track so far, sir. But yes, I think we'll eventually find it.'

'Why?'

Malone hesitated, then dived in, knowing the water would be cold: 'The family. There's enough of them, counting the grandkids, and the more there are, the more likely you'll find a crack sooner or later.'

Zanuch leaned back in his chair, tapped his desk with a silver paper-knife. The seven Assistant Commissioners had their offices on this floor of Police Headquarters and each man furnished his room according to his own personality and taste. Somehow the AC Crime had managed to give his office a distinction of its own. Perhaps it was the small antique book-case, a non-issue item, with its shelves of political biographies; or perhaps it was the silver-framed photograph that stood on a ledge behind his desk, of himself and Prince Charles sharing a joke, laughing mates, Bill and Charlie. Or perhaps (and Malone conceded the point) it was the man himself, with his elegant self-assurance, who gave the room its distinction.

'Certain members of the family have to be protected.'

Malone wasn't sure he had heard aright. 'Sir?'

'Lady Huxwood.'

'You've spoken to her?'

'Yes. And I'm convinced she had nothing to do with her husband's murder.'

'I'll have to interrogate her –'

'Interrogate? There's no need to *interrogate* her –'

'Well, interview her. Just for the record – the running sheets –'

For a moment it looked as if Zanuch was going to over-ride him; then he nodded, though reluctantly. 'Okay, but treat her gently. She's lost her husband, remember.'

Crumbs, how dumb and insensitive does he think I am? 'What about the others, sir? Have you in – have you talked to any of them?'

'Only Derek. I understand you're friendly with him?'

'We're acquainted, that's all. I'm not bringing any bias to this case, sir.' There, the tongue had slipped loose again: the un-co-ordinated Co-ordinator.

'I wasn't suggesting you might be.' Zanuch's tone was sharp.

Malone let that one go past. 'You've read the synopses? Two shots were fired at Jack Aldwych's son. We think there may be a connection – the Aldwych group are in the bidding for Huxwood Press.'

'I'm sure there is. Maybe that's the line to follow.' It wasn't an instruction, but it was close to it.

'We're looking into it.' Malone stood up and stepped back. He was close to the book-case; out of the corner of his eye he caught a glimpse of a book, a biography of Ronald Reagan, *The Role of a Lifetime*. It would appeal to Assistant Commissioner Zanuch, an actor through and through. 'And rest assured, sir – we'll treat Lady Huxwood gently.'

But only if she treats us gently.

He left then and drove back to Strawberry Hills through a day that had turned grey with the promise of rain. For far too long, four years now, there had been promises that had been broken, rain that fell like a whore's kisses, then went away. Out west grass had begun to break through the parched earth, but more protracted rain was needed. He eyed the sky, waiting for the greyness to thicken and drop lower, but he had no faith that it would. Water rationing was still in force and he wondered, abstractedly, how much water the roses at La Malmaison were given. He was certain that Lady Huxwood would feel that rationing of any sort was not meant for her.

John Kagal and Kate Arletti, eating lunch at their desks, were waiting for him at Homicide. 'We've been out at Marrickville,' said Kagal, swallowing the remains of an avocado sandwich. 'Young Dwayne Harod isn't exactly his uncle's favourite nephew.'

Kate, picking at a salad in a plastic box, gave a summary of their visit. 'Then we went up to see the local detectives. Dwayne belonged to one of the youth gangs out there before he went off to Queensland. No convictions, but a suspended sentence for beating up a kid from another gang. He had a reputation for being vicious at times.'

'Hot-blooded?'

'No,' said Kagal. 'Cold-blooded. He was not too popular, even with his own gang. I think we'll have to have another talk with Dwayne.'

'I'll do it,' Malone said, and both younger detectives looked disappointed; Kagal might even have looked resentful. 'I have to go out and see Lady Huxwood before tomorrow – the funeral's then. I can look up Dwayne at the same time,' he added and wondered why he was bothering to defend his authority. 'You two chase up the other grandkids. Russ and I have seen four of them –' He named them.

'What's their attitude?' said Kagal, wiping his mouth of a smear of avocado. He was a health food addict, being particularly addicted to those items that were supposed fattening; yet he never seemed to put on an extra ounce of weight. The mere smell of avocado made Malone feel fat. Kagal began to munch some walnuts. 'Are they money-hungry?'

'One of them is – Ross. The others?' He shrugged. 'I don't know. Not the girl, Sarah – she doesn't want to sell the Press. Check the others.'

'Do we split them between us or work together?' Kate asked.

'Together. You can flatter the boys and John can do the same with the girls. It's the way Russ and I work,' he said with a grin and went looking for his co-flatterer.

Clements was in the filing room, a large windowless walk-in closet. Steel adjustable shelves were stacked with cardboard cartons filled with folders; names were scrawled in blue marking pencil on the boxes; the same name, in some instances, was scrawled on half a dozen of the cartons. This was all evidence awaiting pending cases: the shelves were stacked with murder.

'Five of these cases come up in the next two weeks,' Clements said. 'We're gunna be spending a lotta time in court.'

There was always satisfaction in seeing a murderer brought to trial, but he was a rare cop who enjoyed a day in court. Malone had several times spent a day in the witness box when he had felt that *he* was the accused; defence counsel never treated a cop as a friend and ally. Judges, generally, were sympathetic to the police, but they were all ex-lawyers and some of them could never forget their self-acknowledged superiority.

'Unless I'm absolutely necessary, you take the court duty.'

To his surprise Clements just nodded. 'Okay, I'll do it.'

'Russ —' He leaned against the shelves, against a box marked *Kipsey*, a serial killer of women. 'What's up?'

Clements, too, leaned back against the shelves; he looked suddenly tired. 'Things are a bit difficult with us. Me and Romy.'

Malone almost said, *So soon?* But the tongue was held in check this time. 'I'm sorry to hear that. Lisa will be, too.'

'Lisa knows already, I think. Romy's been talking to her on the phone.' His big shaggy head was pressed back against a carton marked *Cevic*: a wife murderer. On that particular shelf, Malone saw, there was the evidence against four wife killers; domestic murder was common. 'Romy wants a kid. Two, in fact.'

'So what's the problem?' Clements didn't answer immediately and Malone went on, 'What's the matter with you? Crumbs, you *love* kids! You pamper mine —'

'There's a difference. I'm not responsible for your three. I'm forty-four years old, mate. We have a kid, I'll be forty-five, going on forty-six. The kid grows up, gets to university age and I'm sixty-three, sixty-four. Too old to understand him or her.'

'That's the quickest family history I ever heard. How old will he be when he buries you?'

Clements gave him a lopsided grin. 'You're on Romy's side, right?'

'I can only go on my own experience — and happiness. I can't imagine being without my three. The only unhappiness I ever feel is when I think we might lose one of them.'

'Well —' Clements heaved himself upright. 'I'll think about it. In the meantime I'll concentrate on these.' He waved an arm at the cartons around them. 'These were somebody's kids, once.'

There was no answer to that sort of pessimism. 'I'm going out to Vaucluse again.'

'From what Kate and John tell me, there are six Huxwood kids I wouldn't have wanted to father. Good luck.'

Rain spattered the unmarked police car as Malone drove it out to La Malmaison. The police barricades had been removed in Huxwood Road and the Crime Scene tapes had been rolled up and taken away for another scene, another crime. As he got out of the car in the driveway of the Big House, Enrico Quental came out of the house. He wore a tightly-belted fawn trenchcoat and, looking at him as he approached, Malone thought once again that short men should not wear trenchcoats: they looked like brown-paper Christmas crackers.

'Mr Quental, you've saved me a trip. I thought I might have to come out to − where d'you live?'

'Sutton Forest. No, Inspector, we have come up to town for the funeral tomorrow. Linden is inside now with her mother. You haven't finished your investigations here?'

'Not yet. We won't be finished here or anywhere else till we've found Sir Harry's killer.'

'Of course.' Quental appeared to have an unbreakable politeness.

'I understand you and − Linden stayed here the night of the murder.'

'Yes.' They had retreated to shelter beneath the Doric-pillared portico; the rain was falling steadily now. 'I gave all that information to a Sergeant − Takers?'

'Akers. Since then, you haven't remembered something you might have forgotten in the shock of what happened?'

'Such as, Inspector?'

'Oh, anything. The sound of the shot, hearing someone moving around . . . I believe a lot of people who live in the country find difficulty in sleeping when they come to the city.'

'Not me, Inspector. I grew up in a very noisy city, Lisbon. Portugal. Out here at La Malmaison is as quiet and peaceful as our place in the country. Lady Huxwood wouldn't allow it to be otherwise.' For a moment the politeness cracked; then he smiled. 'You've met her.'

Malone nodded, then said off-handedly, 'Do you have a vote in the Huxwood Press set-up?'

Quental's chin lifted as if it had been clipped. 'Of course not! Why do you ask?'

'Just routine, Mr Quental. What about −' He felt awkward: what to call Linden? Quental was stiffly formal. 'Your, er, wife? How does she feel about the proposal to sell the Press?'

'I think you should ask her, Inspector.' The politeness was almost rigid now. 'Will you excuse me? I have to be going.'

And he was gone at a run towards his car, an older model Bentley. It occurred to Malone as the little man disappeared that he had no idea what Quental did for a living, if anything. But, like all the Huxwoods, family, in-laws and *de factos*, he seemed to live well.

When Malone rang the bell, the butler came to the front door. He showed no surprise, no welcome, nothing at all. The detective could have been a door-to-door salesman or a Jehovah's Witness. 'Yes?'

Malone wasn't going to jog the man's memory; or pander to his rudeness. 'I'm here to see Lady Huxwood. And Mrs Quental.'

'Lady Huxwood isn't receiving visitors.'

Listen, Tito . . . But Malone held on to his tongue. 'I'm not a visitor, Krilich —' No *Mr* Krilich: let him know he was a servant. 'I'm a police officer and I'm getting bloody pissed off standing out here in the rain. Tell Lady Huxwood — *and* Mrs Quental — I want to see them. *Now!*'

'This way.' The rebuke washed over the butler as if he were just a stone figure; his square face showed no reaction at all. He led Malone through to the garden room. 'I'll tell Lady Huxwood you're here.'

'*And* Mrs Quental.'

'There is no Mrs Quental,' said Krilich over his shoulder as he went out the door.

Malone was left alone amidst the palms and shrubs; then Dwayne Harod, short garden-fork in hand, stepped out from behind one of the thicker shrubs. He wore a faded Ivy League sweat-shirt; he was one of those who had got no closer to Yale than turning a key in a lock.

'G'day, Inspector. I better get outa here, you gunna see Lady Huxwood.'

'Hold it a moment, Dwayne. Two of my officers have been out to see your uncle and aunt at Marrickville. Your uncle says he hasn't seen you in a week or more, that you weren't home yesterday with a virus.'

The under-gardener looked at the fork in his hand; for the first time Malone saw it as a weapon. 'My uncle'd tell you anything. He don't like me.'

'Why d'you live with him, then?'

'To please my mum. My dad, I dunno where he is, he ran off when I was little. Mum and me lived with Uncle Jack and Aunt Halide, I dunno, six or eight years. Then Mum and me went up to Queensland, Mum's still up there. When I come back to Sydney, she wanted me to stay with them again. They're a pain, Inspector. I tell you, real pains.'

'I'll take your word for it, Dwayne. But then we took your word that you'd been at home yesterday with a virus. Where were you? Why'd you bullshit us?'

'Don't use that sort of language in my house,' said Lady Huxwood, coming in behind him. 'You may go, Dwayne.'

Malone was sure that Phillipa Huxwood had heard much worse language in this house than he had just uttered; she was putting him in his place, a permanent game with her. 'That slipped out, Lady Huxwood.'

'Mother has heard worse,' said Linden (Huxwood? Quental? What name did she go by? Had she been married before?)

He hadn't really looked at her the night before last at dinner. Though she was slightly plump, she was a remarkably good-looking woman: the best-looking of the Huxwoods in his judgment. There was a lazy grace to her, a languidness that suggested she did not take life too seriously. He wondered how seriously she took her mother.

Dwayne Harod was still standing by the door of the garden room that led directly out into the garden itself; the rain had thickened, ran down the huge bay window in a wash that distorted the outside world; it was as if he did not want to go out into it and get wet. Then Malone realized the boy was staring at him, waiting for *him* to dismiss him. 'Righto, Dwayne, I'll see you in a few minutes. Wait for me – is there a garden shed?'

Dwayne nodded, but it was Lady Huxwood who said, 'Yes, there is. Wait there, Dwayne. Inspector Malone won't be long.'

The young Turk turned immediately and went running out into the rain. 'Thanks,' said Malone drily. 'I wasn't sure he understood my instructions.'

Phillipa Huxwood bristled and behind her her daughter smiled, then moved to a chair and sat down. 'Sit down, Mother. I don't think you're making Inspector Malone uncomfortable. He's the one with authority, aren't you, Inspector?'

'Not in this house.' But Phillipa seated herself. 'I think you and I understand each other, don't we, Inspector?'

'Not quite.' Malone sat down on the cushioned couch where Derek Huxwood had sat yesterday. The palm frond that had rested on Derek's shoulder had been snapped off; Malone wondered if it had been the victim of someone's temper. 'I don't think you understand we are investigating a murder — that gives me some authority, a lot, in fact. I'll watch my language, but I'll have to ask questions, when and with whom I like.'

She stared at him and he returned her stare. There was no grief or pain in her gaunt face; whatever she felt about her husband's death had been left upstairs in her bedroom. He did not think the less of her for that: he had witnessed enough tragedy to know that pain hidden was still honourable.

Then she said, 'Go ahead with your questions, Mr Malone.'

'Are you for or against the sale of Huxwood Press?'

She frowned, as if puzzled that that should be his first question. 'I am against the sale.'

'And Sir Harry?'

'He wanted to sell. He told me that the other night, it was the last thing he said to me. The last thing ever —' She bit her lip, the pain abruptly there for the moment.

'Did you quarrel about his decision?'

He got the hard stare again. 'Are you in the habit of disclosing what goes on between you and your wife?'

He was aware of Linden watching the encounter with amusement. He changed tack, slightly: 'Did anyone else know he'd made up his mind to sell?'

'No, he said he hadn't told anyone.' She was still on guard, stiffly upright in her chair. Beside her her daughter lolled at ease.

So, if Sir Harry had told no one of his decision, that meant he could still have been killed by any one of those opposing the sale and also those in favour of it. Except, of course, that Lady Huxwood, an opponent of the sale, would have been the only one to know of her husband's decision.

'How did you feel about what he'd told you?'

'Angry. But not enough to kill him, if that is what you are implying.'

'I'm not implying anything just yet, Lady Huxwood. Not yet,' he

94

repeated, laying bait. Then he turned to Linden, who was as relaxed as her mother was tense. 'And you – do I call you Mrs Quental?'

'No, you call me Ms Huxwood.'

'I never call anyone Ms, since I don't know what it's short for.' The tongue was tugging on its roots: these Huxwood women had a knack for getting under his skin. Yet he should not have been so smart-arse with Linden: unlike the others, she did not seem antagonistic towards him or the police in general. 'For the time being I'd better call you Mrs Quental. That's how you're entered in our running sheets.'

'Enrico, my – my partner will be pleased,' she said with a smile and glanced at her mother, who obviously was *not* pleased.

'Are you in favour of the sale?'

She shrugged. 'I couldn't care less, one way or the other. I've spent most of my adult life abroad, Inspector –'

'Doing what?'

'Doing nothing.' Her smile was mocking. 'A bludger, as the vulgarians say.'

That was twice in two days he'd been grouped with the vulgarians; soon he would be eligible for Canberra, where the politicians set the standard.

'My daughter's ambition always was to be a lady of leisure.' There was no mistaking the mother's disapproval.

'And I'm the only entirely happy one of all the Huxwoods.' The smile this time looked fixed, false. Then she looked back at Malone. 'Don't let us embarrass you –'

'I'm used to it,' he said. 'I've been in more than my fair share of domestics . . . Do you depend on Huxwood Press, or the holding company, whichever, for your income?'

'Of course. You see, Mr Malone, I'm not greedy . . . Neither is my mother, I hasten to add,' as her mother stiffened even more; though Linden herself remained relaxed. 'I've been quite happy with what I've earned. Well, not *earned*. Taken, if you like . . . But some of the others – have you talked to the children, the grandkids?' Suddenly he realized that behind the languor, the good humour, she was a mischief-maker. 'There is enough greed there to throw us back into the Eighties. Everyone a little entrepreneur.'

Not all, he thought, remembering Sarah.

'I think you have heard enough family gossip, Inspector,' said Phillipa Huxwood.

Not nearly enough; but he let it go. 'The under-gardener — who took him on here?'

'I did. Or did Derek? One of us. We advertised for an under-gardener in the *Chronicle*'s classified and he was one of half a dozen who came for interviews. Why? Don't tell me you suspect *him*?' She laughed, a harsh cough. 'You really are too suspicious, Mr Malone.'

'It's inbred,' he said and noticed that Linden smiled. He closed his notebook. 'What does your — *partner* do, Mrs Quental?'

'He breeds stud cattle, Murray Greys. Not really a rewarding occupation, with the drought.' Then she looked out the big bay window. 'Things may be better this year.'

'You have no children, I understand?'

'None that I can recall.' Again the lazy smile.

Does she feel any grief at her father's death? 'How did you get on with your father?'

'I was his favourite.'

'Oh yes,' snapped Lady Huxwood. 'Too true!'

Malone stood up, judging by a split second when Phillipa Huxwood was about to dismiss him; he preferred to time his own departures. 'The funeral is tomorrow, that right?'

'Yes. In view of the circumstances of my husband's death, we want it to be as private as possible. We are forbidding even the *Chronicle*'s reporters and photographers to be there.'

'Good luck, but if I know the media, the others will be there. And we'll be there, the police.'

'Why do you need to intrude?' She was indignant.

'Suspicion, Lady Huxwood. It's what keeps us on our toes. Thank you for your time,' he said and as he turned away and went out through the door into the garden he saw Linden nod and smile after him, almost as if she and he were accomplices.

The rain had eased, leaving the air damp. The clouds had lifted, were flesh-coloured and held aloft by ribs of sunlight. He went round the corner of the house, crossed a gravel path and found Dwayne Harod in a long, glass-roofed potting shed. 'Where's Dan Darling?'

'He's gone to arrange the wreaths for tomorrow's funeral. Lady Huxwood's left it to him to choose the wreaths and flowers. She wants it – discreet, I think she called it. Not too flashy.' He was knocking old soil out of pots. 'How'd you get on with her?'

It's none of your business, son. 'Dwayne, we checked on you with the Marrickville police. You belonged to one of the gangs that were a nuisance out that way a coupla years ago.'

The young man grinned cheekily. 'Just letting off steam, Inspector, you know, waddatheycallit, youthful energy. Nothing serious. You get together in, waddatheycallit, your peer group.'

He's taking the mickey out of me; just like Linden. 'You still haven't told me why you bullshitted us about being home with a virus. Where were you?'

Dwayne ran his fingers through the old soil, crumbling it. 'I just took the day off. I wasn't feeling so good, I been out on the town, and when I heard the news about the Old Man, I thought who's gunna miss me, I don't come in?'

'That was all you felt, a pain in the gut?'

He began to empty another pot. 'What was I supposed to feel? I hardly knew him, I seen him, I dunno, once or twice.'

Malone had seen this callousness before on the part of the young: death was a part of life, at least for old people, what else did they expect? He switched tack: 'What do you know about firearms?'

'Firearms?' His trowel rapped the side of the clay pot.

'Guns.'

'Oh, *guns*. Nothing.'

'What did you carry when you were with the gang?'

He was now carefully scraping the soil from the pot, giving it all his attention, like an archaeology trainee who had just come across an artefact. 'A shiv. But I never used it, it was, you know, just in case.'

'Where do you stay when you're not with your uncle and aunt?'

'Around. Here and there. I got mates, girl friends.' He put the pot beside those he had already emptied, gave Malone his full attention. 'Why are you on at me? Shit, I'm just the fucking under-gardener here!' He was suddenly angry; he had been shaken out of his laid-back attitude. 'What'm I supposed to have done?'

'I don't know that you've done anything, Dwayne,' said Malone mildly. 'Don't get your balls in a knot. Just tell me where we can find you when you're not with Uncle and Aunty.'

97

Dwayne tapped the trowel up and down, up and down, on the bench beside him. The sun had now broken through, came slanting across the harbour into the glass shed; Malone could feel the sweat starting under his armpits, saw the shine on Dwayne's forehead. Then the boy said, 'You can get me at my girl friend's, out in Leichhardt.' He gave an address. 'Her name's Carpano, Sophie Carpano.'

'Italian?' Parts of Leichhardt, named after a German explorer but with no German community there, were known as Little Italy.

'Yeah. A Catholic, too. That's another thing my uncle don't like. You shoulda heard him about Catholics when the Pope was out here.'

'Life's tough, Dwayne. Where does your girl friend work? Come on,' as the young man hesitated. 'Where does she work?'

Reluctantly: 'She works in a fancy shop, you know, cosmetics, perfume, that sorta stuff. In —' He named one of the city's principal arcades. 'You're not gunna embarrass her, are you?'

'What makes you think I'd embarrass her? Relax, Dwayne. Keep gardening — they tell me it's good for the nerves. Maybe I'll see you at the funeral tomorrow.'

He shook his head. 'Not me. I'm afraid of the dead.' He was almost cheeky again. 'I'll stay here and mind the flowers.'

As Malone went back to his car at the front of the Big House he saw Linden coming down the driveway from the front gates. She walked lazily, hips swaying from side to side; the buttons on the slit in her long green cotton skirt were undone and her legs caught the sun as they appeared and reappeared. He was surprised at the thought: what would she be like in bed?

'You look — harassed, Inspector?'

Only because I've just been whacked across the back of my mind by my wife, God love her. 'This is that sort of place.'

She looked around her. 'I suppose so. Maybe that's why I fled it fifteen, sixteen years ago.' Then she looked back at him. 'Do you have to pursue this case so diligently, Mr Malone? It's tearing hell out of my mother.'

'I got the feeling that you and your mother don't get on.' It was cruel, but cruelty opens more wounds than kindness. And he was looking for the wounds in this family.

She didn't respond as he had hoped: 'In the end, Mr Malone, I think all the Huxwoods will stick together.'

'Sale or no sale?'

She shrugged, smiled and walked past him and on down to the house. She was probably right, he thought. Outsiders, police included, would always have to take their chances with the Huxwoods.

3

He drove up over the ridge to Waverley police station, paid his respects to Superintendent Steve Lozelle, the patrol commander, a dour man who seemed a living illustration that a policeman's lot was not a happy one.

'We've set up an incident room, Scobie, and to tell you the truth, I've looked in there only once. Have you had a word from Bill Zanuch? Me too. I'm a year off retirement, headaches are bad at my age.' He allowed himself a rare smile; his broad face appeared to creak with the effort. 'It's all yours, Scobie. You can have the medals and the commendations and the kicks up the bum. I'm generous that way.'

'I've heard that, Steve. All heart.'

'How's it going? Not that I really want to know.'

'We're standing still at the moment.'

'Maybe in the end that'll be the best place to be. Good luck. And take care.'

'Oh, I'll do that, no worries.'

He went back to Homicide, attended to the paperwork on his desk, then got up and walked out into the big main room. He stood at the far end of the room looking out across Prince Alfred Park to the city skyline; this was the opposite end of the skyline he had seen from Nigel Huxwood's apartment on Point Piper. This end of town, neglected for so long, was slowly being reborn. Down below him on the right was Cleveland Street high school, a melting pot where prejudices were slowly being dissolved in the stew of immigration. Immediately below his fourth floor windows were the six Canary Islands date palms in the building's forecourt, immigrant trees that had taken root and somehow survived. Over in the park, beyond the long line of Moreton Bay figs, a wino cavorted like an arthritic fairy, waving the wand of his bottle. Ever since Homicide had moved into this building some months ago Malone had stood at this window in the late afternoon,

99

never really knowing why. Perhaps it was for no other reason than to say farewell to the end of the day, a nod to the dying of the light.

Clements came and stood beside him. 'How'd it go?'

Malone turned from the window; across in the park the wino had fallen in a still heap, all frolic gone. 'Have you talked to this kid, the under-gardener? He rubs me up the wrong way.'

'Half the population do that to me. What's the matter with him?'

'I don't think he could lie straight in a coffin. And he's cheeky.'

'You don't think *he* did it?' Clements looked as sceptical as Lady Huxwood had.

'So far I haven't got a clue *who* did it. But I'm not ruling out anybody, not even our boy Dwayne. Check with Queensland, he lived up there for a while, see if he has a record.'

'It's a long shot. I usually don't back them.'

'Put my money on it, then. I'm going home.' He stopped: 'You go home, too, and get Romy pregnant.'

Clements grinned wryly. 'What if I produced a kid like Dwayne?'

Malone went home to Randwick, to the house that for him had the solidity of unfissionable rock. The three children were home for dinner tonight and he looked at them with heartfelt affection that escaped them; that would have embarrassed him if they had noticed it. His mother had never shown any outward affection for him, but he had known that she loved him; she had had that reticence that had infected her generation, but she had never been a Lady Huxwood. These three of his were the answers to the Huxwoods and the Dwayne Harods of the world.

'You're quiet,' said Lisa from the other end of the table.

'Tired. I had a full day.' Full of lies and evasions and bitterness that soured the spirit. 'What about you? Anyone had an interesting day?'

Maureen and Tom made faces. 'You kidding? School *interesting*?'

'I joined the Lesbians for a Republic today,' said Claire.

'They're taking in straights?' said Malone, worried for a moment.

'So long as we vote for a woman for our first President.'

'Oh gawd,' said Tom, but Maureen shot her fist into the air.

'I went to lunch with Mother at the Sheraton,' said Lisa, filling Malone's plate with a second helping of grilled red mullet with tapen-ade. 'Guess who were just a couple of tables away? Your old criminal chum and his son and the Supples, the English couple we met the other night. They all raised their glasses to Mother and me, and Jack Senior – is that what you call him? – came across and paid his respects. He's an old dear, in his own way.'

'The eleven or twelve fellers he killed didn't think so.'

'How'd he go as President?' said Tom. 'Anyone but a woman.'

Malone poured himself another glass of West Australian sauvignon blanc. Usually he had only one glass of wine at dinner, but tonight he had to be unwound. 'The Aldwyches are part of a consortium that are bidding for Huxwood Press. Maybe they're going to get together with the London crowd. If they do, Huxwood is gone.'

'If Jack Aldwych killed men before,' said Claire, 'would he have had Sir Harry killed?'

She was studying law, God forgive her, though she had told him last year she wanted to go into police work. From which God should protect her. 'Not Jack. He's finished with all that – I think.'

One could never be sure; though he was surprised he was defending Jack Aldwych. But then here he was at the dinner table discussing a murder case with his children, something he had sworn he would never do. He was aware that Lisa was watching him closely, though saying nothing.

'The kids at school know you're on the case,' said Tom, who was in Year Eight at Marcellin, the local Catholic boys' high school. 'They wanna discuss it in drama studies, on video. I'm gunna play you. Inspector Malone, that's me.'

'The lot of you are likely to finish up in Long Bay for contempt of court. Forget it.'

'Why not?' said Maureen, an avid reader of the sensational. 'Everyone had tried O. J. Simpson before he went to trial.' Then abruptly she changed her tone: 'Why don't you retire, Dad?'

She looked genuinely solicitous of him. Normally she was for *action, action*; twenty-five years ago he would have been battling her in anti-war demonstrations. When the Labor Party had recently voted at its annual conference that it should have a thirty-five per cent quota of women MPs, she had at once written off to the secretary of the local branch putting her name down for pre-selection for 2002. Malone loved her, but feared she might become a pain in the butt, especially if she became a Greenie, too. But for the moment she was his loving, concerned daughter.

'Or get a desk job?' said Claire.

'I've got a desk job. Theoretically.' The second glass of wine was unwinding him; he felt an unexpected pleasure that they were all interested in the Huxwood case.

'Our group at uni were discussing it,' said Claire, gathering up the plates of those who had finished the main course. 'The Lefties hope the Huxwood empire goes the way of the British empire.'

'They shouldn't.' For the first time he realized that he did not want to see the Huxwood Press sold; or anyway, the *Chronicle.* He did not care about the radio stations and the television stations in other states, nor about the half a dozen magazines the Press published. 'The *Chronicle* is still more liberal than any of the other dailies.'

'You couldn't call some of its columnists liberal.' Though Lisa had long ago left the diplomatic circuit, she still had the habit of combing the newspapers assiduously; it was she who insisted they bought two daily newspapers and two weekly news magazines. Her education had fine-tuned her mind more than his, but she never flaunted it; she knew that he knew more about human nature than any number of years at finishing school, university and in diplomatic circles could ever achieve. He had waded through the wreckage, the sediment, where muck, when looked at twice, turned into knowledge and understanding. 'Some of them are back in the nineteenth century. They don't know Queen Victoria is dead.'

Like Lady Huxwood.

'Especially some of their sports columnists. Talk about macho male chauvinists!' Claire had brought in the dessert. Dutch apple cake and whipped cream, Malone's favourite. Lisa was clogging his arteries with love, but he couldn't say no, either to the cake or her love.

'I think I'll be a sports writer,' said Tom. 'Sounds interesting.'

Later, in bed, Lisa said, 'Why'd you talk about the case with the kids? You've never done that before.'

'I dunno. I think I just wanted to hear what a family sounded like that didn't hate each other.' They were wrapped in each other's arms and legs; their gift-wrapping, as Lisa called it. He stroked her hair, thick and lustrous again. There was no hint of what she had gone through last year under the knife and chemotherapy; the cervical cancer had not reappeared. She was his old Lisa; or almost. The shadow of the cancer would never entirely go away. 'They've tried to tell me Harry and Phillipa loved each other, but I dunno. Whatever they felt for each other, they seem to have excluded the kids.'

'It happens,' she said sleepily. 'I shan't ever let it happen with us. Get your knee out of my crotch, it's only Wednesday.'

He grinned and kissed her forehead, safe and comfortable in the capital city of the country of marriage. But it was a long time before he fell asleep.

Chapter Five

1

Clements came to him in the morning with a computer print-out. 'Your boy Dwayne has a record up in Queensland. In possession of a firearm, a Twenty-two. With silencer.'

'A silencer? He worked in the canefields up there, he said. What do they do – shoot snakes with a hush-puppy? What'd he get?'

'A fine, four hundred bucks. He said he'd found the gun and the silencer and it actually was registered to someone else, the gun. They couldn't prove he was going to hit someone with it, so the magistrate fined him and let him go.'

'Did he have any connection with anyone with a record?'

'The Queensland boys say no, none they could find. He was a loner as far as they were concerned.' Clements sat down. He looked and sounded happier this morning: like a man on the way to fatherhood? 'If he is the hitman, he wouldn't have done it off his own bat. Someone hired him.'

'Lady Huxwood told me yesterday she and Derek gave him the job. That points the finger at one of them.'

'Maybe. But suppose one of the grandkids wants the empire broken up so that he can take over the radio stations as his share. Then there's the Portuguese, Mr Quental – he's supposed to be stony broke, skint. Maybe he'd like – what's her name? Linden? – to have her share so that he can get himself out of hock.'

'She told me she's always been happy with what income she gets from the family corp. What would she get a year?'

'Your guess is as good as mine. Huxwood doesn't pay big dividends, but every so often it splits the shares. Whatever she gets, it'd make what you and I take home look like petty cash.'

'So how much is Mr Quental supposed to be in the hole?' He knew

Clements would have the answer: figures were the big man's addiction.

'Between fifteen and twenty million.'

Once upon a time Malone's mind would have gone blank at such figures; the nation's bankrupt entrepreneurs had given a new dimension to local finance. 'Where'd he do that much?'

'He got caught up with some of those pirates over in Perth. He's lucky he's not in jail with them.'

'Where do you get all this?'

Clements grinned and winked. 'I have some mates on the Stock Exchange. There are more gossips there than you'd find at a ladies' bridge party.'

Malone got to his feet, reached for his jacket and hat. He was one of the few in Homicide who still wore a hat, though when he had first started in plainclothes hats had been *de rigueur*. He had recently seen a re-run of the old 1960s TV series *Homicide*, filmed in Melbourne; all the actors had worn hats, trilbys with narrow brims, and he had thought they had looked bloody ridiculous, enough to make any crim laugh. But, conscious of his skin cancers, he still wore his medium-brimmed pork-pie. It probably dated him, especially with fashion plates like John Kagal, but lately he had begun to feel dated anyway, with or without his hat.

'Let's go to the funeral, then we'll talk to Dwayne again . . . How're you going with Romy?'

Clements grinned. 'She seduced me.'

'Good. When's the baby due?'

They were at the security door of the big room when Malone heard the phone ring in his office. For a moment he was tempted to ignore it; but Clements, who had opened the door, paused and waited for him. He went back, picked up the phone: it was Jack Aldwych.

'Scobie? I think you and I had better have a talk. I've just got a threatening note.' He laughed, the laugh of a man who had now seen and heard everything. 'Chow Hayes and the old mob must be spinning in their graves, me getting threatening notes!'

The five Huxwood women, all dressed in black, were gathered in the drawing-room of the Big House. Out in the driveway there was a cavalcade of cars and the Huxwood men were there, plus the grandchildren. The hearse stood right outside the front door, as if waiting for the master of the house; but he was already in the hearse, in the walnut coffin with the solid brass handles and his decorations laid on its top like visiting cards that had reached their use-by date. Sir Harry had been released from the morgue, like a man who had done his time, and been brought here by private ambulance and now he was ready for his last journey. Immediately behind the hearse was a second hearse, chockful of flowers and wreaths, a travelling flower stall. The funeral director, in black coat and striped trousers and a solemn decorous air, had bright red hair that looked like a joke on such an occasion. Linden, gazing out through one of the drawing-room windows, would not have been surprised if the director's face had suddenly unfroze and he had turned to the mourners, as in a Dennis Potter film, and asked if they had heard the one about the corpse who . . .

Phillipa Huxwood, seated beneath the stares of the two Renoirs and the Rupert Bunny, here in this room that had been her throne-room, said, 'Where did all those damned flowers come from? I specifically ordered only two wreaths, one from me and the other from all of you. It looks like a damned spring festival, there should be nymphs and dryads.'

'That would please Pa,' said Linden lazily, and instantly could have bitten her tongue. She had promised herself today would be pleasant, as pleasant a day as a funeral could make one.

'The flowers just turned up,' said Sheila. 'From *everyone*. The only one who didn't send any was that horrible man, The Dutchman.'

That was Hans Vanderberg, the opposition Labor leader, who would not have sent flowers to the Virgin Mary if, like Harry Huxwood, she had voted conservative.

'At least he's not a hypocrite,' said Phillipa, who could be fair-minded when she put her mind to it.

Linden turned away from the window and looked around her. She had grown up here and till she was in her early teens she had thought she was happy. She had been unspoiled, despite the family wealth, and yes, happy. There had been the school-days at Ascham, the parties with the boys from Cranbrook: all the privileges of a comfortable existence. The others, she was sure, had been exactly like her; though maybe not Derek, whom she had never completely understood. Then, not suddenly but gradually, she had come to realize there were two families in this house (before Little Houses One and Two had been built). The parents and the four children: Them and Us.

'I still can't believe we're on our way to bury him,' said Cordelia.

She looked older this morning, Linden thought; as if all the aerobics, the beauty salon, the *packaging*, had been to no avail. But why am I being so bitchy? she thought. Cordelia was *not* family, except by marriage, but she had always been honest and generous. She was occasionally less than generous about her mother-in-law, but that only made her even more one of Us. It was Derek who had been the bastard over there in Little House One.

'We should have planned a wake,' said Brenda, being Irish, if only stage-Irish; she had never been to a wake in her life. 'Harry would have liked that.'

'I wouldn't have,' said Lady Huxwood. 'They say that funerals are for the living, a chance to get together, but there are limits. Why aren't we getting started? What's the delay?'

'I don't think Pa will be put out if we're a little late,' said Linden. 'He was never on time when –' She stopped before 'he was alive': that would only bring him back into this room. 'Relax, Mum.'

'I'm always relaxed. I just hate unpunctuality, that always annoyed me about Harry.' She was even more gaunt this morning, bones in black weeds. 'Are all the children here?'

'All of them,' said Sheila. 'On their best behaviour.'

'A change.'

Oh Christ, thought Linden, why doesn't she shut up?

Phillipa was looking out the window, staring at the hearse. There was silence in the big room for almost a minute, then she said, to herself more than to her daughters and her daughters-in-law, 'I'll miss him so. Why did he have to go without me?'

He didn't choose to go . . . Linden caught herself just in time. In that almost-skeletal, once-beautiful face she saw the sudden fierce

107

glow of love, that passion that had locked Linden and her siblings out of what had consumed their mother and father. All at once she felt an immeasurable pity for her mother, only for it to be diluted as she felt pity for herself. Despite all her efforts, she had never found love like that.

'Looks as if we should be going,' said Cordelia, gathering herself together as if there were more than one of her. 'Do you want a hand, Mother?'

'Why should I?' But Phillipa looked unsteady as she rose from her chair. 'Don't *fuss*! What are we riding in?'

'They brought one of those stretch limousines, so that we can all ride together,' said Sheila.

Phillipa stopped, rigid with fury. 'We're going to look like some damned pop group! The Andrews Sisters!'

The Andrews Sisters? thought Linden. When did Mum last listen to a pop group?'

'We can all sing then,' said Brenda, determined to have a wake. '*Don't Sit Under the Apple Tree* or whatever it was they sang.'

Linden had looked out the window again. 'It has those smoked windows. It's fashionable, inconspicuous anonymity.'

'Stop joking,' said Cordelia and looked on the verge of tears, still gathering herself together.

They began to move out of the drawing-room. Linden stopped for a last glance out the window. The mourners outside were standing in a group on one side of the line of cars. Then beyond the cars she saw the young man come slowly down the driveway and pause by the hearse. She wondered who he was, he was a stranger to her; he was in overalls, so perhaps he was one of the gardeners. He stood by the hearse and ran his hand along the glass side, as if trying to reach in and stroke the coffin. He had a thin dark face that showed no emotion, like a man trying to hide grief. Then suddenly he smiled, just for a moment. It was horrible to see and it shook her. Then he turned away and walked quickly out of sight round the corner of the house.

Malone and Clements, getting out of the unmarked police car, saw Dwayne going round the corner of the house. 'You wanna talk to him now?' said Clements.

Malone was about to say No, when he saw Assistant Commissioner Zanuch coming up the driveway towards them. 'What are you doing here?'

'The usual, sir. We always do surveillance at the funeral of a murder victim.' *As if you didn't know.*

Zanuch looked annoyed at being reminded, but he managed to contain his annoyance. 'Well, don't make yourself too obvious. The family want to keep this as private as possible. That's why the Commissioner isn't here.'

But you are, the friend of the family. Malone wondered how thick-skinned the AC was. 'I won't be going to the cemetery, sir. Sergeant Clements will do that. Constables Kagal and Arletti will also be there. I have a few more enquiries to make here.'

Zanuch frowned. 'There'll be nobody here.'

'The staff, sir. I want to talk to one or two of them.'

Zanuch nodded, tried to look as if he commended such thoroughness. 'Have you made any progress?'

'No, sir,' said Malone, straight-faced. 'But it's early days yet. The body isn't in the ground.' There it was again, the loose tongue.

Zanuch looked as if he was about to utter a sharp rebuke, but at that moment the cortege began to move up the driveway towards the big gates. He wheeled quickly and hurried down to a car at the end of the procession and jumped in beside the driver. It was an unmarked police car, one of the larger models, and Malone felt a petty satisfaction to see it at the end of the line, like an afterthought added to the invitation list.

'You sure you don't want to come?' said Clements.

'No, you follow them, make some notes and let me see them. I'm going down to see Dwayne.'

'Can you handle him on your own?'

'I don't think he's got a gun hidden in the potting-shed or amongst the roses. I'll be okay.' The cortege was passing them now, going out the gates. The first three mourners' cars were stretch limousines, all with darkened windows. 'You notice, our funerals are getting to look more and more like Mafia funerals?'

'Everybody wants to be a celebrity. You're in a car with smoked windows, everyone thinks you must be a celebrity.'

Malone couldn't picture Lady Huxwood wanting to be a celebrity. 'Righto, go and get into surveillance mode.'

'Surveillance mode? You've been reading those journalists again.'

The last car drove out of the gates, Zanuch looking out at Malone through clear windows. Malone nodded to him, restrained himself from snapping to attention. Then he went down the long driveway, feeling the sun on his shoulders, hearing the birds singing in the camphor laurels, the black atmosphere of the funeral abruptly gone. At the eastern end of the Big House Dan Darling was working amongst the roses, humming to himself. He looked up as Malone approached.

'I always hum that this time of year. *The Last Rose of Summer*. This was the rose inspired that song –' He gently fingered the pink bloom. 'Old Blush China, it's a hybrid, come out of China about two hundred years ago, but Lady Huxwood tells me it's been raised there for a thousand years. It's one of her favourites, she likes anything that's been around for a long time.'

'Like the *Chronicle*?'

Darling looked at him sideways. 'Yeah, like the paper. You quizzing me or something?'

'No, Dan, I'm going to leave you to Old Blush China. Where's Dwayne the Turk?'

'You quizzing him?'

'Just a few questions. You mind?'

'No. Between you'n me, I don't like him.'

'Why not?'

'The young bugger doesn't have any feeling. I ask him what he thinks of Sir Harry's murder, he just shrugs, says we all gotta go some time. They all like that, the kids?'

'Some. You going to fire him?'

'I'm thinking of it. I'll have to ask Derek or the Old Lady first.'

'What were the others like who applied for the job?'

'A mixed bunch, one or two better qualified than him. But Derek picked him.'

'Well, keep him on for a while, he may change. The atmosphere around here may soften him up. He's never worked in high society before.'

'You think I'm high society?' Dan Darling gave that drought-stricken grin, wiped sweat from his brow with the maimed hand. 'I been here forty years, none of it's rubbed off on me.'

'You love your roses, don't you?'

The maimed hand gently stroked an Old Blush China. 'Indeed I do. So did Sir Harry.'

Malone walked down across the broad lawn to the waterfront. A low stone wall divided the lawns from the tiny strip of private beach; inside the wall was a long strip of garden, no roses but azaleas, gardenias and an assortment of bright border plants. Dwayne Harod was knee-deep in a green surf of azaleas, cutting them back. He was shirtless but in bib-and-tucker overalls and wore a wide-brimmed straw hat that looked brand-new.

He touched the brim of the hat. 'My girl friend insisted she get me a hat, she thinks I'll get sunstroke. A Turk with sunstroke, you ever hear of that?'

'Come to think of it, you're one of the few Turks I've ever met, Dwayne. Do you celebrate Anzac Day? Gallipoli and all that? Your side won.'

'Why would I? Only nuts and old returned soldier farts celebrate war. I'm a pacifist.'

Malone sat down on the wall where a clear patch of lawn ran right up to it. The stones were stained and pitted and he wondered how many generations of Huxwoods had sat here and pondered their good fortune. 'If you're a pacifist, Dwayne, what were you doing with the gun and silencer you had when the Queensland police picked you up a year ago?'

Dwayne paused in his pruning. 'You heard about that?'

Malone nodded.

'Yeah, well, it was all a mistake. I *found* the gun and the silencer. I wasn't gunna do anything with it.'

'The magistrate didn't believe you, Dwayne.'

'Well, I'm a Wog, ain't I? We're only one step up from the coons and the slopeheads.'

Malone had heard this plea before. He looked at the notes he had

111

made from the computer print-out Clements had given him. 'The magistrate's name was Raftopolous. A Greek, I'd say, wouldn't you?'

'Well, there you are —' Dwayne spread his hands. 'He was Greek. Turks and Greeks hate each other's guts.'

Dwayne, Malone was beginning to realize, would always have an answer.

'I remember reading something about that. Cyprus, wasn't it?'

'Nah, long before that. Centuries. My people've been fighting the Greeks forever. My granddad, he used to tell me what he done to the Greeks at Smyrna just after the First World War. He was nearly ninety, a real old man, when he told me, but he remembered everything. Said he used the bayonet like he never used it against the Aussies at Gallipoli. I never asked him why he hated Greeks, he would always say it just happened. I don't think he knew. He used to say there's an old Turkish proverb, *It is not only the fault of the axe but of the tree as well.* You know what that means?'

'Vaguely.' The youth was just talking, trying to get away from the subject of the gun and the silencer. 'Dwayne, what were you going to do with the gun you had? Was there someone you hated? A Greek, maybe?'

Dwayne smiled. 'You're not gunna believe me, are you?'

'No, I don't think I am, Dwayne. The Greek magistrate didn't. What was he, the axe or the tree?'

The boy nodded appreciatively: the young bugger's mocking me again, thought Malone. 'You believe in proverbs, Inspector?'

'No, I don't, Dwayne. For every proverb, there's another one that contradicts it. Or almost. Did you bring a gun to Sydney with you when you left the canefields?'

He said nothing for a moment: the pause was too long, gave him away. 'No.'

'I think you did, Dwayne. You didn't bring a Browning down with you, a Thirty-two?'

'A what? Jesus, why would I wanna bring a gun down to Sydney with me? I got one conviction against me, I get picked up with another gun I'm a goner. Six, twelve months at least.' He shook his head. 'Nah, Inspector, you're barking up the wrong tree.'

'I don't think so.' Malone stood up. 'I've got to tell you, Dwayne. You're high on my list of suspects.'

112

'Ah, come off it! Jesus, why would I wanna kill the Old Man?'

'For money? Someone paid you?'

He had never pursued this line before. He was accusing this young man on no evidence at all, on nothing more than suspicion and dislike of him. And only yesterday he had told Kate Arletti to leave her prejudices at home! Yet he could feel, as surely as the sun-drenched stone beneath his hand, that Dwayne Harod knew more about the murder of Sir Harry than his protestations admitted. The sudden grin on the young man's face abruptly convinced him.

'Bullshit, Inspector. Give a story like that to the *Chronicle* and see if they print it.'

He did it.

'Watch out for the axe, Dwayne.'

He left him on that and walked back up to the Big House. He hesitated on the terrace, then, seeing the door to the garden room open, he went in and through to the main hall. He stood there and, the Celt in him forcing the imagination, felt the ghosts that had inhabited this house, felt the influence they had wielded. Prime Ministers and State Premiers had been adopted here, union bosses and Catholic prelates scorned, the currency devalued: not by the ghosts alone but with the willing co-operation of those who had been invited here. The *Chronicle* had always stood for liberalism, but its owners had often put their own spin on it. Newspapers were a tool and no owner had ever been able to resist the opportunity to use them.

Malone felt no resentment of what his imagination had told him; the *Chronicle* had not killed his father, as it had Kate Arletti's. The paper had at times been critical of police corruption, but more often than not it had backed the police against politicians and public outcry.

He climbed the stairs, his footsteps soft on the thick carpet; the house was silent around him, the ghosts watching. He paused on the gallery, a trespasser: all his years as a policeman had never cured him of his aversion to intruding. Then he thought, What the hell, I'm here investigating a murder. He went into the murder room.

The big bed had been made up, as if Harry would be coming home tonight after the funeral. A silk coverlet matched the drapes on the four-poster; on the heavy dressing-table silver-backed brushes looked as if they had been freshly polished, gleaming in the light from the open window. Malone crossed to the big wardrobe, opened it: the suits and jackets in it looked freshly pressed. Someone was waiting for Harry to come home.

He went to the computer, pressed buttons but got just a blank screen. There was nothing on it of Harry; its memory had been wiped. Physical Evidence would have checked the computer on Tuesday morning, but he could not remember their reporting anything of interest. Perhaps its memory had already been wiped.

'You are looking for something?'

He turned, startled. A slim dark woman in a pencil-striped uniform dress and a spotless white apron stood in the doorway from the gallery. He guessed at once who she was: Mrs Krilich, whom he had not so far met. But she appeared to know who he was.

'I'm Inspector Malone,' he said unnecessarily. 'Has anyone touched this computer since Tuesday morning?'

'I would not know.' She spoke deliberately, as if arranging her English in proper order. 'Sir Harry would never let us touch that thing.'

'Who found him? I mean, who found him – here?' He gestured at the bed.

'My husband. He came downstairs – my husband –' She paused, things falling out of their proper order. She seemed to lose colour, as if she were going to faint; then she recovered. 'My husband was sick. I was the one who had to tell them first what had happened.'

'Who did you tell first? Lady Huxwood?'

'No.' She was composed again. She was a good-looking woman who had settled for plainness. Malone wondered if Lady Huxwood, careful of Harry's attraction to pretty women, had ordered the plain look. 'I came up here and –' she nodded at the open door to Phillipa's bedroom '– and looked in. Lady Huxwood was still asleep. I closed the door –'

'The door was open?'

'Always. Sir Harry and Lady Huxwood slept in separate rooms, but the door between them was always open.'

'What did you do then?'

'I went downstairs and over to Mr Derek's. I told him what had happened and he came running over here.'

'Did he then wake Lady Huxwood?'

'She was awake. She had come in here while I was over at Mr Derek's.'

'How was she?'

Her dark eyes looked at him almost pityingly. 'Do you know what it is to lose a husband?'

'No.' *But I almost lost my wife last year.* 'I know she would be upset, terribly upset. But did she collapse, anything like that?'

'No. She just asked me to close the door.'

'You and Mr Krilich heard nothing during the night? Someone coming up the back stairs?'

'Nothing.'

'Where is Mr Krilich now?'

'He has gone to the funeral.'

'You didn't want to go?'

There was sudden pain in her eyes. 'I went home two years ago to Vukovar to bury my mother and my two sisters, killed in the war. I do not want to go to any more funerals. Lady Huxwood understood. Will you be going now or staying?'

4

He went. It took him twenty minutes to walk up to the top of the ridge where the main road was. He walked up through quiet streets where the houses had the solid, secure look that banks had once had; nothing here went for less than half a million and most of them were in the million-plus bracket. But behind the secure facades he knew there were white ants: of bankruptcy, illness, domestic discord, even thoughts of murder. None of these houses had been as solid and secure as La Malmaison had been, up till last Monday night.

He rarely used public transport, but he wanted to be alone with his thoughts and he did not want to risk hiring a garrulous taxi driver. The Asian drivers were not garrulous, mainly because of the language problem, but they drove like dervishes and he had always been a nervous passenger, even in police cars. He caught a bus.

The bus was full but for one empty seat. He dropped into it and realized at once why it was empty; he was seated next to a bag-lady who smelled like a waste dump. Stuffed plastic bags hung about her

115

like protuberances from her squat body; she carried her home and her life with her; it struck him that she was probably more independent than anyone else on the bus. She was reading a newspaper, a crumpled copy of the *Chronicle* which looked as if she had salvaged it from some waste bin. She turned her ruddy, wrinkled apple of a face towards him.

'Who you gunna vote for?'

He caught a glimpse of a headline: *Premier Slates Opposition* . . . 'I haven't made up my mind.'

'That's the trouble with this country.' She nodded vigorously and the knitted cap she wore slipped down over her brow. She looked around her at the other passengers, all of them well-dressed, none of them smelling like a garbage tip. 'Nobody ever makes up their mind till it's too late.'

He wanted to ask her when she had made up her mind to drop out of society; but he did not want to get into conversation with her. She went back to reading the *Chronicle*, sometimes snorting to herself, the plastic bags heaving as she shifted in her seat. Once, when she had come to the editorial page, she tapped it and looked at Malone. 'He's dead, y'know. Good riddance. We oughta kill more of 'em.'

'Who?' The question slipped out.

'Newspaper owners.'

There was a gasp from the woman seated immediately in front of Malone. The bus slowed to a stop, the woman stood up and Malone caught a whiff of her perfume: Arpège. He bought it every Christmas for Lisa, bought it with love in his heart while the fish-hooks in his pockets grappled with the hand trying to get out the cash. The woman turned and looked down at the bag-lady.

'The police should throw you in jail.'

The bag-lady smiled up at her with broken teeth. 'Oh, they do it regularly, missus. Then they throw me out again.'

Malone hid his smile. He rode on into the city, resisting the temptation to move into the empty seat in front of him; the bag-lady went back to her newspaper and didn't speak to him again till the bus drew into Circular Quay. By then they were the only two passengers left on the bus.

'Look after yourself, love,' she said as he stood up. 'What do you do?'

116

'I'm a cop.'

'You're a gentleman. If that ain't an oxymoron.' She gave him the gap-toothed smile. 'I once had an education. Helluva lotta good it did me. Look after y'self.'

Malone tipped his hat to her, got off the bus and crossed the road to the wharves. He caught a ferry to Manly, sitting outside to catch the breeze that blew across the harbour. He looked south to Vaucluse and caught a distant view of La Malmaison. From the wharf at Manly he caught a cab out to Harbord.

The taxi driver was a garrulous Lebanese. When they pulled up outside the Aldwych home, he looked at Malone with sudden interest. 'You gunna see the old feller, eh? You a cop?'

'No, I'm one of the old feller's oldtime standover men. You're not expecting a tip, are you?'

'Jesus, no! Have a nice day.'

Jack Aldwych lived on the highest point of the small seaside suburb, in a big two-storeyed house set in an acre or two of grounds, where a circus family had once lived and entertained the more bizarre of their performers, including the World's Only Siamese Triplets and a Bengal tiger with two tails.

Aldwych was sitting out on the wide verandah gazing out to sea as if he owned it, King Neptune in a sea-green alpaca cardigan, white trousers and white shoes. He didn't rise but just waved a hand as Blackie Ovens, his general handyman, handy with fists or iron bar, brought Malone up from the gates that kept the Dobermans in and the voters out. 'G'day, Scobie. Thanks for coming.'

'You're a ball of style, Jack. You on your way to the Gold Coast?' The Land of the Great White Shoe.

'My lady is trying to make me young again. She's not having much luck, except for this gear.'

'You've got a lady friend?'

'You met her once. Emily Karp, a real beauty with white hair.'

'Sure, I remember her. Well, she's doing a job on you.'

'You mean you think I look like a lair? Mebbe you're right. I look down at the white pants and I think mebbe I should be playing cricket. Or bowls.'

'I wish you had played cricket, Jack. I'd have bowled bumpers at you and tried to knock your head off. What's this about threats?'

117

Aldwych opened a leather-bound folder on the table beside him, handed Malone a sheet of paper. 'This came in the mail to Jack, at his office. Addressed to Mr John Aldwych.'

'Meant for him?'

'Anyone who knows Jack knows I'm his father. Any threat to him is a threat to me.' For a moment the face hardened; Malone saw the criminal boss of not so long ago. 'Look at this. All the letters cut out of newspaper headlines. I thought that happened only in fillums.'

'Didn't you ever send a threatening note?'

The old man grinned, evil as a cobra. 'I wanted to threaten anyone, I'd send Blackie and a coupla his mates. An iron bar's got more to it than a note. That's amateur stuff,' he gestured at the note. 'I done a bit of investigating. All them letters are cut from the *Chronicle*, it's their type.'

Malone held the sheet of paper by one corner and looked at the message. *You are not wanted. Stay out of it if you want to stay healthy.* The capital letters were arranged neatly, but they somehow made the warning look ridiculous; it was like a warning on a kindergarten blackboard. 'I'll take it with me, Jack. We may be able to lift some prints off it.'

'If you do, they're really bloody amateurs. My dabs are on it and Jack's would be, too. They'd be the only ones – the envelope was marked Personal and his secretary didn't open it. I suppose you've got my dabs on file?'

'Probably. But not Jack Junior's.'

'Well, if you want him, I'll have him call in on you. But there oughta be only three sets of dabs on it – mine, Jack's and the idiot's who sent it.'

Malone folded the note carefully and put it in one of the plastic envelopes he carried. 'Did you keep the envelope it came in?'

Aldwych shook his head. 'Jack didn't think to do that. He dropped it in his wastepaper basket and I guess it got thrown out. Sorry.'

'Can't be helped . . . I got the Ballistic report on the bullets they dug out of the Changs' Mercedes. They came from the same gun that killed Sir Harry.'

'The guy who fired the shots was either cockeyed or they were never meant to go near Jack.'

'They went bloody close to his Chinese neighbours.'

118

Aldwych nodded. 'I still think it was more a warning than any real shot to knock off Jack.'

'Did you know Sir Harry intended to sell Huxwood?'

'Did he? Jack told me he was just a pain in the arse, couldn't make up his mind.'

'He made up his mind the night he was killed. He told Lady Huxwood he was going to vote to sell.'

Aldwych tapped his fingers up and down on the book he had been reading when Malone arrived; it now lay on the small table beside the leather folder. Malone caught sight of the title on the spine: *Whatever It Takes*. The memoirs of a recently retired senator, a man who knew everything there was to know about what it took, a book as cynical as Jack Aldwych himself. But Malone knew that Aldwych would learn nothing from the book that he didn't already know.

'Who else knew besides Lady Huxwood?'

'I dunno. Maybe nobody.'

'So whoever did him in wouldn't have known?' Except Lady Huxwood, who hadn't wanted to sell. She was hard-shelled and, in her own way, ruthless; but would she have employed a hitman to kill her husband?

'I guess that sums it up. We haven't got the sides drawn up yet, those who want to sell and those who don't.'

Aldwych looked surprised. 'I thought you'd have all that worked out the first day.'

'Jack, I'm being ridden from the top. You never had to worry about office politics, did you?'

'Not after I'd eliminated those who tried it.' The smile told you nothing, whether he was joking or not.

A gentle nor'easter was coming in over the cliffs, bringing some gulls riding its currents. They circled the house, alighted in the garden and took off again immediately as the Dobermans tried for a poultry meal.

'You said the other day you had local equity besides your own in the Huxwood bid. Who is it?'

'I can't tell you that, Scobie, not till they want it known.'

'Jack, don't mess me around. This is serious, it's *murder*. Even you in your heyday didn't treat it as just part of a day's work.'

'You're getting insulting now. I thought we were mates.'

'Mates confide in each other. Who is it, Jack?'

Aldwych picked up the book, idly flipped through its pages as if he might find inspiration there; but the Senator had only advice on political murder, which is not an indictable offence but just a headline. 'Between you and me and no further, okay? Nothing in your running sheets or on your computer, whatever you use these days?'

Malone nodded.

'It's Charlie Bentsen. He already owns nine per cent and he's buying more, warehousing the shares till he comes out and announces what he's got. With our other interests, by the time we're finished buying, we'll have forty per cent.'

'Any of the family selling to you?'

'They can't. If they want to sell, they have to sell to someone else in the family.'

'Who's financing all this?'

Aldwych named two prominent, conservatively managed banks.

Malone nodded appreciatively. 'At least those two didn't get themselves into bother back in the boom days. If they're backing you, they must think you're pretty solid. You're going to finish up a billionaire, Jack.'

'Couldn't happen to a nicer bloke.' All smile, enjoying himself. 'I'm honestly rich, I'm friends with a cop – who'd of believed it? There are tycoons over in the West can't say as much.'

'You're still getting threats.' He stood up, putting the plastic envelope in his pocket. 'If you were still in the business, would you hire an untried hitman?'

'You think the job was done by a hitman?'

'Yes.'

'You mean you've got a suspect?' Malone said nothing and Aldwych went on with a hint of exasperation: 'Come on, Scobie – who is it?'

'I don't have a skerrick of evidence, so I'm not saying. It's just a gut feeling and I've never met a judge yet who listens to that.'

'You want me to take care of him?'

Malone couldn't help laughing. 'Jack, it never entered my head. I thought you said you'd reformed?'

'Retired, not reformed. There's a difference. I wouldn't do the job m'self.'

120

Malone looked after the bulky figure walking down towards the mailbox at the gates. 'Blackie?'

'He hasn't lost his touch. It was never delicate, so it would take a lot to lose it.' Aldwych was enjoying himself, reliving memories that could never have him indicted. 'Take care, Scobie. And don't forget – mum's the word on what I've told you.'

'I'll be going to see Charlie Bentsen.'

Aldwych considered that, then nodded. 'I guess you've got to. Just don't tell him you've been to see me. And if you come up with anything on that note, prints or anything, let me know.'

'I'll do that. Look after yourself, Jack.'

'I always have. You got wheels?'

'No, I'll have to call a cab.'

'Nuts to that. Blackie can drive you back to Homicide. I don't think he's ever given a lift to a cop, not an honest one.'

Malone sat down again while Blackie Ovens went to get the midnight-blue Daimler. He and Aldwych discussed the senator's book and sipped iced coffee while the gulls, with reinforcements, came back in on the breeze and fluttered menacingly above the Dobermans, who grew increasingly irritated and frustrated.

'Don't talk to Blackie about the good old days,' Aldwych warned. 'He gets teary and sentimental.'

5

Malone and Blackie Ovens did discuss the good old days, without tears or sentiment. 'There was honest crime then,' said Blackie. 'We knew who you were and you knew who we were. Sure, there was some bent coppers, but we knew who they were and so did youse. We respected each other, right?'

Malone wasn't quite sure his tolerance had gone that far. 'Different generation, different game, Blackie.'

'You can say that again. I'm just glad I never had kids. At least I don't think I did,' he added doubtfully. 'One of Jack's girls tried to con me one time, but I waited till the little bastard was born. Didn't look a bit like me. There was none of them DNA tests in them days, thank Christ. Here you are, Mr Malone. Right to the door. In the

121

Daimler, I hope they don't think it's yours, anyone looking.'

As he got out of the car Malone saw one of the bent coppers from the good old days coming towards him. 'Harry! Just the feller I want to see.'

Ex-Chief Superintendent Danforth pulled up sharply on the other side of a Ford stationwagon. He frowned, looked at Malone, then at the Daimler pulling out of the small parking lot. 'Scobie? They supplying Daimlers now with the new layout upstairs? I just been up there, having a look around. Different to what it was in my day.'

Malone nodded. 'Blackie Ovens and I have just been talking about the good old days.'

'Blackie Ovens, eh? He still working for Jack Aldwych?'

'That's Jack's car.'

Danforth looked at him: *you working for him, too*? Malone read the look, but didn't bite. He was not sure if Danforth had ever worked for Aldwych, but he was sure, with a certainty that was sickening, that Danforth had shot a protected witness on the orders of *someone*. 'How is the old bugger?'

'You wouldn't recognize him, he's so respectable these days.'

'A leopard can never change his spots.'

You'd know. 'You see anyone upstairs you know?'

'Only Russ Clements. He hasn't changed, either.'

'He has, actually. He's married now, to the Assistant Director of Forensic at the morgue. A German lady, a lovely girl.'

'You don't say! German, eh? Not the daughter of that bloke who was killing off people with a poisoned syringe a coupla years ago?'

'You don't miss much, Harry.'

'I read all the papers. I got nothing else to do these days,' he said wistfully.

He had always been overweight, but now he was almost gross; the very quantity of him suggested meals and drinks unlimited. The pink, mottled face was even more pink and mottled; the thin red hair was almost gone. He had been one of those who had benefited from the rule of seniority in the old Force; on merit he would never have risen above constable. All that distinguished him from other bent cops was that, though under suspicion several times, he had always managed to hide his corruption.

'How good's your memory, Harry? Going back twenty-five years?'

122

Danforth was suddenly cautious. 'Why?'

'I'm working on the Huxwood case. Something happened twenty-five years ago, when you were with Missing Persons. A girl who worked for Harry Huxwood disappeared. She was at work one day, gone the next. D'you remember her?' Malone flipped through his notebook. 'Pamela Arnburg?'

Danforth ran his hand over his head, an old habit, as if he were gathering his thoughts; now he was gathering memory. 'No, it doesn't ring a bell. The memory's not what it used to be . . .'

Malone was disappointed, though he should not have placed too much reliance on the older man's intellect and memory: the mind there had never been quick and it had been slowed by too much alcohol. 'Ah well, it was just a hope. I was going to give you a call — you live up the Mountains now, don't you?'

'Laura. The air does the wife good. I don't come to town much, too much effort.' *It would be with all that fat.* 'But I hadda come down today, I thought I'd pop out here and see the new quarters. I get nostalgic for the old days, y'know . . .'

Another one. But Malone couldn't see himself coming back to Homicide after retirement. 'I've still got a few years to go —'

'You'll be glad to pack it in?'

'I dunno, Harry. If I'm stuck in a desk job the last few years, I think I might be.'

'You should make Chief Superintendent, like me.'

Not the way you did, Harry.

Danforth had unlocked the door of his stationwagon, was about to get in when he straightened up and looked at Malone over the top of the car again. 'I remember that girl going missing now — her name meant nothing when you said it. She worked for Harry Huxwood, you said?'

'At the *Chronicle*, yes. She was the librarian. She was also rumoured to be his girl friend.' He had hesitated for a moment before voicing that. But (his own memory clearer by the moment) he remembered Harry Danforth had always responded to gossip.

'She was?' Danforth thought about that, looked regretful that he hadn't known it at the time. 'Well, well . . . I was on the point of leaving Missing Persons around then, I'd been moved to, I dunno, Vice, I think . . .'

'I was told that the file on the girl was closed, all of a sudden. She was never heard of again and nothing was done about her.'

'I wouldn't know about that. Like I told you, I'd moved on. Try Bill Zanuch, he took over from me. He'd of been the one who shut down the file.'

Chapter Six

1

Sir Harry Huxwood was buried in a small cemetery high on a ridge between the sea and the harbour. The view was magnificent but wasted; Sir Harry Huxwood would have been the first to laugh at the irony of it. Indeed he had, when his father had been buried in the same vault. Vault, perhaps, was an under-statement; it was more a mausoleum. Another prominent newspaper family had a vault in the same cemetery, but wisely had not attempted to rival the Huxwood grandeur. The bones in the mausoleum were no better than theirs or anyone else's. Skeletons only have value in closets.

Though the ceremony had been kept as private as possible, there was still a large gathering. Neighbours had come in their discreet best, out of respect and curiosity: you never knew whom you might see. They did see the Premier and the Opposition Leader, both with one eye constantly looking sideways for a photo opportunity; the election was only two days away and their minders rarely had the chance to show their charges in sober mode, as the captions next day would say. Neither of the politicians approached the widow for fear of being brushed off in a manner that nobody could mistake. Assistant Commissioner Zanuch, in full dress uniform, stood out amongst the funeral weeds. The State Governor, a modest man, regretted for a moment that he had chosen to come in mufti.

Though there was to be a memorial service in St Andrew's cathedral in the city in two days' time, the minister conducting the burial service was determined to get in his eulogy, two single-spaced pages of it. His voice droned on and Phillipa Huxwood, eyes sharp as needles behind her black veil, took stock of those close around her. None of the clan was missing; none of them would have dared risk her wrath. Her daughters and daughters-in-law all wore hats; the granddaughters let their hair blow in the wind. So did some of the grandsons; they all looked so *untidy*, she thought. Her eyes passed over both the Premier and the Opposition Leader; she ignored the little nod each of them gave her. Three strangers stood at some distance from the grave, half-hidden behind statues of angels like minor devils. They were vaguely familiar, but she was too short-sighted to be able to recognize them. She took her glasses from her handbag, lifted her veil and put them on; if they were reporters from the *Chronicle* she would have Derek dismiss them at once. But they were not from the paper: two of them were detectives who had come to La Malmaison on the day after Harry's – *murder*: it was a word she could not say even in her mind. The third man she did not recognize, but since he was with the woman detective she guessed he also was from the police. She was angry: did they have to continue their investigation at such a moment?

She was about to take off her glasses when she saw the woman in a dark suit standing not far from the police officers. She was half-hidden by a large Celtic cross that topped a hip-high vault; she wore no hat and her dark hair was blowing across her face and her dark glasses. Phillipa's first reaction was to curse her own glasses; if she had not put them on she would not have recognized the woman. Even after twenty-five years there was no mistaking Pamela Arnburg.

The minister finished his eulogy on a rising note that was swept away by the wind as if it, too, had lost patience with him. Sir Harry Huxwood went into the mausoleum to join his ancestors; Derek, standing next to his mother, knew how crowded it was in there. There would be room for his mother, but those following her would have to find their own final resting places. Looking around him, he decided he would be cremated, preferably in the middle of the night and not far from here. Then, as the door to the mausoleum was gently closed, he was surprised at the tears that blinded him. He was going to miss the Old Man: love temporarily demolished him. All the bitter rancour of the past two years went away on the wind.

'Wait for me at the car,' said his mother, moving away from him. 'I have to speak to someone.'

He watched her go, puzzled as she walked through the crowd of mourners, acknowledging none of them. She walked right by Bevan Bigelow and Hans Vanderberg as if they were no more than statues amongst all the other statues and continued on to a woman standing

126

some distance from the Huxwood mausoleum. Then people were crowding around him, offering condolences, and he lost sight of his mother.

Phillipa stopped a few feet short of the woman, separated from her by the low vault. 'I recognized you. Did you expect me not to?'

'I really didn't care. I didn't mean to intrude.'

'You haven't changed.' She managed not to sound envious, though she was.

'Oh, I have, Phillipa.' She tapped her breast, hinting at secret changes. 'We all do, it's inevitable. Even you, I guess.'

'Why did you come back? Revenge?' She didn't know what prompted her to make the last remark.

Pamela Arnburg smiled, took off her dark glasses and wiped one of her large dark brown eyes. She is still beautiful, thought Phillipa; though there were age lines round those eyes. She would be – what? – fifty now? She still had a good figure, slightly more rounded now perhaps, and the jawline and the neck had not yet been lost in the erosion of age. Phillipa couldn't remember what her voice had been like, but there was now a slight American accent to it, soft and drawn-out.

'My husband died six months ago. I just suddenly felt – well, lonely. You'll know the feeling soon.'

'I already do.'

They were speaking across a long-dead couple: George and Myrtle Frasa had died on the same day, December 24, 1913. In an accident? By common consent? Or had one murdered the other and then committed suicide? Phillipa knew she would never enquire.

'How long were you married?'

'Fifteen years. It took me ten years to get over Harry.' Pamela said it without malice or resentment, though Phillipa was sure there would be enough of the latter.

Phillipa took off her glasses, dropped her veil; from behind it she said, 'How long have you been back in Sydney?'

'A month.'

'Did you see Harry before –?' She gestured, her gloved hand like a black claw.

'No. We made a bargain. I kept it.'

Phillipa was not sure whether to believe her; they really were

127

strangers to each other, though they had fought over the same man. 'Where have you been all this time? Did you go to America?'

Pamela put the dark glasses back on; it was if she had taken them off to reveal to Phillipa what Harry had once fallen in love with. 'Yes. I lived in New York, I worked there as a librarian, I had no trouble getting a job after I got my visa. Thank you for arranging that.'

'It was no trouble.' She knew how to wield influence even with foreign consuls.

'I invested our – our arrangement and I lived very comfortably for ten years. Then I met my husband, Harry Stockton. No, I didn't marry him because he was another Harry. We went south, to Charleston, South Carolina. You'd be at home in Charleston, Phillipa.' She smiled again. Her teeth were white and even: American teeth, thought Phillipa, all that expensive dentistry. 'The Daughters of the Confederacy would elect you chairwoman, even though you are a foreigner. They love autocrats. Or do I mean aristocrats?'

'Have you any children?'

'No. When I had the abortion, they ruined my insides.' The smile had gone, there was bitterness now. 'If I'd had children, I wouldn't have come back. I owe you a lot, Phillipa.'

'Have you come back to make trouble?'

'No. I told you, we made a bargain.' Then she looked towards the Huxwood mausoleum and said wistfully, 'Did you keep him happy till the end?'

'We loved each other. You probably never understood that.'

They were still standing on either side of the vault; Harry had joined the Frasas, whoever they were. 'I did understand, Phillipa. What you never understood was that Harry could love both of us. Some men are capable of that. Some women, too.'

Not me, thought Phillipa; but didn't voice it. 'Are you going back to America? To Charleston?'

'Yes, next week. I have no one here. You were very fortunate I had no one back when –' She paused a moment, then went on, 'My parents were dead and I had no brothers or sisters. It made it so easy for me to disappear. Made it easier for you, too. I was surprised no one ever tried to trace me. The police –'

Phillipa glanced back towards the mausoleum. Dimly she saw that the crowd had dispersed; only the family remained beside their cars. 'I must be going. I can't say, welcome back.'

Pamela smiled again, a little ruefully. 'I never expected you to. Don't worry, Phillipa, I haven't come back to whip up an old scandal – our bargain stands. But tell me – who killed Harry?'

'I wish I knew,' she said and left her, stumbling a little as she brushed her knee against the vault and almost falling. 'Goodbye, Miss Arnburg.'

'Mrs Stockton.' But the wind caught those words, too, and they were gone.

Phillipa made her way cautiously between the graves towards those waiting for her. Derek came forward to take her arm. 'Who was that?'

'An old – friend.' He had never known Pamela Arnburg; he had been working in the *Chronicle*'s London office during those years. 'Let's go home. I'm tired.'

2

Malone looked at the flow-chart of the Huxwood homicide. There was as much flow in it, he mused, as there had been in the western rivers during the recent four-year drought. It amounted to not much more than a list of names; he was tempted to draw a red line under Dwayne Harod's name but resisted the obvious. Instead he wrote down a list of those who had not yet been interviewed:

Colin (Derek's son), Camilla (Sheila's daughter), Ivor and Beatrice Supple, Charlie Bentsen.

He paused and looked at the names, then added two more: Sophie Carpano, You Know Who.

He went back to his office and rang Superintendent Lozelle at Waverley. 'Steve, this is as far as we've got –' He gave the senior man a rundown. 'Not far, as you can see.'

'That should please You Know Who. He was on to me this morning, said he was going to the Huxwood funeral and he didn't want the cemetery over-run with my men.'

Malone grinned. What would AC Zanuch say if he knew that his junior officers bandied his name about like this, even if they never actually mentioned his name? 'Steve, can you spare me some men?

I want twenty-four-hour plainclothes surveillance on the under-gardener at the Huxwoods'. A kid named Dwayne Harod, a young Turk.'

'A Young Turk? I thought you only got those in political parties? Wasn't our PM one of those once?'

'I doubt if this kid would ever bother to vote. I've got no evidence on him, Steve, just a gut feeling he knows more than he's letting on.'

'Scobie, I've spent half my service life relying on a gut feeling.'

'How often has it let you down?'

'About half the time.' There was a chuckle at the other end of the line; then Lozelle said crisply, 'Okay, you'll get your surveillance. I can only spare one man at a time, though. I'll give you three. You want them to contact you direct, something happens? What are they looking for?'

'What he does in his spare time, who he meets with.'

'Is he dangerous, likely to trouble my men?'

'I dunno, Steve.'

There was silence on the line, then Lozelle said, 'You think he did the murder.' It was a statement, not a question.

'I don't know that, either, not for sure. But yes, I've got my sus-picions. Not off his own bat, someone paid him, I think.'

'He's a hitman? A professional?'

'I don't think so. But maybe he is. He's only young, twenty-one, but how old do you have to be to be a hitman?'

'These days, soon's your voice breaks.'

Malone hung up and sat back in his chair and looked out through the glass partition at the main office. Most of the desks were empty. There had been three more murders in the three days since the Hux-wood homicide; his resources were stretched thin. Three men besides Russ Clements were on stand-by to appear in court to give evidence on older murders. Sydney's homicide rate was as nothing compared to, say, Detroit's or Washington's, but that was little comfort to the man in charge in Sydney.

He picked up this morning's *Chronicle*. The Huxwood murder had disappeared from its pages. But the main editorial talked of law and order, said that it and the environment were the main issues of the coming election. Malone wondered if Sir Harry, amongst his roses, had ever given a thought to the environment. Probably not. The *Chron-*

icle, for all its professed liberalism, had always been pro-development. The paper had as many contradictions as Sir Harry, it seemed, had had.

Clements came in and slumped down on the couch by the window.

'Nothing at the funeral. Some of the women were weeping, it all looked pretty genuine. Even the men looked properly upset.'

'How was Lady Huxwood?'

'Stiff as a post. Does she ever unbend? She put her glasses on and gave me and Kate and John the once-over. When it was all done she went across and spoke to some woman, just the two of them on their own.'

'Who was the woman?'

Clements shrugged. 'I dunno. I got to one of the grandkids – Sarah? One of the better-mannered ones, she apparently doesn't hate cops. I asked her if she knew who the woman was, but she hadn't a clue. I wouldn't make much of it. People like the Huxwoods would know hundreds of people. I was surprised the crowd wasn't bigger. Zanuch was there, all done up in his silver braid. Made you feel proud to be a cop,' he said straight-faced. 'How'd you go with Dwayne the Turk?'

'He did it, all right. The question is, do I spread the word? *My* word.'

'You don't need to. Kate already thinks he's the one. She told me so at the funeral. Suspicion, she says, is an Italian trait. She's not sure whether it comes from the Mafia or Machiavelli.'

Malone had learned long ago to be cautious about his suspicions. He remembered a proverb he had once seen in a book of Lisa's: Suspicion is no fault, but showing it is a great one. 'Where's Kate now?'

'I told her to go back to the Huxwood house. Not to talk to anyone, just to check if anything out of the ordinary happened. I don't expect it to, but you never know. They looked a pretty sad lot, like at most funerals.'

Malone looked at his watch. 'She's taking her time.'

'She's probably gone to lunch. That's where I've been. Are you doing a time-and-motion study on us?'

'Do I sound that shitty?'

'Yes.'

Malone sighed, felt tension run out of him that he had hardly been

131

aware of. 'I got back here half an hour ago. There was a message to ring Greg Random – I did. One of the Minister's minders has been on to him, leaning on us to get a move on. He wanted to know, didn't we know there was an election on in a coupla days? I never knew before that solving a homicide was good election stuff. As if Bev Bigelow himself had jumped in and helped us solve it.'

'Law and order,' said Clements, gesturing at the newspaper on Malone's desk. 'It's always good election stuff, every time.'

'A homicide like this has nothing to do with law and order.'

'Do you think the ordinary voter works that out for himself? Out there in the file room we've got nine unsolved murders, plus the five we've got coming up in court next week. The voter lumps them altogether, along with the muggings, the rapes, the poofter-bashings –'

Malone waved him quiet. 'Righto, I know, I know. That's not all. I'd no sooner hung up on Greg than I got a call from Zanuch – he was on his car phone, on his way back from the funeral. He wants me to let him know next time I'm going to talk to Lady Huxwood.'

Clements bit his lip, his old habit when confronted with a new hurdle. 'He's telling you to stay away from her?'

'He didn't spell it out, he's too smart for that, but he knew I'd get the message.'

'So what are you gunna do?'

He was silent a while, then he said flatly and quietly, 'When I have to talk to her again, I'll do it. I may or may not let him know, I dunno.'

'I think you've always had your heart set on Tibooburra.'

Tibooburra was the remotest posting in the service, in the far north-west of the State, out where the rabbits and kangaroos roamed, where never was heard a discouraging word, at least not from Sydney.

'I'll take the risk. The Minister doesn't know it, but he's on my side.'

He looked out into the main room. Kate Arletti had just come back. He gestured at her and she came into his office, rolling up a sleeve that had come down. Her blouse was soaked, and two buttons were undone. She looked as if she had been caught in a bargain sale mêlée.

'I got caught in the rain, without a coat or an umbrella.'

Out beyond the windows the rain was falling steadily, the clouds sitting like elephants' bums on top of the city. The drought had truly broken, the farmers and graziers would be jumping up and down in

132

the paddocks, squashing the frogs that had come out into the open, hoping to learn to swim again.

'Anything to report?'

She looked at the chair opposite him, he nodded and she sat down. She did up the buttons on her blouse and smoothed down her bedraggled hair. 'There was a bust-up outside the front door of the Big House when they got back to the cemetery. Derek and Quental had words, then Derek threw a punch.'

'He's twice the size of Quental!'

She nodded. 'Practically everyone had gone inside except a couple of the grandsons, Michael and Colin. Quental ducked under the punch, then gave him one back, in the gut. It looked to me like a real boxer's punch, you know —' She shot out a straight left.

'Remind me not to argue with her,' Malone said to Clements. 'What happened then?'

'The two grandsons got into the act, separated them. Then they saw me up at the top of the drive and I thought it was time to make myself scarce.'

Malone looked at Clements. 'Looks like the war has started.'

'Do we go and ask them about it now?' But Clements didn't stir from the couch.

'Do you want to?'

'No. I might run into Lady Huxwood — she's your pigeon.' He grinned and then did stand up. 'I'm staying inside for the time being. Sorting out the law and order. Remember what they said to Lazarus — things will get worse before they get better.'

'Up yours,' said Malone, and saw Kate smile. He waited till Clements had gone, then he said, 'I want you to come with me in to the Strand Arcade, we're going to have a word with Dwayne's girl friend, Sophie. She works in a cosmetics and perfumery shop called —' He flipped through his notes. 'Janus? Isn't Janus supposed to be two-faced?'

'That's what make-up is all about,' said Kate, who wore little of it. 'Maybe the owner has a sense of humour.'

The Strand Arcade has had a chequered history. Over a hundred years old, it has thrived, been neglected, been refurbished, had a disastrous fire and been refurbished again. Now it resembles its original Victorian style, a quiet retreat from the brash streets at its either end. True, one or two of the brasher tenants have tried to jazz up its atmosphere, but the arcade usually wins out. There are no fast-food outlets, no CD or video stores, no discount houses: nothing bought here has ever fallen off the back of a truck. There are four floors to the arcade, with galleries running round in front of the shops and a clear uninterrupted view from the ground floor up to the vaulted ceiling.

A shoeshine girl, at work in front of a heavy padded chair such as one used to see in old-time barbers' shops, was a reminder of times gone by. The occasional group of youths, passing by in their Nikes and Reeboks, looked at her as if she were some medieval craftswoman. What's she doing, man? Shining shoes, for Crissake?

The Janus perfumery was squeezed between a nut-and-candy shop and a tea and coffee merchant's. The owner with the sense of humour was not present. Behind the counter was an attractive dark-haired girl in a pink uniform that showed more cleavage than Malone wanted to see while he was working.

'Miss Carpano?' He showed her his badge.

She looked both puzzled and afraid, as if she had been expecting them. 'Police?'

'We just want to ask you a few questions about Dwayne Harod,' said Kate Arletti. Malone had told her to do the questioning, on the premise that Sophie Carpano might respond better to a woman than to a man. 'You are his girl friend, we understand?'

'I was.'

'Was? You mean you've broken up with him?'

Sophie Carpano nodded. She was wary of the two detectives, her eyes flicking from one to the other like two black beetles ready to take off. She was an averagely pretty girl turned into a beauty by make-up; Malone wondered if she'd peeled off the artificial face when she had been alone with Dwayne. She looked too good for him, a class above him; but that was taking them at, well, face value.

'When did this happen?'

'Why are you asking me these questions?' She had picked up a perfume atomizer, was holding it as if it were a weapon. Malone grinned at the thought: he and Kate were going to be Maced with Chanel No. 5 or whatever.

'You know that Dwayne works as a gardener for the Huxwood family, the media family? You know Sir Harry Huxwood was murdered three nights ago?'

Miss Carpano had very severe, natural eyebrows; the make-up artist, if there was one, had not been allowed to touch them. They came down suddenly in a frown that made her look older. 'What's that got to do with Dwayne?'

'Nothing, we hope,' said Kate. 'We just wanted to check with you that he was with you on Monday night. Was he?'

The shop was small; there appeared to be no store-room or toilet facilities; one presumed Miss Carpano locked up and went elsewhere for that relief. All the stock was on the surrounding shelves or in the glass display counter. All the brands, familiar perhaps to Kate but not to Malone, were there.

Miss Carpano saw Malone looking at the perfumes. She said, an obvious attempt at escape, 'Could I interest you in some perfume for your wife or girl friend?' She looked sideways at Kate.

'She's not my girl friend,' said Malone with a grin. 'But my wife likes Arpège.'

'No offence to your wife, sir, it's still a lovely perfume. But it's old hat these days.'

So much for the only perfume he would ever recognize, whose signature was in his nostrils.

'We cater mostly for tourists, the Japanese mainly. They like the fruity perfumes, Calvin Klein, Issey Miyake, Asja by Fendi, those sort.'

There were none of the cheaper brands; Janus, evidently, catered for the carriage trade, as it used to be called. Then, as if on cue, the carriage trade was at the door: a dozen Japanese, let loose from a tourist carriage.

Malone and Kate moved out into the arcade. The shoeshine girl looked enquiringly at Malone, but he, an old-fashioned type who cleaned his own shoes every morning, smiled and shook his head.

Through the shop window he watched Sophie Carpano with the Japanese; she was a good saleswoman. She flirted with the men, but gave most of her attention to the women. She knew who would be wearing the make-up and the perfume.

'What d'you reckon?' he asked Kate.

She had been watching the way the Italian girl was handling the customers. 'Why would she be interested in someone like Dwayne?'

'We don't know what yarn he spun her. He's a born liar.'

'Do I ask her bluntly if she's ever seen him with a gun?'

'Why not? Just let's find out a little more about her first.'

At last the Japanese tourists came out of the shop, carrying their bags like looting soldiers. The shoeshine girl stood up, holding up her brush as if it had value the Japanese men couldn't resist; she was an attractive blonde with a wide smile and at once three of the men lined up to sit in her chair. A middle-aged woman said something to the tour guide, a young girl, and the latter burst into laughter. Kate, close by, looked at the guide, who seemed ready to share the joke.

'She said the men think she is an Australian geisha.'

'Oh, we're all like that,' said Kate and she and the guide laughed, ignoring Malone.

He, who wouldn't have known what to do with a geisha if he found one, went back into the shop. Sophie Carpano was re-arranging her stock. 'You seem to have done well,' he said.

'We always do with the Japanese. They can't believe our prices.' She turned back from the shelves, still wary of him. 'You said Dwayne worked as – a *gardener*?'

'He's the under-gardener, assistant, on the Huxwood estate. What did he tell you he was?'

'He said he worked for the *Chronicle*, on the business side.'

Kate had now come back into the shop; the tourists were still out in the arcade, making Japanese jokes about the men in the shoeshine chair. 'Where did you meet him, Sophie?'

'At a disco.' She seemed more relaxed with Kate; Malone stood back. 'You know how it is, you meet a guy – you don't check his credentials first time out, right?'

'How long ago did you meet him?'

'A month ago.'

'You've been going with him regularly ever since?'

She nodded. 'Two or three times a week, sometimes more.'

'Dutch shout or was he paying all the time? An assistant-gardener's wages wouldn't go far if you were out two or three times a week. What? Discos, movies, dinner?'

'All of them. We'd go to a disco at least once a week, dinner a coupla times. He always seemed to have enough money. Not a lot, but enough. You know what guys are like today, young ones. Some of 'em make money you wouldn't believe.'

'Not assistant-gardeners,' said Malone. 'Do you live alone or with your parents?'

'I have a small flat in Stanmore, my parents help with the rent. They didn't like the idea at first – they're Italian –'

'So are mine,' said Kate. 'Were. Things are okay with them now? How did they take to Dwayne?'

Sophie Carpano hesitated, then said, 'They met him only once, they didn't like him. Plus the fact he's a Muslim – though he says he's nothing. My mother's a strict Catholic, when the Pope was out here last month she was on her knees all the time he was here.'

'Praying for you?'

'How'd you guess?'

Malone was content to stand back; the two girls were now almost like old schoolchums. 'Did Dwayne ever spend the night at your flat?' said Kate.

The severe brows came down again. 'I think that's my business –'

'He told us he spent the night with you last Monday night, that's why we're asking. We're not passing judgement on what you do with your life, Sophie.'

Then Malone decided he had better ask the blunt question; he did not want the fragile rapport between Kate and Sophie abruptly spoiled: 'Did you ever see Dwayne with a gun? Did he ever talk about guns?'

The question was almost too blunt; her head reared back. 'A *gun*? Why would he –?' Then the reason behind the question straightened her even more: 'You mean you think Dwayne might of done the murder? Oh shit! No, he couldn't of –' But it was evident that she suddenly had doubts.

'Why did you break it off with him?' Kate said gently.

Sophie looked out into the arcade, as if willing the Japanese to come bursting in again; but, all shoes shined, they were now moving

137

off, the shoeshine girl farewelling them with her brush held up like a flag. Then she looked back at the two detectives. 'We had a fight Monday night. He hit me – it was over sex –' She looked at Malone. 'I'd rather talk to her alone.'

Malone nodded and went out into the arcade again, leaving Kate with Sophie. The shoeshine girl gave him another inviting smile and again he shook his head. If he went home and told Lisa he had paid to have his shoes shined, he would be the butt of jokes from her and the children for the rest of the week. They would never forgive him such extravagance, he who thought a fifty-cent tip made him a phil-anthropist.

Inside the shop Kate and Sophie Carpano were in deep conversation, woman to woman, no histrionics. Then Kate patted the other girl's arm; Sophie smiled as if in gratitude. She picked up the atomizer, sprayed Kate's wrists and behind her ears and the latter came out of the shop smelling of innocence and violets; which showed how the nose could play tricks.

'He tried to sodomize her, but she wasn't having any. She said she is covered in bruises all over the lower part of her body – I didn't ask for a look, not in there.' She nodded at the shop and its lack of privacy. 'I'm beginning to think our Dwayne is a real shit.'

Malone nodded in agreement, then tipped his hat through the windows to Sophie and he and Kate walked out to the Pitt Street Mall. It was still raining and a wind blew up the narrow mall, looping the rain in gusts. People held their umbrellas against the wind, sometimes walking into each other like colliding toadstools. A Hare Krishna member stood under an awning, his shaven head covered by an oilskin hat, his yellow robe the only spot of colour in the grey day.

'Go back to the office, Kate, and make up your notes. Don't put them into the computer, not yet anyway. I think we owe Sophie some privacy, maybe we can keep her out of all this. Her mother would die if she learned what Dwayne tried to do to her. Did she say what time Dwayne left her on Monday night?'

'He took her to dinner, then left her about eleven o'clock. She said he came back about one-thirty, she'd given him a key. He was on a high of some kind, she said, almost as if he was on drugs, though she said neither of them ever used them. Maybe killing someone gives some people a sexual high?'

138

'It does,' said Malone, remembering past murderers. Kate, he realized, still had a lot to learn about killers.

'Do we bring Dwayne in, then?'

'Not yet, we need more than we've got so far. We've got him under surveillance, that'll have to do for now. I don't think you could ever belt a confession out of him. But he pulled the trigger. All we have to do now is find out who paid him. I'll see you back at the office. Tell Russ I've gone to see someone at the *Chronicle*.'

He found a public phone and rang Beckett at the newspaper. 'Is Derek in today, Os?'

'He's just come in, he's here for the four o'clock editorial conference. There's another one at seven, but I dunno he'll stay for that. He looks pretty buggered. You coming in?'

'Yes. But keep it to yourself, okay?'

There was a dry chuckle from Beckett. 'I'm almost tempted to come back on to police rounds, just to cover this one. Drop in and see me when you come in.'

The rain suddenly eased and Malone decided to walk uptown to the newspaper's offices. He noticed, as he had several times before, how once he passed south of the Town Hall, the city, even the people in the street, seemed to change. It was hard to point a finger at the difference in the people, but it was there. This was the less affluent end of town, there were no fancy perfumery shops here catering to tourists; maybe that was it – the people here had to be careful with their money, no shoeshine girl would ever make a living this end of town. It was also kids' end of town: the cinema complexes, McDonalds, Pizza Hut, game parlours. He passed one of the cinema complexes, where teenagers were queueing up to see *Love and a .45*. There was another queue for *Pulp Fiction*, a movie he had seen, where the crims all talked like no crims he had ever known.

The guardian at the gate of the *Chronicle* recognized him. 'Who this time, Inspector?'

'Mr Derek.' He guessed that in dynastic empires the boss was always Mr Derek or Mr Charles or Mr Whatever.

The guardian made a phone call; then: 'Top floor, Inspector.'

Malone rode to the top floor, found Derek waiting for him when he got out of the lift. 'Come in, come in.' He led the way past a

139

receptionist into a large panelled office, the windows of which looked out on to the back end of Chinatown. The rain had started again, but there was no wind down this part of town and it just fell straight like a bead curtain. 'This was Dad's office. I'm just in here sorting out some of his things. You got anything to report?'

'Not really. I'm here to ask questions, Derek.'

'Ah.' Derek went round and sat down behind a large leather-topped desk and waved Malone to a chair opposite him. Portraits of other Huxwoods hung on the panelled walls; Malone did not know the artists, but there was a Dargie, a Longstaff, conservative artists at home in a boardroom. The portrait of Sir Harry showed none of the pain and strain that Malone had seen in the handsome face on Monday night. 'Am I a suspect or something?'

Malone ducked under that one. 'I understand you and Enrico Quental had a bit of a barney this morning. You threw a punch at him. Care to tell me why?'

'Oh, I care very much. No offence, but it's none of your business, Scobie.'

'All right. Another question. Your under-gardener, Dwayne, told me it was you who put him on. He couldn't have been the best of those who applied for the job.'

'He wasn't, there were two others with better references.'

'So why did you give him the job? A cane-cutter. Are you thinking of growing sugar?' He said it with a smile, to show they were friends, almost.

Derek was sitting back in the high-backed leather chair that had once been his father's throne. Here, Malone guessed, Sir Harry had been his own man, had not been threatened by Lady Huxwood. Derek, on the other hand, did look threatened; or perhaps it was just exhaustion. His smile was the wry one of a dying man whose humour had almost dried up. 'Perversity, Scobie. To spite my mother.'

Malone said nothing, waited for him to go on.

'She belongs to the old school, the sort of Australians who are dying out, thank Christ. She can't stand Wogs, Chinks, Dagoes, any sort of immigrant. Though she's too well-bred to use terms like that.' Again the wry, even sour, smile. 'She tried to get Dad to run anti-immigration editorials, but he wouldn't listen to her. Mum and I haven't been on the best of terms for some time now. When Dwayne turned up, I gave

140

him the job. As it happens, he's turned out to be a good worker, so Dan Darling tells me. The surprise is, my mother has come to accept him. He flatters her, I think. He can be oily when he wants to be. Why your interest in him?'

'We're interested in everyone out at La Malmaison. That's the way we work. We start out with a crowd and just keep eliminating. Much like choosing a cricket team.'

'And you're going to finish up with eleven suspects? That's not a good analogy, Scobie. Don't let's revive the old mates' act. It didn't work at last Monday night's dinner, did it?'

'No, it didn't.'

'I was going to write you, an apology. But then . . .' He stopped. The pain in his face was stark. Malone saw it and, against the grain of his training, crossed Derek off his list. He might have killed in anger, spontaneously, but he could never have cold-bloodedly hired someone else, *Dwayne*, to do the killing. He recovered and went on, 'Why do you suspect our gardener?'

'I told you, he's one of several. All of you, if you want the truth.' *Better include him, if only for appearance's sake.*

'It could have been an outsider, some burglar Dad disturbed.'

'It could've been.' But his tone implied he didn't believe it had been. 'Were you at odds with your father over the sale of Huxwood?'

'Yes and no. Dad couldn't make up his mind. He was always like that, just between you and me.'

Didn't he know that there were others on the *Chronicle* staff who knew Sir Harry's failing?

'He was distressed that some of the family wanted the sale. But he recognized that it happens, that in − dynasties, if you like, there's not the same loyalty when it gets down to the third, fourth or fifth generations.'

'He'd made up his mind to sell the night he was murdered. Your mother told me that.'

Derek nodded. 'She told me, too.' He was silent a moment, then he said, 'You have a piece of our notepaper, my brother-in-law Ned tells me. You didn't show it to me.'

'That was an oversight,' Malone admitted. 'I think I was paying too much attention to Mr Van Dieman at the time.'

Derek grinned, but with little humour. 'Yeah, he can get under your

141

skin. He gets under mine occasionally . . . I think the paper was a scrap from a memo I'd left in Dad's room — I gather most of it had been torn off?'

'All of it, except for a scrap with the word No scrawled on it in red marking pencil. Exclamation mark. What was in the memo?'

'You don't have it?'

'It's back in what Sergeant Clements calls his murder box. The computer has taken over practically everything in a homicide investigation, the old running sheets, the checking of records, everything like that. But you still can't store *physical* evidence in a computer. Not without buggering up the works,' he added almost with relish. He knew already that he would never be able to read the signposts on the information superhighway.

Derek nodded again. 'I feel the same way about our VDTs. They're necessary, it's progress, but I miss the old ways. We ran a feature on Bill Gates when he was out here and when I read it, for me it was like the Coming of the Apocalypse . . . Anyhow, the memo. It told Dad that if he couldn't make up his mind, I was going to ask our institutional shareholders, who are our biggest shareholders outside of the family's holding company, I was going to ask them to invite Kerry Packer in as a buyer. I'd rather him than an overseas buyer, even one like Metropolitan. As soon as the Poms took over, they'd have their own men in here, trying to turn us into a Fleet Street tabloid.'

'And your father would prefer them to Packer or Rupert Murdoch or any other Australian buyer? I thought he'd be more nationalistic than that.'

'The truth is, I don't think Dad knew what he wanted. Lately, his mind seemed to be elsewhere. I dunno where, but elsewhere. Would you like to see the *Chronicle* sold?'

Malone realized it was more than an idle question; it was personal, not the sort of question put by a survey poll. 'Me? You mean a reader's opinion would count in a — what's the figure? Two billion? In a sale like that?'

'No.' Again the tired smile. He waved a hand at the window behind him. 'I'd like to know someone out there was on my side.' But if there was anyone out there, the rain hid them. It was falling now like a tropical downpour.

'I think most of your readers would be on your side. I would be,' he said and realized how much the *Chronicle* was part of his life. 'I grew up with it. My dad was – *is* – a real old-time Labor socialist. He'd bring home *The Worker* each week, but every day we got the *Chronicle*. Yeah, I'd be against selling it. I think most people would be.'

Derek shook his head. 'Not *people*, Scobie. Our readers maybe, but not *people*. Most people don't read newspapers any more. Sixty-five per cent of them get their news from radio or TV. What sort of news is that? Illustrated headlines, that's TV. Verbal headlines, that's radio. The world is filling up with news illiterates. Political editorials don't hold any clout any more. The dills of the world, and there's too many of them, they vote on the image, what they see on TV.'

The two of them sat in silence, troglodytes in a cave where presses rather than lions used to roar, while outside the dills of the world sat in a spreading harvest of television sets and radios blared, the new band of angels.

Then Malone said, 'But why would your father be against selling to Packer or Murdoch? I've seen pictures of them together, better mates than you and I.'

'Ouch,' said Derek, but grinned, with a little more real humour this time. 'Of course, the cross-media ownership thing could stop them. But as for the pictures, never believe one of newspaper proprietors together. They never love each other. It's an emotional impossibility, worldwide. In Britain Northcliffe, Beaverbrook, the Astors, they were never bosom buddies. In the US the same – Pulitzer, Hearst, MacCormick, they never sent valentines to each other. They were the old-timers, but the latest batch are no different. Look at the price war between Murdoch and Black in London a year or so ago . . . Dad had an ego as big as any of them, as big as those of my grandfather and my great-grandfather. He just hid it better than some. If you're a gentleman – and Dad always was – most people never think of you as having an ego.'

'All right, who do you think was your father's biggest enemy in the extended family?'

Derek didn't hesitate: 'I was. We've done nothing else but fight the last two years. Him and my mother.'

'Over what?'

'A lot of things. The way the paper was run, the staff we employed.'

143

He leaned forward, almost as if he were still arguing with his father. 'Newspapers have changed, have *had* to change. People no longer want just *news*, they want – I hate the bloody word, but they want *infotainment*. Compare the *Herald* or the *Australian* with what they were like even just ten years ago – you wouldn't think they were the same papers. We've had to go the same road – and Dad hated it. So did I, but I had to be pragmatic, you don't make money running against the traffic. So I went shopping for columnists, writers who could entertain as well as inform. I had to start paying salaries that gave Dad a heart attack – well, not actually.' He sat back, the wry smile in evidence again but not sour this time. 'Of course, we've now got so many columnists they're trying to shoulder each other aside. We've got so many columnists on the sports pages they look like one of those American gridiron teams running out to play, two hundred of them all dressed up for the occasion. I hate it all, but as the kids say, it's the way to go. But Dad never saw it that way.'

'Did anyone know of your fights?'

'No, we tried to keep them as private as possible. Of course, some of the editors knew, that was unavoidable.'

'What about your wife? Your kids – you have three, that right? You never took your troubles home?'

'Do you?'

'Most of my troubles have to do with murder, Derek. That's a bit different from office politics.' *But yes, last night I did take my troubles home.*

'Well, okay, yes, I did discuss them at home. With Cordelia, once or twice with the kids when they were at dinner with us. But I never made an issue of it, tried to get them involved.'

'How do your kids feel about the sale?'

Then there was a knock on the door and a secretary looked in. 'They're waiting for you downstairs, Mr Derek. The four o'clock conference.'

Derek stood: a little too quickly, Malone thought. 'You'll have to excuse me, Scobie. I've missed the last three conferences, this morning and yesterday. I'm still executive editor. I'm glad we had this talk. Though I don't know I've been any help?'

Malone didn't answer the implied question. 'We'll talk some more, Derek. Take care.'

Derek looked at him sharply, pausing as he rounded the desk. 'You think I should?'

'You never know.'

He said it only to keep stirring the pot. He might have made a good columnist, even in a crowded field.

4

When Malone got out of the lift on the ground floor he saw Alexandra Huxwood and a tall young man coming across the lobby. He waited outside the lift, holding the door open. 'Miss Huxwood, could you spare me a few minutes?'

'What's this about?' The young man was as tall as Malone, broad-shouldered and upright. His long dark hair was held together in a pony-tail; he wore a dark-blue double-breasted suit and a tieless white shirt. He had a reasonably good-looking face that at the moment was hard with aggression. 'Who are you?'

'He's Inspector Malone,' said Alexandra. 'A friend of Dad's.'

'Almost,' said Malone. 'You're Colin?'

Colin Huxwood just nodded, still plainly hostile.

'I'd like to talk to both of you,' said Malone, still holding open the lift door while people on floors above buzzed for it. 'Where can we go?'

Alexandra looked as unfriendly as her brother. But she glanced at her watch, then said, 'Dad will be at the four o'clock conference. Let's go up to his office.'

They rode in silence up to the top floor, Malone relaxed and the two Huxwoods stiff with antagonism. Their attitude did not worry Malone, but he was not going to be patient with them, even if they had just come from the funeral of their grandfather. He was running out of sympathy for the Huxwood clan.

Alexandra strode past the enquiring look of the receptionist at the desk between Sir Harry's room and the adjoining one. 'We shan't be long, Sheryl. Dad won't mind.'

Colin Huxwood closed the door behind the three of them, sat down on a green leather couch beside his sister and waved Malone to a matching chair that half-faced the couch. Malone's peripheral vision

145

had already told him this was a smaller version of the chairman's office: the same panelling, the same leather and antique timber. The portraits of the ancestors were missing and in their place were framed front pages of past *Chronicles*.

Colin took off his jacket, took a dark tie from one of the pockets and threw the jacket and tie over the side-arm of the couch. 'What's this about? This is hardly the day to be worrying my sister, is it?'

Malone was tired of explaining that homicide investigations didn't conform to social niceties. 'Do you work here, Colin?'

'No, I don't. I work for —' He named one of the biggest advertising agencies in the city.

'A copy-writer?'

'No. I'm an account executive.'

How old would he be? Twenty-five? 'It's a young man's game, I gather.'

'We get our positions on ability, not seniority.'

'It's like that in the Police Service.' *Now.* 'How do you two feel about your grandfather's murder?'

Alexandra gave a low gasp and even Colin seemed surprised by the bluntness of the question. 'Christ Almighty, how do you think we feel? We're both — shattered.' He felt for and squeezed his sister's hand. 'Yeah, shattered. There's no other word for it.'

Malone could now see the resemblance of the young man to his younger brother Ross; resentment of any sort of authority seemed to be endemic in the Huxwood grandchildren. 'Have you thought about why he was murdered?'

His use of *murdered* was deliberate, it had more punch than *killed*. He hoped Colin, a man selling words, would appreciate that.

'Why do *you* think he was murdered?' Alexandra, it seemed, was more controlled than her brother.

'Oh, I think it's perfectly obvious, don't you? Someone resented your grandfather's approach to the selling of Huxwood Press. How do you two feel about it?'

'I'm against it,' said Colin, still belligerent.

'Alexandra?' Malone looked at her.

She took her time; she was never going to be rushed for a reply. 'I've thought a lot about it. I couldn't care less one way or the other. I'll still be a Huxwood.'

She is her grandmother's granddaughter, he thought; some day she would be just as imperious. 'The family name means a lot to you?'

The hard look seemed to soften. 'Yes.'

'What about you, Colin?'

'The same.' He, too, looked a little tense now, less aggressive. 'We're a —' He hesitated.

'A dynasty?'

'Well, yes. Except it sounds a bit high-flown.'

'I didn't think that would upset an advertising man.' But he grinned when he said it and Colin appeared to accept that there was no malice behind the remark. 'Alexandra, were you — are you planning to make a career here at the *Chronicle*?'

'I don't know, the way things are.' She had taken her time again about answering.

'Do you find it difficult being the boss's daughter?'

Brother and sister looked at each other, then she nodded. 'Is there ever any nepotism in the police force?'

'I think that's one handicap we've managed to dodge.' *But I could tell you of dozens of others, scores of them.* The police culture of not blowing the whistle on one's workmates was a variation on nepotism. 'Colin, what about you? You've never wanted to take over the *Chronicle* from your father?'

'No, I'm not a newspaperman, I don't think I ever could be.'

'You're an advertising man?'

Colin hesitated a moment. 'No, not really. I'm learning the ropes. I'm lucky, I seem to have a knack for it.' There was no aggression now. 'No, eventually I'm going into TV, it's the way to go.'

Out there catering for the dills of the world.

'You'd like to run one of the Huxwood channels?' He had looked up the extent of the Huxwood empire. There were two television stations, one in South Australia, the other in Queensland. The cross-media laws did not allow for ownership of a television station and a major newspaper in the same State, so Huxwood had no television interests in New South Wales. The cross-media laws were irksome to the tycoons, a constant rash that was anti-capitalist.

'Yes.' No hesitation this time.

'Where did you go to school?'

'Cranbrook.'

147

'Kerry Packer's old school?'

'I'm a great admirer of Mr Packer.'

'Did your grandfather know that?'

'Ye-es.' Reluctantly.

'If Huxwood is sold lock, stock and barrel, you could never buy back one of the channels, could you? Not with your share of the sale.'

'You seem to know a lot about our share of the estate,' said Alexandra. 'How do you know what we'd get and what a TV channel would cost?'

'I do my homework.' Actually it had been Clements who had done it. 'I understand if the sale goes through each of you will get around fifty, sixty million dollars each.' He said it as if he were accustomed to quoting that sort of money every day in the week. 'I don't know what a TV channel in South Australia or Queensland would cost, not the ones Huxwood owns, but Alan Bond paid a billion dollars for Channel Nine here in Sydney and Kerry Packer bought it back from him for around five hundred million. It was looked on as a bargain, the buy-back.'

'You sure have done your homework,' said Colin.

'Did you ever discuss the sale of Huxwood with your grandfather?'

'I didn't.' Colin looked at his sister. 'Did you?'

'Yes.' She took her time; this girl, Malone decided, was never going to be hurried. 'He told me he was not going to sell.'

'He was definite about it?'

'Yes.' She pushed back a strand of hair that had fallen over one eye. She had rather small eyes and Malone decided that that was where her lack of real beauty lay; the rest of her features were not bad. Her eyes were grey and, at times, seemingly opaque, bits of glass behind which her mind had retreated. 'Why do you ask?'

'Oh,' he was off-handed, 'I'd heard he could change his mind from day to day.'

'Who'd you hear that from?'

'Here and there.'

'Rosie Gilligan?' He could hear the venom in her voice.

'No, not her. What do you do for Miss Gilligan?' He was aware of Colin watching them closely.

'I'm her general dogsbody, her go-fer. I arrange her interviews, our own fashion shoots – we do four a year for special issues. I do *every-*

148

thing except get my name in the paper.' The venom was there again.

'Where do you two live? Out at Vaucluse?'

'Alex does,' said Colin, taking over; he's protecting her from herself, thought Malone. 'She lives at home with Mum and Dad and my brother Ross. I have a flat in Bellevue Hill.'

'I have to ask this – where were both of you last Monday night?'

'Jesus, you don't think we killed Pa, do you?' He looked at his sister and they both shook their heads and smiled at each other at the stupidity of the question.

'No,' said Malone, keeping his temper. 'But I'd like to know anyway. Where were you?'

'I had dinner with a client, at Merony's.' Colin seemed to appreciate that Malone was in earnest, that the question had *not* been a joke. 'I was there till, I dunno, ten-thirty, I guess. Then I went home and went to bed. I didn't go to sleep right away, I sat up in bed watching the cricket from the West Indies. I've subscribed to pay-TV.'

'And you, Alex?'

Again there was the deliberate pause. 'I was home all night, at least till eleven o'clock. Then one of Ross's rugby friends called me to say Ross was at the Royal Oak at Double Bay, pretty drunk and making a nuisance of himself. I got my car and went there to pick him up and bring him home.'

'Did you get him home before your mother and father came across from the dinner party at the Big House?' Derek and Cordelia had said they were back in their own house by eleven-thirty.

'No. There was a bit of a scene . . . Ross has told me you know about him and Rosie.'

'How long did the – the scene last?'

'I don't know. I went up to bed, I'd done my bit for the family's reputation. Ross has been picked up by the police several times for making a nuisance of himself.'

He could see her going up to her room, detached from whatever had gone on between Ross and his parents. He stood up. 'Righto, I think that's all for now. I may have to talk to the two of you again.' He looked at one of the framed front pages above the heads of the two young people. 'That was an interesting day.'

'The day I was born,' said Alexandra, standing up and looking at the page behind the glass. She appeared much more at ease, even

149

friendly: or is that because I'm leaving? Malone wondered. 'Amongst other things. I just didn't get a headline.'

Malone leaned closer. August 10, 1974, said the dateline. FORD SUCCEEDS NIXON, said the main headline. There were other, lesser stories. Bread had gone up another two cents a loaf to thirty-seven cents. A million State workers had been granted four weeks' annual holiday. Two men had robbed a betting shop of eight thousand dollars. Malone straightened up. 'Who had this office before your father became executive editor?'

'Grandfather,' said Colin. 'He'd have been editor-in-chief when that page appeared. That was what he was called in those days, they hadn't invented the word *executive* then. Dad told me Pa wrote the editorial on the Nixon resignation. I've read it, it's a beaut. Giving the man his due for what he did on foreign affairs, but scathing about him as a man. Pa had pretty high standards on how a politician, particularly a president or a PM, should behave.'

Malone wondered what Sir Harry would have written about his own behaviour with Pamela Arnburg four years earlier. But then, he guessed, editors-in-chief or executive editors, whatever one called them, never wrote anything about themselves.

Chapter Seven

Malone rode down to the fourth floor with the two Huxwood siblings, got off when they did. Alexandra looked at him in surprise. 'You're getting off *here*?'

'I'm seeing Ossie Beckett.'

'What is he, your mole?' The aggression was back, like a flash of temper.

'Alex!'

She looked at her brother, then back at Malone. Unexpectedly, her apology sounded sincere: 'I'm sorry, Inspector. I shouldn't have said that.'

'No, Alex, you shouldn't. Ossie Beckett and I are old acquaintances, that's all. Have a nice day with Rosie.'

He found his way through the maze of desks, most of them now occupied. Some of the journalists were frowning, suffering shock waves, as if confronted with another cliché: what was another word for mode? they asked their VDTs, but the machines had no answer. A young reporter Malone recognized as the State political roundsman looked bored: what was new that could be said about yet another election, where was a grain of truth to be found in the quarry-ful of press releases? The financial reporters, though, were busy, leaning forward into their VDTs like kids in a game parlour: the possible sale of Huxwood could now be written about. Malone went into Beckett's cubbyhole and no one questioned his presence.

He sat down and waited. It was another fifteen minutes before Beckett appeared. He was in dark suit trousers, a white shirt and a black wool tie. 'I've been to the funeral,' he said, squeezing in behind his desk.

'I didn't think people wore black ties to funerals any more. I saw a picture recently of a feller wearing a Sydney Olympics tie. I wondered if he was going to long jump over the grave.'

'Was he burying an old athlete?'

'No, it was his grandmother.'

'Maybe she'd been a discus thrower at the Berlin Olympics.'

It was all chit-chat, confetti tossed into the breeze as they worked their way towards the real reason why Malone was here. Now Beckett said bluntly, 'You wanted to see me? This is a busy time, Scobie.'

'You *asked* me to drop in and see you, Ossie.'

'Did I?' Beckett looked at a large notepad he had brought in with him; then he pushed it away from him, sat back in his chair. 'Did you see Derek?'

'Yes. He's got a lot on his mind.'

Beckett nodded abstractedly, as if Derek was not on *his* mind. Then he said in his usual flat voice, 'Pamela Arnburg turned up at the funeral today.'

'Oh? Did you speak to her?'

Beckett shook his head. 'She and Lady Phillips had a little conflab, then she disappeared. I thought about chasing her, but decided that wouldn't go down well with the Old Lady.'

'Were you surprised to see she's still alive?'

'I dunno. I guess so. What did you think had happened to her, after I told you about her?'

'I hadn't made up my mind. Fifty per cent of the people who disappear, never to be heard of again, chances are they're dread. Yes, I thought she was probably dead.'

dead

'Murdered?'

'I don't know I was prepared to go that far. But yes, I guess I thought it was a possibility. How did she look?'

'Still a dish, considering she's twenty-five years older. She's worn well, that's how I recognized her. Not at first, she had on dark glasses, but when she took 'em off, yeah, it was Pamela, all right.' He wobbled his head in appreciation of Pamela Arnburg. 'God, she looked good! As a man gets older, older women look better. Some of them.'

'My wife loves a chauvinist like you,' said Malone. 'I want to talk to her, Os.'

'So would I. What a story —' He wobbled his head again. 'I don't know where she is, Scobie. Do your own dirty work.'

152

'Righto, tell me where to start?'

'I haven't a clue. Why do you want to see her? She's ancient history.'

'To ask her why she came back from wherever she's been all these years. Revenge, the woman spurned, all that.'

'I didn't know you read Mills and Boon. Harry didn't *spurn* her. It was Lady Phillipa who screwed her. If you'll forgive the expression.'

'How do you know it was Lady Phillipa?'

Beckett drew the notepad towards him, as if to say the conversation was over; then he pushed it away from him again. 'Okay. Rosie Gilligan came to me once, asked me what I knew about Pamela Arnburg – she was before Rosie's time here. She said Harry had let his hair down once to her, said he'd had an affair years ago with a girl who worked here, that his wife had broken it up. That was when Rosie decided to break it off with Harry – she didn't want Phillipa's knife in *her* back . . . Are you hinting Pamela came back to kill Harry?'

'Not personally, no. But she could have come back and paid someone to do it.'

'You think it was a hit job?'

'We don't know.' *To show suspicion is a great fault.* 'Where do I start to look for Pamela Arnburg?'

'I really don't know, Scobie. Like I told you, evidently she had no family, no parents or brothers or sisters. Nobody.'

'*Someone* must've known her.' Malone got to his feet. 'I'll find her. I just hope she did have nothing to do with Harry's murder. If she did, you're going to have enough dirt to turn the *Chronicle* into a scandal sheet. Like *Beckett's Budget* back before World War Two.'

'You're too young to remember that. Even I am.'

'We hear a lot of old scandal in the Police Service. We sometimes have to look up those old papers like the *Budget* and *Truth*. I hope you're no relation to *Beckett's Budget*?'

'No connection. Jesus, I'd hate dirt like that to come out – I mean about Harry and Pamela.'

'Prepare for the possibility, Os. What's the score on the takeover of Huxwood? Has it been put off because of the murder?'

'Derek didn't seem to think so. The wolves are at the door. A bit of blood only excites them.'

Malone thought that was going too far in describing Beatrice Supple

153

and Metropolitan Newspapers. 'I'll let you know if I manage to trace Miss Arnburg. If she gets in touch with you . . .'

'Why would she do that? I won't wish you luck, Scobie. I'd rather keep the dirt out of the *Chronicle*. A man my age has to have a few things left to believe in.'

Malone left him to his shredded beliefs. On his way through the newsroom he saw Alexandra on the far side of the room. He made a gesture of farewell, but there was no response. It struck him that no one in the big room was looking at him with any friendliness. He was on a par with the other wolves at the *Chronicle* door.

2

Malone called a cab from the Chronicle's lobby and went back to Homicide with a cab driver who welcomed the rain with as much fervour as any farmer. 'Great for business! Days like this I wish I had a licence for a bus instead of a taxi. Look at 'em,' he said gesturing at waving people under shop awnings. 'Hands up like a classroom of kids busting for a piss. Great day!'

Malone didn't spoil his great day by giving him a tip. He got out of the cab, ran through the rain and went up to his office. As soon as he had taken off his wet jacket he called in Phil Truach, who had worked in Missing Persons before he had come to Homicide. 'Phil, when a file is closed at Missing Persons, what happens to it?'

Truach bounced his cigarette lighter in one hand; he was always on his way to a smoke or just coming from one. He had a voice coated with smoke and the skin of his lean face had a yellow pallor, yet Malone had never seen him out of breath or known him to take a day off through sickness. His shirt should have been covered in tobacco company logos.

'Now they're on computers they probably don't close a file for ten years. Maybe more, I dunno. When I was with them we still had filing cabinets and manilla folders. What's the problem?'

Malone explained whom he was looking for, without explaining why Pamela Arnburg had disappeared. 'All I know is that the file was closed a week after she disappeared.'

'Give me five minutes.'

'Take ten. You look as if you're dying for a smoke.'

Truach grinned, nodded and tossed the lighter in the air, caught it deftly. 'You're a civilized man, Scobie. I'll be back.'

He was back in ten minutes; the lighter was no longer in sight. 'Their files only go back to 1975. In theory, they said, the files are supposed to be kept forever, if the missing person isn't found, but that's only theory and you know what happens to theory. It gets burnt, along with all the other trash. Incidentally, it's no longer Missing Persons. It's the Community Tracing Section, as of a coupla weeks ago. The name-changers are at it again, making work for themselves. When do you think they'll find a new word for Homicide? Community Disposals, maybe?'

Malone grinned. 'Any day now. Thanks, Phil.'

'You don't want me to follow it up?' Truach didn't look enthusiastic. He was up to his neck in another murder, a domestic that had brought about the deaths of an immigrant woman and her two small children. Other religions, other customs were widening the education of those in Homicide.

'No, I'll handle it.'

When Truach had gone back to the main room Malone looked at his phone for fully five minutes before he picked it up. Even then he hesitated before he asked for Assistant Commissioner Zanuch.

'Yes, Inspector?' Zanuch was always formal on the phone.

'Could I come and see you, sir? Something has come up on the Huxwood case.'

'It's late, Inspector. I have to go to a reception.' A funeral and a reception all in one day; Assistant Commissioner Zanuch hardly had a moment to himself. 'All right, be here in ten minutes.'

In peak hour traffic? What does he expect me to do, use the siren?
'Yes, sir. I'll be there.'

He was two minutes late, arriving at Police Headquarters just as the rain stopped; he did a U-turn through three lines of traffic and parked the car in the police zone outside Headquarters. A grizzled sergeant, older than Malone, grinned at him as he went through the front doors. 'That's the stuff, Scobie. Why didn't you give 'em the siren and the flashing light?'

'G'day, Barry. And give the Service a bad name?'

Zanuch looked at his watch as Malone entered his office, but said

155

nothing. He was in mufti this afternoon, Zegna-suited (though no label showed), the silk police tie flat against a pale-blue shirt with a wide-spread collar just like that worn by Prince Charles in the photo behind him. AC Zanuch was never buttoned-down.

'What is it, Scobie?' He looked at his watch again. 'Ten minutes is all I can give you.'

Malone told it as flatly as he could. 'A woman appeared at the Huxwood funeral this morning. She remained apart, but Lady Huxwood went across to speak to her. The woman was a Pamela Arnburg, who used to work at the *Chronicle* as a librarian and disappeared twenty-five years ago.'

'Yes?' The long-fingered hands were steepled together.

'I understand you were the sergeant in charge of Missing Persons when she disappeared.'

A small frown was the only reaction. 'I dimly remember the case.'

Is he telling me to forget it? 'I understand you closed the file after a week.'

'You're talking of twenty-five years ago. If I closed the file, as you say, there must have been a good reason for it.'

'I want to trace the woman, sir. She's on my list now.'

'List?'

'Of suspects.'

The fingers were untangled, he leaned forward on his elbows; the body language was four-lettered. Malone waited for the explosion, but the Assistant Commissioner had too much control for that. 'You actually think this woman might have murdered Sir Harry? You really are stretching it, Malone.'

'Maybe, sir. I don't think she would have pulled the trigger, no. But she could have paid someone to do it.'

'Now you think it was a hit job?'

Don't sidetrack me. 'Yes. The woman had no family, no relatives at all, it seems. But she must have had *someone*, a friend of some sort, someone whose name was on that file.'

Zanuch sat back, but didn't relax. 'You don't expect me to remember a detail like that, do you?'

'No, sir. But I thought Lady Huxwood might know something about her, something that would help me trace her.'

'Why would Lady Huxwood know anything?'

156

'Because —'

He hesitated, then plunged in: Tibooburra, he could see, was just over the horizon. He told Zanuch what Beckett had told him, without revealing where he had got his information.

'Where did you get all this?'

Name no names: 'People who were working on the *Chronicle* at the time.'

'It could be just office gossip —'

'No, sir. It's a fact.'

Zanuch sat absolutely still, like a man who suddenly had had a glimpse of rigor mortis. Christ Almighty, thought Malone, all he's thinking about are his connections out at La Malmaison! 'Why would this woman — Arnburg? — why would she have Sir Harry killed?'

'Revenge, maybe. I have a list as long as my arm of women we've arrested for revenge murders. And men, too.' He had almost given up: somehow or other Zanuch was going to deny him interrogating Lady Huxwood on the matter.

Then, making no attempt to hide his reluctance, Zanuch said, 'Okay, talk to Lady Huxwood. But go gently with her.'

'I'll do that, sir. I hope I haven't kept you too long from the reception.' What social alp was he climbing this evening?

Zanuch looked as if he were searching for sarcasm; but Malone remained bland. 'No. No, it's all right. One can never be too late at a reception, unless it's for oneself.'

'So I'm told, sir.'

When Malone had gone Zanuch sat at his desk, all at once in no hurry to go to the reception at the Conservatorium, where Bev Bigelow, who didn't know Mahler from McCartney, was to hand out something called the Mozart scholarships. He sat there for fully five minutes, then he reached for the phone.

'Phillipa?'

3

'I was expecting you, Inspector.'

'I thought you might be, ma'am.' They were in the library. The rain had gone, the clouds had risen and broken up. The last of the sunlight slanted in through the windows to give a golden sheen to the brown room. 'It's about Pamela Arnburg.'

Phillipa Huxwood made no pretence that she did not know who Pamela Arnburg was. 'Where did you get her name?'

'You really don't expect me to tell you that.'

'No, I suppose not. But I can guess.' A look of pain crossed her thin face; or perhaps it was shame. She was wearing a high-necked dark purple wool dress and looked as if she were feeling cold. She wore a minimum of make-up and just a silver brooch at her throat. 'Is it common knowledge in the office?'

'The *Chronicle*? No. It wasn't passed on to me as gossip, Lady Huxwood, and I'm sure most people there know nothing of what we're going to talk about.'

'You're sure we're going to talk about it?'

'I'll just keep coming back —'

'Yes, I think you might . . . If you find Pamela Arnburg there could be headlines. They're worse than gossip.'

'Do you want us to find who killed your husband?' He did his best to keep the bluntness out of the question.

'You don't really think Miss Arnburg killed Harry. She would never have known how to get into this house.'

'She might've employed someone to do it.' *Someone who works here.* What would her reaction be if he told her the killer was her under-gardener? Would the racist in her abruptly re-emerge? 'I'm not saying she did. But I have to talk to her. Do you know where I can find her?'

She was sitting at the desk where her husband had sat on Monday night; looking, Malone thought, as ghastly as Sir Harry had in the yellow light of the desk lamp that night. 'Twenty-five years ago, Mr Malone, I had the worst experience of my life. What would you do if you were about to lose your wife to another man?'

'I don't know. I've never considered the possibility.'

'Lucky man. Lucky, too, that you don't sound smug about it.' She turned away from him and gazed out the big window. 'My husband, Mr Malone, was the perfect imperfectionist. If there was any way of upsetting the balance of things, he would find it. Not out of malice or a sense of destruction. It was just — *him*. From the day we were married, it was I who kept the balance.'

158

Malone sat still, remained silent. When had this tortured woman last made a confession like this and to whom? Was he, a stranger, the first?

She swung her chair back to face him. 'I bought Miss Arnburg off. I gave her a hundred thousand dollars, which was worth much more than it is today, to leave the country. She went to America and I heard no more from her till I saw her today.'

'Did Sir Harry ever hear from her?'

The question obviously hurt. 'I don't know.'

'Do you know where I can find her?'

She was looking at him but not seeing him. She turned her head and looked around her, at the bookshelves where there appeared to be not even space for another single book. This had been her husband's room, his retreat, Malone thought; where, perhaps, his imperfections had been safe. He wondered how many hours Phillipa Huxwood would spend in here in the future. In here, at that desk, Sir Harry may have written notes to Pamela Arnburg; he wondered if Lady Huxwood had been through the drawers of the desk looking for evidence. But he knew, as if she had confessed it to him in so many words, that no matter how much jealousy poisoned her blood, she would always love Harry, living or dead. All at once he saw the possessiveness, the fierce passion that had bound the elder Huxwoods, that their children and their grandchildren had apparently never understood and had resented.

The myopic eyes got him into focus again. 'She married while she was in America. She would be Mrs Harry Stockton. I wrote the name down,' she said, and he could imagine her doing just that.

He wrote it down himself. 'You're sure?'

She snapped, 'Of course I'm sure! Dammit, Mr Malone, I'm not one of those old women who can't remember what they were doing five minutes ago. My memory is perfect,' she said, but he knew she could not remember where she had put the piece of paper on which she had written the name. The loss of memory was there in her face and she seemed suddenly frightened by it. Then, with an obvious effort of will, she recovered: 'Her name, if she is using it out here, is Mrs Harry Stockton.'

'Harry?' His tongue slipped.

'Yes,' she said and if her sight had been longer her look would have killed him. 'That will be all, Mr Malone.'

159

He stood up, smiling. 'I wish I'd met you under better circumstances, Lady Huxwood. You and I could have had some entertaining arguments. I'm not used to being dismissed, except by senior officers.'

She stared at him, then he saw a faint smile, the first he had seen on that gauntly beautiful face. 'How do you respond to Mr Zanuch?'

'Politely, ma'am.'

The smile widened, took some of the gauntness out of her face. 'Wise, Mr Malone. Yes, I think it is a pity we didn't meet under different circumstances. You'd make quite an opponent. I always look for people who will argue with me. I can't stand sycophants, the world has too many of them. Especially towards women like us . . . I can't tell you where Pamela Arnburg, or Mrs Harry Stockton, or whoever she is, I can't tell you where she is. But I can give you a hint. Harry – *my* Harry – told me she liked the good life, the best of everything. She is going back to America next week, so if you go looking for her, don't look in second-class hotels or cheap apartments. Good luck – no, I shouldn't wish you that. It will be better if you don't find her.'

4

When Malone got back to Homicide most of the staff had gone home. The Unit did not carry a night staff, but there was a roster from which detectives could be called at any hour. The pager, calling a detective to sudden duty, was sometimes a danger to health: one man had sustained a hernia when his pager beeped during orgasm.

Andy Graham, the youngest officer, was still at his desk, scribbling furiously as always, as if a despatch rider was waiting at the door to carry the desperate plea for reinforcements; he worked with an enthusiasm that would have had cattle and sheep dogs crawling away with their tails between their legs. Russ Clements, too, was at his desk, doing what he called tidying up, though no one, looking at the desk, would have known what he meant. He looked up enquiringly as Malone came in.

'I thought you'd finally made Tibooburra. We were going to send food parcels.'

'I almost did.' He gave a quick rundown on how he had spent the afternoon. 'I'll put it all in the running sheets tomorrow. I'm buggered now, I'm going home. You in court tomorrow?'

'Not till the afternoon. The Beemer case.' A boy who had held up a service station and shot dead the night attendant. All for thirty-three dollars and a few cents.

'Righto, do some leg-work for me, without moving your legs. A Mrs Harry Stockton, the woman you saw talking to Lady Huxwood at the funeral this morning. She's the girl who went missing twenty-five years ago, Pamela Arnburg. Check all the first-class hotels, the city travel agents, Qantas and United, the better estate agents around the Harbour –'

Clements shuffled some papers into order, put them down on his desk and somehow managed to have them at once slide apart into an untidy heap. 'That could take all day –'

'Not with your contacts, all those girls you know –'

'*Used* to know. I'm a married man now, maybe a father-to-be. Talk about unsafe sex . . .'

'Congratulations. Where are you going?'

Clements had stood up. 'Over to tell Andy what I want, so's I can give it to you tomorrow morning. It's called delegation, in case you've forgotten. All sergeants do it, you used to, too. He can start on the hotels and serviced apartments tonight. He wasn't going out tonight.'

'How do you know?'

'I'm going to tell him.'

Malone left him and went home to Randwick, to the family where the squabbles were minor, where he and Lisa loved each other passionately but never to the exclusion of the children.

He put his car away in the garage, then stood for a moment in the front garden. The rain had gone completely now, but the soil and the shrubs still smelt of it. The azaleas had started to blossom again, their colour pale smudges in the twilight. He looked at the house, built at the turn of the century; it was probably fifty years younger than La Malmaison, but just as solid. More solid: there was no white-anting family inside it.

After dinner, when Maureen and Tom had gone to their rooms to do their homework and Claire had gone out with her latest boyfriend, Lisa and he sat in front of the television set and watched *NYPD Blue*. The series was almost a season old and the red-headed actor who

161

played Detective John Kelly (Malone could never remember TV actors' names, but he could name every bit-part actor in old late-night movies) had not yet been replaced by some other actor whose name he also couldn't remember; Maureen, the family TV critic and columnist, had announced there would be changes soon in *NYPD Blue* and *Law & Order*, his other favourite viewing. It was Lisa's choice, too, so Thursday night there was no argument. There was only argument when he and Tom wanted to watch the cricket and Lisa and the girls wanted to watch something that featured women with problems. As if cricketers didn't have problems.

'A good day?' Lisa said during the first commercial.

'Good enough. I'm getting nowhere, yet somehow I don't feel I'm standing still.'

'I often feel like that in the kitchen. You should come home some time and try it. So what happened?'

He told her of Pamela Arnburg's appearance at the funeral; then the commercials finished and he said, 'Sh-h. I'll tell you later.'

So she got the story of his day during the commercials: *Carefree* sanitary pads wafted in the background like bodyless gulls while he told her of his encounter with Zanuch; Pizza Hut offered The Works for six dollars ninety-five while he told her of his meeting with Lady Huxwood. She sat up and looked hard at him when at last he said, 'What would you do if I fell for another woman?'

'I'll think about it,' she said as *NYPD Blue* resumed.

The red-headed actor was being screwed. Internal Affairs had put the knife into him; he was being transferred, out of the precinct, out of the series. Malone felt sorry for the poor bastard. He remembered now that Maureen had said the actor was leaving the series for much, much more money in Hollywood; but that didn't obscure the fact that Detective John Kelly had been shafted. The actor could look after himself, but Detective Kelly had got the rough end of the pineapple. Any cop had to feel sympathy for him.

NYPD Blue finished and Lisa sat up once more. She said without preamble, 'I wouldn't touch you, but I hate to think what I might do to her, whoever she might be.'

'You wouldn't touch *me*? But I'd be as much to blame as her.'

'Of course. And I'd never let you forget it, if you ever brought her up again. But I'd still have you.'

162

'Even if I'd said I was in love with another woman?'

'You'd still be in love with me. It wouldn't be the same as it is now, but it would be enough.'

He kissed her. 'You sound just like Lady Huxwood.'

'There are more Lady Huxwoods running loose than you know. Your trouble is, like most men you don't appreciate how much pain a woman can take for love.'

'The feminists wouldn't agree with you.'

'Not publicly, no. But political correctness isn't a thing of the heart.'

He kissed her again, held her to him while *Law & Order* came up on the screen. He was not a chauvinist, but as soon as he saw the word *feminist* in print he turned to another page. He skirted the New Age as if it were a bottomless swamp. But if, tomorrow, he found Pamela Arnburg, he might ask her how long the pain had lasted. And feel pity for her.

Chapter Eight

⁓

1

Friday morning, as soon as he got to his office, Malone checked with Superintendent Lozelle at Waverley.

'The first summary of your boy Dwayne has just landed on my desk, Scobie. They picked him up at La Malmaison – the wife wants to know why we don't have a name like that for our house. She thinks it has more tone than Number 42 – they picked him up when he knocked off work and tailed him out to Dulwich Hill –'

'He lives out there with his uncle and aunty. I gather they all hate each other's guts.'

'From there he went to a flat in Stanmore –'

'His girl friend, probably.'

'Then she must be the one he had the argument with. At her front door. He tried to force his way in, but she slammed it in his face. He left there –'

'How does he get around? Has he got wheels?'

'A BMW 318 –'

'An under-gardener? On what, three-fifty, four hundred bucks a week?' The smart-arses could never resist the mistakes they made.

'Whatever.' The shrug was almost visible down the line; Lozelle was another who had given up trying to understand the young. 'From Stanmore he went to a McDonalds, at the Hoyts complex in George Street. He parked the car in the QVB. From there he went out to Double Bay, to the Royal Oak –'

'The pub? Did your man see him talk to anyone there?' *Like Ross Huxwood, for instance?*

'My feller kept losing him in the crowd. He finished the night by going home with some girl in Bronte. He stayed the night –'

'Is he at work this morning?'

164

'I guess so. We still have the tail on him, the latest summary isn't in yet. Anything happens, I'll be on to you, Scobie. You getting anywhere?'

'The gut feeling is still there, that's all.'

He hung up as Clements came in and sat down on the couch. 'Before you start . . . Get a warrant to search Dwayne Harod's car, his uncle's house, his girl friend Sophie Carpano's flat —'

'What are we looking for?'

'A Thirty-two calibre gun, the one that shot Sir Harry.'

'Okay, but won't that tip him off we think he's the one?'

'Of course it will. But we've got a tail on him and if he does a bunk when we tell him about the warrant, then we know he's our man. I don't think he's mug enough to have the gun in his car, so start out at Dulwich Hill first, then Sophie's flat, *then* the BMW.'

'He drives a BMW?'

'It's probably second-hand, but it makes you think, doesn't it? On his wages. Now, have you got anything for me?'

'Mrs Harry Stockton is staying at Wharf West, she's been booked in there for the past month. Andy tells me he tracked her down in five phone calls. The boy's a genius.'

'I'd better get down there before she gets wind from the reception desk that the police want to talk to her.'

'I told you, Andy's a genius. He said he was from a travel agency, wanted to send her an itinerary. We don't give the boy enough credit.'

'I do. So do you. But he's just so bloody tiring —' He stood up, put on his jacket and the pork-pie hat.

'You want me to come with you? I'm not due in court till two —'

'I'll take Kate. I don't want to frighten the lady.'

Kate Arletti drove him in an unmarked car down to Wharf West. On the way, as she carefully threaded her way through the traffic, she told him of her and John Kagal's efforts yesterday afternoon.

'We interviewed the other Huxwood grandkid, Camilla. She's harmless, I'd say. She'd go with the flow.'

'You mean she'd vote with the majority on the sale?'

'I think so. She's not Mr Custer's kid, her name is Fyfe, F-y-f-e. I haven't yet found out what happened to Mr Fyfe.'

'He died, lost at sea in a Sydney to Hobart yacht race. I've checked on everyone who's married into the Huxwoods, or lived with them.

165

Except Linden – God knows how many live-ins she's had. The ex-Huxwoods are a pretty mixed lot, but at this stage I don't think we have to complicate things by trying to find out if one of them wanted Harry bumped off. Let's stick to those we have in sight. Including Mrs Stockton.'

Wharf West was a high-rise block of serviced apartments on the ridge that led up to the southern end of the Harbour Bridge. It had gone up in the last four or five years when developers began to realize that visitors to the city might want something more than the cramped quarters the newer hotels were offering. It had a marbled lobby and a staff who came of a new mutation of the natives, young people who didn't think service and a smile cost them their dignity.

'Police?' The brunette in the tight uniform behind the desk managed to contain her curiosity. 'I'll have to announce you, sir. It's our policy – security, you know –'

'By all means. Inspector Malone and Detective Constable Arletti.'

The girl picked up the desk phone, not taking her eyes off Kate, who smiled and tried not to look an oddity. She was neat today, every button done up, and Malone had never seen her looking more attractive. The Huxwood case was obviously agreeing with her, despite her prejudice against the family.

'Oh, Mrs Stockton, we have two detectives down here would like to speak with you . . . No, Mrs Stockton, not *private* detectives. Police . . . She says to go up –' She gave them an apartment number. 'There'll be no trouble? If there is, I can ask our manager –'

'Nothing like,' said Malone. 'It's just a social call.'

Going up in the lift Kate said, 'Do you think she was expecting a private detective?'

'We'll ask her. Nicely.'

Mrs Harry Stockton, née Pamela Arnburg, opened the door as Malone reached a hand towards the ornamental knocker. She was wearing a coffee-coloured silk shirt, a pale beige skirt and she was, as Ossie Beckett had said, a looker. Still.

Malone introduced himself and Kate. 'We have just a few questions to ask you –'

'Come in. I suppose I should have been expecting you. You were at the funeral yesterday, weren't you?' She looked at Kate as she

166

waved the two detectives to chairs in the living-cum-dining room. 'I've just made some coffee. Would you like some?'

'I'll get it,' said Kate, and Pamela Stockton did not look displeased at a stranger taking over her small kitchenette. Malone wondered if she was accustomed to servants back home, wherever that was, a maid who always *brought* her her coffee.

'Did Lady Huxwood send you to see me? Phillipa always had a talent for twisting the knife.' There was a faint American tinge to her voice, not harsh but soft: Southern? Malone wondered. 'But if you've interviewed her, you've probably noticed that.'

Malone dodged the question by taking the cup of coffee Kate gave him. His quick eye had taken in the apartment. The furnishings were what he thought might be called Swedish modern, comfortable but anonymous, designed not to clash with whoever came into the apartment. A big wide window looked out on to the harbour, like a large poster of what the city had to offer the visitor. Mrs Harry Stockton sat in the middle of it all, identified by nothing that surrounded her. He wondered who she had been, what had identified her, in the twenty-five years since she had been Sir Harry's lover.

'I understand you've been back in Sydney a month. Did you see Sir Harry in that time?'

She sipped her coffee. 'I'm sorry I can't offer you a cookie or something − I'm not very good at housekeeping − there are some nibbly things in a rack over the fridge −'

'No, thanks. Sir Harry?'

She took another sip of the coffee. She had her own way of taking her time, but it was not as irritating as Alexandra Huxwood's had been. 'Yes, I saw him.'

'Once, twice? Several times? Here?'

'Twice. Yes, here.'

'What was the − the reunion like?' said Kate.

Pamela Stockton's hand shook a little; the cup rattled in its saucer and she put both of them down on the table beside her. Malone was surprised at the reaction; she had seemed imperturbable. 'I don't think I have to answer that.'

Kate looked at Malone and he said, 'Not if you don't want to, Mrs Stockton. But wouldn't it be better for you to answer questions like this, just between us three, rather than for us to take you back to

Homicide and question you there, with your lawyer, if you want one, listening in on all of it?'

She seemed to look at the two detectives with new interest. 'Do you suspect me of something? Not – ?'

'Of killing Sir Harry? Mrs Stockton, everyone closely connected with him is on our list. What was the reunion between you and Sir Harry like? Was it friendly? Did you still think of yourself as lovers?'

'How much do you know of Harry and me?' She was treading carefully, as if Malone and Kate were laying mines for her.

'We know you were lovers. We know Lady Phillipa paid you a hundred thousand dollars to disappear –'

He had put none of what Lady Huxwood had told him into the running sheet and he had neglected to mention the bribe to Kate on their way down here. He felt her look at him, though she was beside him and just on the edge of his vision. Pamela Stockton looked at Kate, then back at Malone. 'Phillipa seems to have let her hair down. She never used to be like that.'

'She's just lost her husband.'

'Is she on your list?' Then she shook her dark head and waved a hand in a vague gesture. 'No, I shouldn't have said that.'

Though she had appeared composed when he and Kate had entered the apartment, almost unsurprised to see them, Malone saw now that she was under strain. Her face and her body in the last minute seemed to have sagged, as if whatever had been holding her together had snapped.

She said, letting her own hair down, 'I was pregnant to Harry. I had an abortion that he paid for – Phillipa knew about it, after it happened. The abortion was botched, I almost died – it ruined me for having children in the future. I loved Harry and he loved me – but he couldn't make up his mind between me and Phillipa. But . . . Yes, since you ask, we saw each other after I came back. We didn't go to bed –' She nodded towards the bedroom off the living-room. 'If that was the next question you were going to ask. The old spark, as they call it, wasn't there any more. Not for me. It may sound cruel, but in those twenty-five years Harry had become an old man. And I had been truly in love with my husband. But, if you must know, I wept all night Tuesday when I read that he was dead.'

The confession seemed to exhaust her; she sighed and shrank in

168

her chair. Kate said, 'Did you ever correspond during your separation?'

She shook her head. 'He wrote me, but I never answered. Then when I married, I was in love with my husband – he didn't know about Harry Huxwood and I never told him. I was very happy with him till – till he died.'

'Did Sir Harry ever come looking for you? He would have made a lot of trips to America over the years, business trips.'

'He may have. I don't know. When I was living in New York I never went near the *Chronicle*'s office there. I'd been there a year when Derek, the eldest son, came across from the London office. I don't think he ever knew what went on between me and his father, but he would have recognized me.'

'Ossie Beckett recognized you at the funeral yesterday.'

'Good old Osbert.' She was re-gathering her strength, sat up again in her chair. 'One of my favourites, back then. I think he knew about Harry and me, but he kept his mouth shut.'

'He did,' said Malone. 'When we were downstairs you asked the girl on the desk if we were *private* detectives. Have you hired a private detective?'

She smiled, some of the age slipping out of her face. 'Lawdy, no!' Lawdy? thought Malone. The last time he had heard that was in *Gone With The Wind*. 'I thought Phillipa might have hired one. She won't be happy till I'm on the plane for home, a long way away so that no old gossip can be revived.'

'Where is home?'

'Charleston, South Carolina. I'm happy enough there. Harry would have been, I think. Phillipa, too. Charleston likes to think it's the last aristocratic capital in the United States. There are customs there, still, that we have never had here in Australia. The St Cecilia's Ball – my husband's father was on the committee for that. It was run entirely by men, the ball. No actors or actresses could ever go to the ball, no divorced woman. Things may have changed, my husband was never interested in it and I was never one for balls and dances.'

She would have been a decoration at any of them, thought Malone.

'I like Charleston, the pace of living suits me – I'm basically lazy, I suppose – and I like the people, the ones who aren't snobs and trying to live in the past. The odd thing is, Phillipa would have fitted in there, exactly, as if she were born to it.'

169

She had regained her composure, looked ready for more questions. Malone asked her, 'Did Sir Harry ever discuss the sale of Huxwood Press with you on those two occasions you met?'

'Once, on our last meeting. He said he was at the end of his tether, trying to do something that would please everyone. He said he had had a fierce row with one of his grandchildren, one of them who wanted to sell.'

'Which one?'

'He didn't say. He seemed very upset by what was going on in the family. He asked me what life would be like for him in Charleston.'

'What did you say?'

'I put him off. It might have been just an idle question, but I wasn't going to encourage him. Love may not die, Inspector, but sometimes it is better to let it sleep.' She smiled again, looking better by the minute. 'I was a librarian once. I don't remember whether I read that or whether it's original. Proverbs stick to us like burrs, they're an occupational hazard.'

'If you had encouraged him, would he really have gone to live with you in Charleston?'

She gave that long thought; then nodded. 'Yes, I think so. He said that if ever he agreed to sell Huxwood, that would be the end of his life with Phillipa.'

2

Derek could not remember a gathering of the family such as this, except at Christmas and on the golden wedding anniversary of his parents. They sat about the long dining-room table with a mixture of expressions, none of them joyous but some of them (and this disturbed him) not exactly morose. There were the four Huxwood senior siblings, their spouses, legal or otherwise, and the six grandchildren. And his mother, the matriarch, the one who had called this gathering.

'No,' she had said last night when he had protested about calling the family meeting, 'we must have it *now*. I haven't seen your father's will, but I know what was in it — we wrote our wills at the same time. Unless he changed his,' she said, as if to herself, and looked puzzled,

170

as if unable to understand something so underhand. 'Perhaps we had better have the will read first.'

'It's a bit sudden, isn't it?' He didn't know why he had said that; he had had no experience of the reading of a will.

'No more sudden than his death.' She said it almost masochistically. Why is she torturing herself? he wondered. 'Get Alan Van Dieman.'

'Now? It's after nine –'

'*Now.* We pay him enough for his services.' She never quoted sums of money, that was vulgar, but she demanded value for whatever was spent.

Derek went out into the hall and rang Alan Van Dieman. '*Now?*'

'I'm afraid so, Alan. She wants to see Dad's will – now.'

There was silence on the other end of the line but for laughter in the background. Then Van Dieman said, barely controlling his irritation, 'I'll have to go into the office to get it. I'm in the middle of a dinner party –'

'Tough titty, Alan,' said Derek, suddenly feeling his own irritation. 'But you know what Mum is like.'

'Indeed.' Then Van Dieman obviously had second thoughts about the remark: 'Sorry.'

'It's all right. Make it as soon as you can.'

He hung up and went back into the library. There was a phone on his father's desk, but he was glad he had gone out to the phone in the main hall. He had not been sure how much argument he might have got from Alan Van Dieman. But, of course, he had forgotten how much weight his mother wielded.

'He'll be here as soon as he can. He has to go into the office to get the will.'

'He should live closer.'

Van Dieman lived at Killara on the North Shore, an area so populated with lawyers and judges that the garbage men's Christmas boxes were usually tied with legal pink tape and had a note attached that stated the enclosed was given without prejudice or admission. It would take the lawyer at least an hour to get into the city and then out to Vaucluse, probably more. Derek sat down to wait, picking up a book from several on the table beside his armchair. His mother, as if alone, was already reading one of the leather-bound volumes she had taken from the library's shelves.

171

He sat a moment watching her. As far back as he could remember, she had been absolutely sure of the power she had. She had come from a family that had money and political influence; she had married money and media clout. There was a certainty to her existence that few had these days; part of it was due to her own certainty of mind. She still believed in a social system that was crumbling all round her; she was a standard bearer in a world where the flags were tattered or lowered. In her younger days she had been chairwoman (*not* chairperson) of the committee of the Black and White Ball, the city's premier charity function; she had resigned when the New Lot (her term) had come in with nothing to recommend them but their husbands' new wealth. She did not believe in entrepreneurial wealth, political correctness, feminism or Labor governments. Yet isolated though she was in the world as it stood, she still wielded power, in the family and in Huxwood Press. He was just glad that she would be on his side in the coming battle over the sale of the empire.

He looked at the book on his lap: *Barbarians at the Gate.* His father must have taken it down to re-read it in the few days before his death.

Alan Van Dieman arrived at ten-fifteen. He made no apology, but came bustling in as if determined not to be delayed more than was absolutely necessary. 'You're lucky. I had the will out on my desk only this afternoon. I really shouldn't be doing this, I'm not the executor –'

'Have you read it?' said Phillipa Huxwood, marking her book with a leather bookmark and putting the book down carefully on the desk in front of her.

'Yes.' Van Dieman sat down opposite her, glanced sideways at Derek, who had remained in his armchair. 'There's nothing surprising in it. In the will itself.'

'Everything is left to me?' said Phillipa: it was a statement as much as a question. 'The same as mine, leaving everything to him.'

'Well, not exactly. I said in the *will* – but there's a codicil.' Was that a small smile of satisfaction, Derek wondered. 'Harry added the codicil, dated –' The lawyer looked at the papers he held. 'Dated a month ago. His share of the holding company is to be divided equally amongst the six grandchildren.'

'Who witnessed the codicil?'

'I and one of my partners.'

'So you knew what Harry intended to do?'

'Yes.' There was just the slightest hesitation.

'And you didn't see fit to tell me?'

The hesitation was just that much longer: 'He told me not to. I assumed he was going to tell you himself.'

There was faint antagonism in the lawyer's tone and Derek resented it. He said, 'Is there any mention of my brother and my sisters in the codicil?'

'None, I'm afraid.' The voice was flat this time, no hint of satisfaction. Derek had never heard the soft voice raised in anger but he had heard it insinuated into arguments, demolishing them like water crumbling a dike. 'I queried him on that, Derek, and he said you would all be well looked after with what you already hold. And,' he looked back at Phillipa, 'with what you will leave them in your will.'

Phillipa sat without moving. Derek remembered she had been a loving, caring mother when he and his siblings had been young; the rigidity in her manner and outlook had come only in her middle age. It had happened — what? Twenty-five years ago? — and it had stiffened as she grew older. Abruptly she said, 'That will be all, Alan. Leave the will and the codicil.'

'I can't do that, Phillipa, not yet.' He stood up. He looked less grey this evening; or perhaps it was the flush from his dinner drinking. 'I'm sorry this has been such a shock to you, but Harry was, as they say, of sound mind, et cetera. He gave me no reason for what he was doing, just asked me to draft it and witness it.'

'Thank you,' said Phillipa and swung her chair round and stared out into the night.

Van Dieman raised his eyebrows at Derek, said, 'I'll let myself out,' and left the room.

'You can't blame Alan for what Dad did.'

It was almost a minute before she swung her chair round to face him. In the light from the desk lamp she looked skeletal, *ancient*; he could not bear to see her looking like that and he got up and switched on the ceiling light.

'Why did you do that?'

'Because I want a little more light between you and me.' He sat down on a chair across the desk from her, the seat of it still warm from Van Dieman's backside. He reached across and switched off the desk lamp; she abruptly lost several years. 'I know nothing about what

Dad planned in his will or the codicil, but I'm not surprised. About me and Nigel and the girls. Especially not about me. Dad and I haven't seen eye to eye for a long time now. The night he was – killed, I left a memo on his desk, right there –' He gestured. 'Telling him I wanted to invite Packer or Murdoch in as buyers, to cut off selling to Metropolitan.'

She gazed steadily at him, but he could not be sure whether she was studying him or collecting her thoughts. Then she said, 'What about the others? Charlie Bentsen and whoever he is with?'

Derek shook his head. 'They know nothing about newspapers. They're only interested in the money they can make out of it. I'd blow up the *Chronicle* before I'd let Charlie get near it. Or his partners.'

'Do you want to sell at all?'

'No. But if I'm – if *we* are to be out-voted, I want to see everything go to someone who knows newspapers, who is Australian.'

'I admire your nationalism.' He wasn't sure of hers. She was a monarchist through and through; the Queen had been to a private dinner here at La Malmaison. 'Your father wanted to sell to Beatrice Supple and her crowd. He told me so on Monday night. He'd made up his mind to sell.' She was silent a while, raising a hand of bones to stroke her forehead; she was losing some of her stiffness. 'I saw your memo.'

He frowned. 'How? Did he show it to you?'

'No, I tore it out of his hand.'

'You *what*?'

'It was I who found him.' She paused, blinked; the rigidity was flowing out of her face like blood. 'I went into his room as I always did – I always woke before him. He was lying there –' She stopped.

'Why didn't you scream or something? Jesus, Mum, you just *stood* there?'

'I'm not the screaming sort.' She was almost reproachful. 'I saw the paper in his hand – at first I thought it was a suicide note. Suicide? My Harry? I tore it out of his hand – he didn't want to let go . . .' She let out a sharp sigh; recovered: 'Then Stefan came in with the morning tea. I let him – raise the alarm, I mean.'

'Did you tell him not to let anyone know you'd found Dad first?'

'Ye-es.'

174

'Why, for Crissake?'

'Because of that damned piece of paper!' For a moment there was a flush in the gaunt cheeks. 'And what your father told me the night before. Sell, sell — that's what you both wanted! And I shan't ever allow that!'

He said gently, 'Mum, I've never wanted to sell. I've wanted to *change* the paper — I've argued for two years with you and Dad about that. But I never wanted to sell, not really. That memo, that piece of paper, was a — a surrender. I felt I'd lost the war and, if I had, I wanted to see the paper still owned by Australians.'

She sat unmoving for a long moment; then she reached out a hand for him across the desk. He took it: it was the first gesture of affection between them in God knew how long.

'We'll keep the paper, Derek, it and everything else. We'll fight for it together.'

'We're going to have opposition, a lot of it. Christ knows how the kids will vote when they learn what they've inherited.'

'We'll tell them —'

'Should we do that? Alan said something about the executor —'

'We'll do it,' she said. 'That way we'll find out who is for and who is against the sale. But in any event, we shan't sell. No way,' she said, though she was not given to modern expressions.

He had to smile. The rigidity of her might prove their biggest lance.

Now, on this Friday morning, they were all sitting round the big dining-room table; there were no lawyer advisers, no non-family board directors, no outsiders at all. This was the battlefield and these were the combatants who mattered.

'Let me begin by saying we are not going to sell Huxwood.' Phillipa sat at the head of the table, where her husband had sat; she had moved, the gesture speaking for itself, into the chairman's chair. She was dressed in black, but she was the only one who was.

'Isn't this all a bit premature?' Nigel was in open-necked shirt, blazer, jeans and boat shoes; ready, it seemed, for a day on the harbour. 'Shouldn't we have the full board here?'

'Whatever the full board says has no weight. The power is here with us.'

She should have been Prime Minister, thought Derek. She was not afraid to use the word *power*. Her use of it was the only thing she had

175

in common with the master of it down in Canberra. That and a taste for Mahler, though any discussion between her and the PM would have been as discordant as anything by Schoenberg. There would certainly be some discordance this morning.

'The voting strength lies here.' She looked round the table, particularly at her grandchildren. She had no favourites amongst them, just one or two she liked less than the others. 'Last night I saw your father's and grandfather's will. And a codicil. It was not what I expected,' she confessed, and Derek was surprised that she revealed herself so much. She looked again at the grandchildren in turn, passing over their parents as if she did not see them. 'Your grandfather has left all his shares in our holding company to be equally divided amongst you six. Nothing is official yet, but each of you will have equal voting power.' There was the word again.

'Dad left nothing for us?' Sheila waved a hand at her sister and brothers. 'Nothing?'

'Nothing,' said Derek from the other end of the table, his mother's old place. 'None of us is exactly destitute,' he said and avoided looking at Enrico Quental.

'Jesus,' said Nigel, 'this is unbelievable!'

'Linden?' said Derek, looking at his sister but still avoiding looking at Quental, who sat beside her.

'I'm disappointed.' She was sitting forward, not at all languid this morning; her hand felt for Quental's. 'It means I may change my mind about something.'

'What?' said her mother.

'About selling Huxwood.'

She has to bail out bloody Enrico, thought Derek; and tasted the bile of hatred. Not of Linden: when they were younger he had always protected her. He had defended her when she had made a fool of herself over men, when she had drifted off to Europe and God knew where. He had defended her again when she had reappeared with Quental; but he had never taken to the Portuguese. Now he suddenly hated him for the influence he had over Linden.

Phillipa stared at her daughter; then looked down the table again, taking them all in, rounding them up with her eyes. She was wearing her glasses this morning, designer-frames that somehow hid her

176

gauntness; she was not risking missing anything that might pass between those she ruled. 'Let us draw up a list. Who is for the sale and who against?'

Again Nigel protested. 'Mother, this is too premature –'

'You like that word, Nigel. I don't. Nothing is premature if one's mind is made up.'

'But that's it! Some of us haven't made up our minds –'

'You surprise me. It's been under discussion for a month now . . . Derek, take count.'

'Excuse me,' said Michael, in banker's grey the only formal-looking one of his generation of the family, 'but how much does each of us, the grandchildren, inherit from Pa's will?'

'It's too early to tell and in any event it's immaterial. It is what your share amounts to in votes. Make the list, Derek.'

He drew a sheet of paper towards him, the same sort of sheet on which he had written that last memo to his father. He ran a line down the middle of it, wrote *For* and *Against* at the head of each column. 'Those against. I'll start with Mum and myself. Anyone else?'

Sheila looked at Ned Custer, who nodded. She raised her hand. 'We are against it.'

That surprised him; he had expected Ned Custer to be well and truly rid of the family. But he showed no expression. 'Anyone else?'

There was hesitation right round the table. Then two more hands went up, those of Sarah, Nigel's daughter, and Colin, his own son.

He had a sinking feeling: his mother and he were going to lose. His mouth felt dry as he said, 'No more? Then those for the sale?'

Nigel's hand shot up like a leaping fish. Linden sat still, but Derek saw Quental press her hand and then she raised the other one. Three more hands went up: Ross, his other son; Alexandra, his daughter; and Camilla, Sheila's daughter. He wrote down the names, feeling treachery like more bile in his mouth. What the fuck were Ross and Alex up to?

'Michael?'

'I'm sorry, but I haven't made up my mind. I want more time to consider.'

He's showing a banker's caution, thought Derek; or what used to be a banker's caution. The Barings bank collapse was still in the headlines and the *Chronicle* had heard from its European correspondent that Credit Lyonnais was heading for *les roches*. 'Have you been talking with Lester Kohn?'

It was a moment before the boy nodded. 'Yes.'

'What does he advise?' Kohn, so far in meetings, had advised against selling. But one never knew with bankers these days. Flash enough money at them and they would leap off cliffs, hoping there was water and not rocks below them.

'He told me I had to make up my own mind. Which I'll do.'

'When do you think you can favour us with your decision?'

'Don't pressure him, Uncle Derek,' said Camilla unexpectedly.

She was the family airhead, a pretty brunette with seemingly nothing between her ears but a vocabulary such as *incredible, fantastic, fabulous*, all flung out with exclamation marks. She worked at one of the Huxwood radio stations and, he gathered, spent all her time with disc jockeys and pop stars whose vocabulary was as extensive as her own. She was the last one he had expected to contribute anything at all to the discussion, limited though it had been so far.

'Okay, Michael, in your own good time . . .' He looked down at the list. 'Five for, five against. With Michael to come.'

Brenda spoke for the first time. 'Can we in-laws vote?'

'No,' said Phillipa.

'Thank you,' said Ned Custer, sober, almost pale-faced this morning. He was dressed for the office but without his jacket and looked business-like; but so far he had said nothing. 'That clears that up, Mother Huxwood.'

'You're welcome,' said Phillipa. 'But not to call me Mother Huxwood. I'm not something out of a fairy story.'

'My mistake,' said Custer and grinned, but got no answering smile.

Derek looked around the family and, for the first time that morning, opened the door on the question that he had kept from himself. Who here at this table had had Dad killed? When Scobie Malone had raised the possibility, he had found it almost impossible to accept. For several years now the family had been divided, though it had always presented a united front to outsiders. But to consider the idea of murder by one of them? Certainly, ruthlessness had come and gone in the family of the past; but that had been political and editorial murder. He knew the family history better than anyone and there was no record of violence in it. Almost without realizing it, he found himself looking at the outsiders.

Ned Custer? He had never got on with either Harry or Phillipa, had been flamboyant, sometimes drunkenly so, in his independence of them. But a murderer? He had seen Ned in a terrible rage while drunk, but he could not imagine him cold-bloodedly planning a killing. Unless he would do it for Sheila's sake?

Brenda? An actress in her every waking moment (and probably in her sleep, too); she might have been influenced by Nigel, who made no secret of their desire to go back to Europe, to the 'civilized world'. Brenda had no money of her own, had come from a background about which Derek knew nothing. Nigel had always been the family bludger, taking his dividends and contributing nothing; his earnings as an actor would have been less than his dividends. Perhaps Brenda had hopes of a richer life?

Cordelia? His own wife, who had no secrets from him, including her strong dislike of his mother. But she had loved his father, had sometimes taken Harry's side in the rows between his father and himself. He felt ashamed that he had even included her amongst the others.

Enrico? Ah, there was someone who might have had his reasons. Their brief stoush yesterday after the return from the funeral had blown up out of nowhere. Enrico had asked how soon was the will going to be read and he, still full of grief for his father, had erupted. He couldn't remember what he had said, but he had thrown a punch, missed and been hit in the gut by a fist that had seemed to come out of Enrico's pocket. It was only then he had remembered something Linden had told him: Enrico had been a boxer, the Portuguese lightweight champion, before he had become a businessman. The punch had suggested he had been a better boxer than a businessman.

Enrico was broke now, desperately so. But was he so desperate that he would hire someone to kill Dad? Or do it himself? He and Linden had stayed in the Big House on Monday night; their bedroom had been on the same floor as Harry's. But that suggested Linden would have had to be an accomplice, and he could not believe that of his favourite sibling.

179

Phillipa stood up. 'That is all for now. Till Michael makes up his mind. Perhaps Lester Kohn will help you there?'

'No, Grandma,' said Michael. 'I have a mind of my own. It's a family trait.'

She had taken off her glasses. He was at the far end of the table and she could barely see him. But she gave a thin smile at the dim silhouette of him. 'I'm glad to hear some Huxwood traits are still alive in you. They may influence you not to sell.'

She went out of the room, not sweeping out of it because her myopia did not allow that, but still giving the impression that she was making a theatrical exit. Nigel, if no one else, noticed it.

'Just like Maggie Smith,' he said, giving the impression that he had acted with Dame Maggie innumerable times.

'How would you know?' said Brenda, sounding bitchy.

Everyone waited for the actor and the actress to get even bitchier; but Nigel disappointed them by choosing to make his own sweeping exit. Brenda went out at a more leisurely pace. At the door she paused and looked back, theatrically.

'Do make up your mind, Michael darling.'

He smiled, not taken in. 'You'll be the first to know, Brenda.'

That quickened her exit: she obviously would have liked the last word, the exit line.

The others rose to leave, but Derek, remaining seated, said, 'Don't go, Alex. Ross. Stay a minute.'

Cordelia looked at him, but he shook his head and she went out of the dining-room after the others.

Colin stood hesitantly, but Derek said, 'I'll talk to you later.'

'I'd like to stay, Dad –'

'No,' he said adamantly, and the boy, after another hesitation, followed his mother.

Alexandra and Ross moved down the long table towards their father. 'Dad, I have to go to work –'

'Ten minutes won't matter, Alex. I'm the boss now and you are the boss's daughter. The women's page can get along without you for ten minutes more. Sit down, both of you.'

They sat down, the boy slumped in his chair, his long beefy legs thrust out in front of him. 'What's this about, Dad? Are you shitty because Alex and I voted against you?'

180

'I guess that's one way of putting it. Yes. But as Michael said, you have minds of your own. I'd just like to know why you voted for the sale?'

'I want my own money,' said Ross. 'I don't want hand-outs from the family.'

'Hand-outs? You get — what? — twenty-five thousand a year in dividends? Not a bad hand-out for a twenty-year-old, someone still at university.'

'The dividends are always so bloody low! I see the profits every year — after all, I'm doing Economics at uni —'

'If you read the annual reports, you'd know it's always been the policy to plough the profits back into the company. We haven't built Huxwood into what it is now on hand-outs. Alex?'

She was less sullen, less aggressive than her brother. These were the two he had always had difficulty in rearing; they had always been more rebellious than Colin. Latterly, preoccupied with the battles with his father, it seemed that he had grown away from them. Cordelia had warned him of it, but he had not taken the warning seriously. And now he was confronted with a son and daughter who wanted to destroy everything he worked for. *Believed in.*

'I want my own radio station,' said Alexandra. '2HP.'

'Christ Almighty! You're only twenty-one!'

Her ambition shocked him. At twenty-one his own sole ambition had been to play for the State at cricket or rugby; he had had no thoughts of where he would go in the family empire. The Sixties had been in full swing, he had worn his hair long, smoked pot, dislocated a disc to the Rolling Stones. But serious ambition?

'You think the staff at HP are going to work for a twenty-one-year-old boss?'

'You obviously haven't been near HP in years.' Despite his irritation (anger?), he had to admire her coolness; she was not attacking him, just educating him. 'Most of the staff aren't much more than twenty-one.' He knew it was an alternative music station, whatever that was, with a solitary talk-back host: 'Except for Russ Jorgensen.'

The fifty-year-old hippy who, Cordelia had told him, lived in a time warp, who had been at Woodstock and, apparently, was still there. 'What about Camilla? Do you think she'll want to work for you? Or is she in cahoots with you?'

181

'Yes, she is. We've been talking about it for six months.'

Kids running a radio station; the air pollution would be appalling. 'I thought your interest was with the paper?'

'Working for Rosie Gilligan?' He noticed she avoided looking at her brother. 'No, thanks.'

He gave up on her and turned to Ross. 'What will you do with your money, if you get it?'

The boy shrugged. 'I dunno, yet. I might buy into computers. The information highway is the way to go.'

'Spare me, no commercials. Anyhow, computer firms have been going broke all over for ten years now.'

'Not all of them. They made Bill Gates a billionaire.'

The *Chronicle* had run a flattering full-page interview with Gates during his visit earlier in the year; Warren Gates, the managing editor, had planned that one, as if seeking to relate himself to his famous namesake.

'He's a genius. You're not ...' He decided to surprise them. 'Grandpa was for selling, did you know that?'

He had surprised them. They looked at each other, then back at them. 'I don't believe it,' said Alexandra. 'You've been saying for months he would never make up his mind.'

'He made it up the night he was – murdered. He told Grandma just before he went to bed.'

'Jesus!' Ross slapped his thighs. 'Then everything would have been all right!'

'All right? What do you mean?'

The boy gestured vaguely. 'I mean that would have settled all the arguing. With his vote, the sale would've gone through.'

'Probably,' Derek conceded. All at once he felt weary, his mind, his flesh collapsing about the bones of him; only his bones were holding him up. He could barely raise his hand in dismissal. 'Okay, you can go to work. We'll talk more about it later.'

'What's to talk about?' Alexandra did not sound aggressive, just curious.

He looked up at both of them; he had the odd feeling that they did not belong to him. Had he failed them, as he had often thought his own father had failed him? What small wars lay ahead between him and them?

'You seem to forget,' he said carefully, 'there's no decision yet on whether we sell or not. Not till Michael makes up his mind.'

'That stuffed shirt,' said Ross. 'A stuffed-shirt shit.'

'I shouldn't call him that,' said Derek, abruptly weary this time of his son. 'He might vote against you, if he heard you.'

Chapter Nine

1

'He's here,' said Clements.

'Who?'

'Dwayne the Turk. Our suspect.'

'Here? What the hell's he want?'

'I dunno. He rang from downstairs and I sent Andy down to get him.'

Malone got up and looked out through the glass wall of his office. Dwayne Harod sat at Clements' desk in the main room, gazing around him as if he were sizing it up before making a bid for it. Several of the detectives were at their desks and when they would look at him he would nod affably and, in the case of Kate Arletti, give her a wide smile.

'Does he know we've got the search warrants?'

'Maybe. John and one of the Marrickville Ds are out at his uncle's house now. Maybe they phoned him, the uncle or aunt.'

'Righto, bring him in.'

When Clements brought in the young Turk there was abruptly no smile, no affability; he was here on business, you'd better believe it: 'Someone's following me, Inspector.'

Malone looked at Clements; both men made a good pretence of puzzlement. 'Following you, Dwayne? How do you know?'

'They're not your guys, are they?'

'No,' said Malone truthfully: nobody from Waverley was one of his guys.

'Then it must be a fucking private eye!' Dwayne did his own acting; he made a good pretence of looking angry.

'A private eye? You've been reading too many books, Dwayne. Or looking at too much TV. Why would a private eye be following you?'

184

'Christ knows. But it makes you think, doesn't it?' He was now inviting them to be on his side.

Malone looked at Clements again and the latter said, 'Yeah, I guess it does. Have you heard from your uncle and aunt this morning?'

'Uncle and —? You mean you think they've got someone following me? Ah, come on! Why would they do that?'

'I don't think that's what Sergeant Clements is suggesting,' said Malone. 'Right now two detectives are out at your uncle's place in Dulwich Hill with a search warrant. They were picking up either your uncle or aunt and taking them out there.'

The tanned face abruptly darkened; there was no pretence now. 'What for?'

'Just routine, Dwayne. We're looking for the gun that killed Sir Harry.'

'Fucking routine? Bullshit!' For a moment he looked as if he were about to leap out of his chair; then just as quickly he had a change of mind, a change of character. He sat back: one could see the control taking over. 'You doing that with everyone? A routine search?'

This bugger is too clever for his own good. But Malone had seen it all before: the crim who couldn't resist going to the very edge, who had to prove, if only to himself, that he was smarter than those trying to catch him. The ploy sometimes worked, but not always: ego was a bell that often cracked.

'Yes, we're getting the warrants now.' Lies might not be as legal as warrants, but they were useful.

'Dan Darling? You getting one on him? You've gotta go to a judge or magistrate, haven't you?'

'How'd you know that, Dwayne?' said Clements. 'Most people wouldn't have a clue how we get a warrant.'

'It must be like you said, I guess I watch too much TV.' He didn't smirk, but something played along his lips.

'You mentioned Dan Darling. You think Dan might have a gun? That he might've killed Sir Harry?' Malone glanced at Clements. 'We hadn't thought of that, had we, Sergeant? Maybe we should go back and see Dan, tell him the finger's been pointed at him.' He looked back at Dwayne. 'If you're wrong, Dwayne, it could mean your job. Or are you after his job, you want to be head gardener? That might impress the girls more than just being the under-gardener. Someone like Sophie Carpano.'

'You've been to see her.'

'She told you?'

'Yeah.' He was silent a while and the two detectives said nothing. Then he looked up at them: 'Forget what I said about Dan. He's okay . . . You're not gunna find any gun at my uncle's. You oughta left them alone, I'm in the shit enough with them.'

'We've got a warrant to search Sophie's flat. And your car. Is the BMW downstairs?'

'How d'you know I drive a BMW?'

That was a mistake. 'One of our men saw it out at La Malmaison.'

'I don't drive it to work, so they didn't see it there.' Then he shook his head, not in anger but in admiration; or what looked like admiration. 'Jesus, it's you guys who've been following me!'

'As if you didn't know, Dwayne, once you'd cottoned on to them. I warned you – watch out for the axe.'

'You really think I killed the old guy?'

'Yes,' said Malone, 'I really do.'

Dwayne looked from one to the other; there was no hint that he was upset by the accusation. Despite himself, Malone had to admit the boy had control. It was not disguised as cockiness, though that was what had brought him here; it was the confidence of someone who had thought everything out right down to the wire.

'You think that, all on the fact that I was pinched up in Queensland for being in possession of a gun? Shit, that's stretching it, ain't it?'

'Dwayne,' said Clements, lolling on the couch as if this was just a pleasant little chat, 'why'd you come in to see us? Did you think we were gunna pick up some private detective for following you? We've got better things to do with our time than that.'

'I didn't think it was a private eye.' His own eyes had a private look to them. He's measuring whether he's done the right thing coming here, thought Malone. 'I thought it was youse guys all along and I was right.'

'So you thought you'd challenge us on it, that right?'

'Yes.' Then he had second thoughts; his mind was sliding from one gear to another: 'Well, no. Not *challenge* you. Why would I wanna do that? I just wanted to find out what's going on.'

186

'Now you know,' said Malone. 'What do you think about the possible sale of Huxwood Press?'

'Why would I be interested? Nobody's gunna sell the rose garden.'

'Nobody from the family's talked to you about it?'

A firm shake of the head. 'Nobody. D'you think they're gunna come out and talk to someone like me, the *under*-gardener, about something like that?'

He had a point: he had a lot of points, it seemed. 'Well, we're still looking for the gun, Dwayne.'

The control broke for a moment; or perhaps it was faked. 'If you think I did it, why for Crissake don't you pinch me? I'm here. Arrest me and charge me.' At least he didn't put out his wrists for the handcuffs; the control was still there, there were no theatrics. 'No, you can't, can you? Your suspicions are just so much shit, right?'

'Watch out for the axe, Dwayne,' said Malone and stood up. He had had enough of the young man. 'We'll be following you.'

Dwayne Harod got to his feet, unhurriedly. He was dressed in denim overalls and a white T-shirt; Mick Jagger peeped over the bib of the overalls; the Rolling Stones were due in town next week. 'You're making a mistake, Inspector. You watch out for the axe, too. You might chop off your own foot with it.'

'That a threat?' Clements had got up from the couch; against the midday light he looked big and threatening.

Dwayne looked up at him, unafraid. 'No, I was just talking metaphorical, like. Inspector Malone understands me.'

'Have you got the BMW downstairs?' said Malone.

'No. I've got the estate ute – I been taking garden rubbish out to the tip. You gunna let me know when you wanna search my car?'

'Where is it now?'

'Out at my uncle's, parked in the drive. It's got a cover over it, I look after it.'

'Then it's probably already been searched.'

Dwayne was suddenly concerned. 'Shit, I hope they haven't ripped it to pieces!'

'They'd only do that if they thought you had a gun hidden in one of the doors. Or behind the upholstery.'

'I can sue you, you know –'

'Do that, Dwayne. Go and dump your rubbish.'

187

The boy paused in the doorway; he wanted the last word but couldn't think of anything better than: 'You guys gunna keep following me?'

'Just keep an eye out. You'll know whether they're on your tail or not.'

Clements escorted the young Turk down to the ground floor; strangers were not allowed to roam around loose in the building. When he came back, Malone was standing at his office window, gazing across towards the other wing of the building, where the Fraud Squad was in business.

'Do you wonder sometimes if life wouldn't be easier in other sections? No blood, no danger, maybe some pressure from Upstairs but not much?'

'We'd never have the pleasure of meeting shit like young Dwayne.'

'We might. Over in Fraud they get to meet a lot of Big Shits.'

But in his heart he knew he would leave Homicide only when Administration, in its misguided wisdom, insisted on his transfer. Bringing murderers to justice was more rewarding, even though it might look like a blood-sport.

Then his phone rang and he picked it up. 'Inspector Malone? . . . Scobie, this is Derek Huxwood.'

'What can I do for you, Derek?' His tone was flat, but he felt a flutter of hope. Was Derek going to offer him some clue?

'We had a family meeting this morning – about the sale of Huxwood. I don't know whether I'm being alarmist, but –'

There was a long pause and Malone waited patiently. 'Go on, Derek,' he said at last.

'Well, as I said, maybe I'm being alarmist –' He sounded tentative, uncertain, something Malone had not expected of him. 'We had a vote on whether we should sell, an informal one, the full board weren't there. There is a deciding vote still to be cast – Michael's. My brother Nigel's son. The boy – no –' Again there was a long pause.

'Don't hang up, Derek. You're suggesting whoever killed your father might have a go at Michael? That's not alarmist – it could happen. You have no idea which way he's intending to vote?'

'None. Michael, more than any of the kids, always plays everything close to his chest. He's like my mother, in some ways.'

Malone thought a while. 'If whoever killed your father doesn't know which way Michael will vote, then he should be safe. For a while, anyway. Don't tell anyone you've been in touch with us, least of all Michael. Leave it with us. We'll have someone keep an eye on him till he makes up his mind.'

'Thanks, Scobie. I hope I'm not being melodramatic . . . I'm still trying to come to terms with what's happened this week.'

Malone hung up, looked at Clements. 'You got the gist of that?'

Clements ran a hand through his tousled hair. He was sitting beneath the light from the window and flecks of grey were very evident. Only that morning Malone had scrutinized himself in the bathroom mirror and noted the grey streak or two in his own thick crop. Maybe it came with the job . . .

'Michael the banker? What's he been up to?'

Malone told him. 'I dunno what's gone on over at Vaucluse this morning, but Derek thinks Michael might cop the next shot.'

'I'll get someone to keep him company. Kate?'

'No,' Malone said adamantly. Last year he had lost a woman detective, Peta Smith, shot coldbloodedly by an ex-KGB man who had apologized later but said it had been necessary. He was not going to risk losing another woman, not to a hitman like Dwayne, who would never apologize. 'Not Kate.'

Clements understood; the two of them had worked together so long they often shared a common antenna. 'Okay, I'll send John Kagal — he won't look out of place amongst the bankers.'

'We don't want Michael to know he's being watched.' Then he abruptly changed his mind: 'No, why not? If he knows how important he is, his vote, maybe he'll give it a lot of consideration.'

'What I saw of him the other day at Point Piper, he'd give a lot of consideration to picking his nose . . . What about our mate Dwayne? I think we should double the surveillance on him.'

'We'll have trouble digging up enough men. Ask Steve Lozelle to ask Randwick if they can spare someone. While you're at it, get Kate to call the Queensland cops. Have them check if they have any unsolved homicides on their books, ones that they think might be professional hit jobs. It's a long shot, but Dwayne might've been earning money on the side while he was cutting cane.'

'Why'd he bother to come up here complaining about being followed?'

'Cheek. He's a smartarse, Russ. He figures if he keeps tabs on us, he's going to be okay. He was enjoying himself while he was here.'

'Till we mentioned searching his BMW. He'd come gunning for *us* if we ripped the guts out of his toy. Another question – why's he still hanging around?'

'A couple of possibilities.' Malone, on his morning walk round Randwick racecourse, had considered the possibilities. 'One, if he skips, that's an admission he did it and he knows we'd pick him up eventually. If he hangs about, waits us out, we have to come up with evidence to nail him – and he knows as well as we do, that up till now we've got nothing on him . . . Two, maybe he hasn't been paid yet. He'd have got a down payment, but there's more to come. Maybe a lot more, considering how much is at stake. This is more than a ten thousand or twenty thousand dollar job.'

'We're assuming whoever paid him wanted the sale to go through.'

'Of course. What's in it for whoever hired him if the sale doesn't go through? You don't hire a hitman to save an institution. You hire him to get rid of it.'

'I dunno. Bev Bigelow has had his hitmen out this week trying to save his institution, the Government.'

'Who said politicians are like the rest of us? I meant to ask Derek who voted *for* the sale this morning. Get on to him and ask him.'

'Why don't you call him? You're his mate.'

Malone had looked at his watch. 'I'm going to lunch with Ivor Supple and his missus.'

'To talk about cricket?'

'I doubt it. Not if Mrs Supple is there.'

2

The Sheraton-on-the-Park was one of the latest of the five-star hotels that had gone up in the city in the past three years. Due to bankruptcy it had already changed hands and had its name changed twice; manufacturers of brass name-plates were said to be on constant stand-by. It was a towering cliff of windows and had a lobby that looked like a temple; there were marble pillars and a curving stairway where vestal virgins, an unknown quantity in Sydney, should have been standing at every step.

No deity was waiting for Malone, just Ivor Supple. He was dressed in a dark grey suit but was wearing his MCC tie, possibly the worst colour combination since the first artist mixed some ochre and blood and tried painting a mastodon on his cave's walls. 'I thought we'd have a drink, a word together, before lunch.'

He steered Malone towards the bar and the latter, suddenly cautious, had the feeling he was being shepherded. Towards what or from what? 'I'll have a light beer.'

Supple ordered a gin-and-tonic for himself, a drink that seemed almost to have died out here in the colonies. Supple looked across the narrow table at Malone and smiled. He had always had a charming smile, Malone remembered; he had seen it on television clips, though smiles had not been exchanged when they had been playing cricket. Now it looked rather weary.

'Gin-and-tonic – we cling to it in England like some sort of elixir . . . I never thought we'd meet again like this. Were you a police officer when you played against me?'

'Yes, I was on the beat in uniform in those days. I never thought of you as a politician.'

'Neither did I. I did history at Oxford. I had a vague idea I might teach. Then someone convinced Maggie Thatcher I might lend a sporting image to the Tory benches – Maggie didn't know a late cut from a hair-cut, but it didn't matter. Image is everything these days.'

'You sound disillusioned.'

'I am.' He sipped his drink again. 'I have to go back to London tomorrow. The PM was on the blower last night, seems I'm needed.'

'What do you do, Ivor? I'm sorry, I'm not very up on British politics – I have enough trouble worrying about our own –'

'Don't apologize, old chap. Most people would rather ignore them, including half the voters back home. I'm the junior Sports Minister. I thought it would be a breeze, a bit of a loaf – you know, opening sports grounds, presenting a cup to some winner . . . I'm lazy, y'know.' Again the charming smile.

'That's what got you out most times. You played as if you'd suddenly fallen asleep.'

'I'm not going to get much sleep when I get back. There's no fun in the Ministry of Sport. A cricket team that couldn't beat their grandmothers, soccer hooligans everywhere – ' He took another drink, a longer mouthful this time. 'And now this soccer bribery scandal. One couldn't be blamed for thinking we're going to the dogs. Scandals in the City, politicians who can't keep their trousers up . . .'

Malone took a long swallow of his beer. Though he was and always had been a republican, he took no pleasure in Britain's woes. 'What does your wife – Beatrice – think?'

He smiled again. 'Beatrice is Mother England, she's Boadicea without the knives on her chariot wheels – she's certain we'll pull through. All we have to do is hang all the miscreants. Or transport them to the colonies. But don't misunderstand me – I love the dear old thing. Which brings me to why we're in here – ' He waved a hand at their surroundings.

'I wondered when we were going to get to that.'

'You were suspicious? Is that the cop in you or the fast bowler?'

'You know that fast bowlers have always been open, take-me-at-face-value fellers.'

'Yes, that was what Andy Roberts said when he hit me in the throat with a bumper . . . No, you've been invited to lunch as a cop, Scobie. We're having it in a private room upstairs.'

'Now I am suspicious. Just the three of us?'

'No-o. Charlie Bentsen is joining us. And a father and son, the Aldwyches. I haven't met them, but Beatrice has.'

Malone put down his empty glass. 'Are you trying to use me for something, Ivor?'

'My dear chap – ' But Supple looked as if he had been sent on an expedition for which he hadn't volunteered. 'No, no. All I think they want is advice.'

'What advice do they think I can give them? I'm a cop, Ivor, not a lawyer.'

'Well, I'll let them explain. You can always say No.' He looked relieved to be passing the buck back where it belonged; Boadicea would have to climb up on her chariot. 'Shall we go up? I've ordered the lunch. Beatrice tends to think anything built around brussels sprouts is gourmet stuff. She's still at Roedean, gastronomically speaking.'

Malone's immediate impulse was to get up and walk out. But the thought of seeing the mix of Jack Aldwych with Beatrice Supple and

Charlie Bentsen was too inviting. However: 'Is there going to be anyone else there? A banker, a lawyer?'

'No. Beatrice has Metropolitan's lawyers and a banker here, but I told her I thought they would frighten you off.'

'They frighten me as much as batsmen who used to drive the ball straight back at me.'

'The good old days,' said Supple. 'Shall we go up?'

The private dining room looked out on Hyde Park, where the Archibald fountain caught the sunlight in its bows of water and old men sat on benches, their eyes glistening with either rheum or lechery, and watched the young girls swing by. Some of the trees had already begun to thin, an early surrender to autumn, but others still clung to summer, great green balloons only faintly fading at the edges.

Beatrice Supple was in a dark green wool suit with a white silk blouse and a single strand of pearls. She looked businesslike today: one could imagine her telling the cleaning woman not to go lightly with the Windolene on the 'glass ceiling'.

'Mr Malone! How nice to see you again. You know Mr Bentsen. And this is Mr Aldwych, Jack Senior and Jack Junior.'

'We've met before,' said Jack Senior. 'How are you, Scobie?'

'You were a cricketer too?' said Beatrice.

'No,' said Malone. 'We were in complementary trades.'

'Oh, you were in security, Mr Aldwych?'

'Sort of,' said Aldwych.

'Shall we sit down? I let Ivor order the menu. God knows what we'll get. Some of the worst meals I've ever had in my life I've had at the MCC.'

As they sat down Malone glanced across at Supple, at the MCC tie. He wondered if the tie had been worn as part of the bonding process, the cricketers' old mates act.

Talk during the first course was idle, as smooth as the excellent oyster soup. Then Charlie Bentsen, with a builder's bluntness, thick with the trowel, said, 'You know we're trying to buy out Huxwood Press? But at the moment we're up in the air. This business out at Vaucluse is hanging over the deal like – well, like a corpse.'

There was a gentle clatter as Ivor Supple's spoon clanked against the side of his soup bowl, but no one else seemed put out by Bentsen's bluntness.

193

'What we'd like to know,' said Beatrice Supple, 'is whether you, the police, are close to arresting Harry Huxwood's murderer? There's been nothing in the press, but perhaps you are close to closing the case?'

The cream in the oyster soup was beginning to curdle. 'You don't expect me to give out information like that.'

'Well, actually, I thought you might,' said Beatrice.

Malone looked at Jack Aldwych. The two Aldwyches did not look out of place at the table; both of them were dark-suited, sober-tied, white-shirted, discreet gold links in the cuffs. Both were handsome, though Jack Senior's features were chipped and there was a faint scar on his right jawline where a razor, not his own, had nicked him. Jack Junior was taller than his father and the bulk of the two men, sitting side by side, was formidable.

'Did you think I would, Jack?'

'I'd of been surprised if you had . . . Mrs Supple —'

'Beatrice.' She said it as if handing him a decoration.

'Beatrice.' The old crim smiled, to himself and to Malone more than to the company. He was wondering how the sly-grog and brothel queens like Kate Leigh and Tilly Devine, the crowned heads in his early days, would have handled Mrs Supple. 'I came along to this lunch because I know Scobie better than any of you. He's not a dumb cop.'

'I never suggested he was.' Beatrice bridled.

'I'm not saying you did. But I've known cops all my life and only the bent ones give out information and always for a price. Scobie isn't bent.'

'Thanks, Jack,' said Malone; then looked back at Beatrice and Bentsen. He had the feeling that Ivor Supple was embarrassed at the way the conversation had gone, but he did not look at the junior Minister for Sport. 'I think I should tell you that you were both on our early list of suspects for the murder.'

That did curdle the soup. 'Jesus Christ!' said Bentsen, and Beatrice Supple reared back so that she seemed to grow taller and bigger. Ivor Supple said, 'I say, old chap —' and then said nothing more.

'Did Sir Harry ever tell you that he intended to sell?'

'No,' said Beatrice. 'I've never met anyone so hard to pin down. It was like dealing with the Arabs.'

At the other end of the table her husband shook his head and smiled indulgently. Boadicea had no time for foreigners.

'Was that why Harry was killed? Because he'd made up his mind not to sell?'

'We don't know.' Malone made up his mind he would be candid, up to a point; you never knew where it might lead. Candidness was supposed to be a native trait, but foreigners too often mistook it for rudeness. Not, he thought, that Beatrice would mind a little rudeness. 'He might've wanted to sell or he might not have – the killer might not have known.'

'It's immaterial now, isn't it?' Jack Junior would never have the ruthlessness of his father, but there was no point in being delicate, not in business. Malone began to have the feeling he was lunching with sharks, including a female white pointer. 'The vote will lie with someone else now. They're the ones we've got to stroke, get on side with.'

'All of them?' said Beatrice. 'They're worse than the damned Royal family.'

'Careful, old thing,' said her husband. 'There's a member of Her Majesty's loyal government down this end of the table.'

'I wasn't talking of Her.'

'If I read you right, Mr Malone,' said Bentsen and Malone knew the tycoon could read a balance-sheet at a hundred paces; reading a cop at close quarters was no strain at all, 'you're a long way from an arrest. It could be weeks, even months off. Am I right?'

'No,' said Malone. 'But that's all I'm going to tell you.'

A waiter had come in and taken away the soup plates. Malone noticed that the questions had not stopped while the waiter had been in the room; it was as if he were seen as deaf, dumb and blind. The waiter came back in again with the main course, but Beatrice seemed unaware of him.

'Then we are to assume that you have someone in mind as the killer? Anyone here?'

The waiter's eyes were hanging out on his cheeks.

Malone smiled at his hostess. 'Beatrice – may I call you Beatrice?'

'Do, by all means.' She sounded more gracious, less patronizing than before.

'Beatrice, you are off our list.'

195

'And us?' Bentsen waved a hand at himself and Jack Junior.

'Do you want me to spoil your lunch?'

As the waiter served the last plate of the main course, grilled lamb cutlets, and went out of the room Malone saw him look back, eyes and ears wide open. He was falling over himself to come back and refill the wine glasses.

'I have a cast-iron stomach,' said Bentsen. 'I'm sure Jack has, too.'

'Not me,' said the younger Aldwych. 'Dad has.'

'I haven't enjoyed lunch so much in years,' said Aldwych senior and cut the cutlet as he might have a competitor's throat back in the good old days.

'Well,' Malone told Bentsen and Jack Junior, 'let's say you're at the bottom of our list.'

He looked across the table at Aldwych, who grinned and nodded his head in appreciation. 'You haven't lost your touch, Scobie.'

Malone put down his fork and knife, gave his attention to Beatrice Supple and Charlie Bentsen; he decided that the Aldwyches were the junior partners in the consortium. He just wondered why Jack Aldwych had not told him their partners were Metropolitan Newspapers.

'Has anyone approached you, outside of Derek Huxwood and Sir Harry?'

'You mean someone else from the family?' said Bentsen and glanced at Beatrice. She gave him an almost imperceptible nod and he went on, 'Yes.'

'Who?'

Aldwych said, 'We invited you here, Scobie, to get information outa you. Now you're screwing it outa us.'

'Like you said, Jack, I haven't lost my touch. Mr Bentsen?'

There was no invitation to call him Charlie. 'We've had a couple of approaches. Nigel Huxwood came to see Beatrice and Enrico Quental came to see me.'

'Asking for what?'

'Asking how high we were prepared to go in price.'

'Both of them have inflated ideas how much Huxwood is worth,' said Beatrice.

'The last I'd heard of your offer was that it was eleven-fifty. This morning the market price of the shares is thirteen dollars.'

196

'You follow share prices?' Bentsen made it sound as if Malone were running a prostitution protection racket. One never knew what cops got up to these days.

'No, but my senior sergeant does . . . What were Nigel and Mr Quental offering?'

'They weren't in a position to offer or ask for anything. They just offered to work on Sir Harry, get him to make up his mind our way.'

'Work on him? In what way?'

'I don't know,' said Bentsen, who had, in his earlier days, worked on strikers who had tried to picket his jobs.

'They were working together?'

'I don't think anyone in that family works together,' said Jack Junior, who had done his homework.

'We assumed they were together,' said Beatrice. 'Spurred on, no doubt, by their wives.'

She had picked up a cutlet and was devouring the last of the meat on the bone; her little finger was raised, so that she at least looked genteel. Malone could imagine her chewing up recalcitrant share-holders of Metropolitan or misogynistic MCC members in the same way. Yet there must be another side to her: there appeared to be genuine love between her and Ivor.

'We took no notice of their offer.' She put down the bone, wiped her fingers on her napkin. 'The only one who was going to influence Sir Harry was Lady Huxwood.'

She glanced down the table at her husband, who raised his fork in salute. 'It's the way of the world, old dear.'

Everyone, including Beatrice, laughed, and the waiter, coming back with more wine and further curiosity, found the conversation had lapsed into remarks about the weather and tomorrow's State election, subjects too boring for words. Then cheese and crackers were served and Malone, a sweet-tooth man, decided that Ivor must not like desserts. The cheeses, he noted, were all English.

Over some Stilton he said, 'Did any of the grandchildren approach you?'

'The grandkids don't count,' said Bentsen, as if the young had no more clout than family pets.

Little do you know, Charlie. 'I think you'd better look into it.'

'Do you know something we don't know?' said Jack Junior.

197

'I'm not sure. And that's all you're getting out of me. Nice cheese, Ivor. This what they serve at the MCC?'

Lunch finished and Malone, not wanting to be buttonholed further by Beatrice and Bentsen, was the first to rise. 'I have to be getting back —'

'I was hoping we could have a little more time together,' said Ivor. 'Talk cricket —'

But Malone had caught the glance between Beatrice and him. 'Sorry, Ivor. Good luck back in London. I think your soccer hooligans are a bigger problem than your cricket team. All you need is a captain with some git-up-and-go in him and a coupla batsmen who can use their feet. Like you used to ... Thanks, Beatrice, for lunch. Watch out for the grandkids.'

'Mine? Oh, you mean the Huxwoods?' She seemed off-balance that he was escaping so easily.

'Tell me something,' said Bentsen in the doorway. 'Are you in favour of the sale?'

'No,' said Malone. 'But I'm just the public.'

While he was waiting for the lift Malone was joined by Aldwych. 'Jack Junior is staying behind. You gave 'em something to think about, Scobie.'

'I told 'em nothing, Jack.'

'It's what you didn't tell 'em that's got 'em thinking. They're not dills, least of all Jack Junior. As for Beatrice, I think she could have manhandled Churchill.'

'And Bentsen?'

'He doesn't remember me, but when he first got started, I had Blackie and some of my fellers go in and disrupt things — the union was having trouble with him and they paid us to influence him.'

'Did you?'

Aldwych smiled, shook his head. 'One of my few failures. You care for a walk? I like to walk a meal off.'

Malone looked at his watch. 'Twenty minutes. Let's go over into the park.'

Aldwych signalled to Blackie Ovens in the Daimler to wait, then he and Malone crossed the busy street as jay-walkers, Aldwych not bothering to hurry as traffic bore down on him. Once in the park

Malone said, 'Why did you lie to me, Jack? You never mentioned you were in with Metropolitan.'

'Why did you lie to us back there? You've got someone lined up that you're gunna nab. We're not on the list of suspects, never were.'

'You didn't expect me to come out with the truth, the whole truth and nothing but the truth, did you?'

'Of course not. I been reading cops' minds for years, Scobie, longer than you've been alive. But why do you expect the truth, the whole truth and nothing but the truth in business? You're not that naive.'

'I thought we were supposed to be mates?'

'We are – or I like to think so. But I'm mates with my son, too. It's our money – *my* money, if you like – that's in this deal. It adds up to millions –' He stopped as a wino approached them, one hand holding an almost empty bottle, the other held out in supplication.

'You look like a coupla kind gents –'

'Do you take American Express?' said the elder kind gent and walked on. 'This will cost millions, Scobie, and I'm keeping an eye on it every inch of the way.'

'Somehow I can't see you as a press baron.'

'I'll be well in the background. But you think I'd be any worse than Ezra Norton?'

'Before my time, Jack . . . Have you had any more threats?'

The lunch crowd in the park had gone back to their offices and stores; the pigeons picked their way amongst the crumbs. The day was warm, muggy, and Malone took off his jacket; but Aldwych stayed in his three-piece, not a gleam of sweat anywhere on him. His silver hair glistened in the sun and two women in their thirties, passing by, looked back at him and remarked to each other that sometimes there was something to be said for older men. Especially older, *rich-looking* men.

'None. Jack's been keeping an eye out for them, but there's been no more. I think it was just a one-off. Maybe they've backed off, in case I'm still the same as I used to be.' He smiled, enjoying his past.

'Talking of who you used to be – do you still have any contacts?'

Aldwych shook his head. They had crossed Park Street and were in the southern half of the park. They passed a group of men playing draughts on a bench, kibitzers standing behind them like political minders. The Anzac Memorial was on their right, now seemingly a

199

relic; the natives were not ones for revering their monuments. Half a dozen Japanese tourists stood on its steps while another of their party photographed them. Malone looked around, waiting for some veteran to spring out of the bushes and attack them; but there was none. Only Aldwych, who had dodged the draft and spent the war making money, not munitions, looked disapproving.

'That's pretty insensitive,' he said, then gave his attention again to Malone. 'No, I don't have any contacts any more, not the way I used to. All the honest crims you and I used to know, they're gone now. What did you wanna know?'

'I want some word on a hitman. This is between you and me, okay?' He had to be cautious. In the new politically correct world police were not supposed to ask criminals, even retired ones, for information. 'We're mates?'

Aldwych grinned. 'I won't even mention it in my prayers. Who's the guy?'

'A kid named Dwayne Harod, works as an assistant-gardener out at the Huxwood place. I've got no hard evidence, but I *know* he's the one who pulled the trigger.'

'You think he's a pro?'

'I don't know. Maybe he's just a learner. He's been up in Queensland for the last twelve months. He has a record up there, in possession of a weapon plus a silencer –'

'Plus a silencer? And you dunno whether he's a pro? You're slipping, Scobie. How old is he?'

'Twenty-two, three. He's a Turk.'

'A Turk? Dwayne? Whatever happened to Abdul and Mustafa?'

'Don't laugh. We arrested a kid this week named Django Muldoon.' They had reached the end of the park, stood for a moment looking across Liverpool Street at the Connaught, a huge block of apartments. 'Dale Flannery lived there.'

Flannery had been the city's best-known hitman. He had left his apartment one day nine years ago and had never been seen since; he was said to be part of the foundations of at least seven major developments in the city. 'Did you ever use him, Jack?'

Aldwych looked hurt. 'What a question!' They turned to retrace their steps. 'If you're so sure this kid did the hit, why don't you verbal him?'

200

'That doesn't work any more, not since we've used video in the interview. I never used it, anyway,' he said piously. 'But sometimes I think it had the right effect. I saw something the other day about "noble cause corruption".'

'I like that, it has a nice unethical ring about it. What's it mean?'

'It means that cops, not just here but everywhere, are fed up with lawyers using loopholes to get their clients off. Your lawyers got you off at least a coupla times when you should've gone down.'

Aldwych looked hurt again. 'You've been going back over my record?'

'Jack, I just have a good memory. Do you really think the justice system is a search for the truth? That was what it was designed to be, but now it's just a matter of one side winning and the other losing. It was wrong, but in the old days verballing made the weights more even for us against the lawyers . . . I'd verbal this kid if I could, but it's a no go.'

'You asked me if I still had contacts. What about your own gigs?'

Malone grinned wryly. 'You wouldn't believe it, but they're all doing time at the same time. Where's Doodles Leyland?'

'Doodles?' Aldwych smiled to himself as if remembering a favourite pet. 'Was he ever one of your gigs?'

'No, but several others told me he was a mine of information.'

'I'd have cut his throat if I'd known that.' Then Aldwych smiled again. 'Figuratively speaking . . . He went up to the Gold Coast. He was always a good con man and he thought he could make his fortune up there amongst the honest crooks selling shonky developments and phantom blocks of land.'

'Did he?'

'They did him for everything but his white shoes. Last I heard of him he was selling racing tips to mug punters.'

'Can you get in touch with him?'

'No problem.' Malone would not have been surprised if Aldwych had said he could get in touch with the Pope or Elvis Presley. 'What d'you want?'

'I want to know if there was a hitman for sale up there. Up to, say, two or three months ago. If there was, ask what price.'

Aldwych nodded, but said, 'I dunno why I'm doing this —'

'Yes, you do, Jack. One lot of bullets was fired at Jack Junior and his wife. Next time the feller's aim may be a lot straighter.'

201

Osbert Beckett sat in his cubbyhole reading this morning's election-eve editorial. It was bland to the point of boredom; he was ashamed that he had written it, though, being an editorial, it had no by-line. It had been written as it was at the insistence of Derek, who had over-ridden Shoemaker, the editor, and Warren Gates.

'If things were different,' Derek had said, 'we'd go to town for the Coalition. But with Dad's death and the paper maybe going to be sold, I don't think we can tell the voters what to do.'

'Why not?' Shoemaker had said. 'The polls say there are nineteen per cent I-don't-knows out there. Someone has to make up those nongs' minds for them.'

'Not us,' said Derek adamantly. 'Make it noncommittal, Ossie. Reasoned, I think is the word.'

Beckett looked now at the scraps of paper with quotes on them that he had intended incorporating in the editorial. There was one from Charles de Gaulle: *Since a politician never believes what he says, he is always surprised when others believe him.* And one from H. L. Mencken: *A politician is an animal that can sit on a fence and keep both ears to the ground.* And even one from Nikita Krushchev: *Politicians are the same all over. They promise to build a bridge even when there is no river* . . . He had looked forward to using those gems, but to no avail; he would have to save them for another election, maybe the Federal one in less than a year's time. If he lasted that long. If the paper came under the hammer, maybe the new owners would not want an associate editor so close to superannuation.

He glanced out into the newsroom where the reporters and columnists were beginning to straggle back from lunch. At least half of them were glowing with health rather than with liquor. In his days as a reporter lunchtime was always spent up the road at the Great Southern, where the *Chronicle* staff, reporters and printers, held up the bar like human scaffolding. Nowadays most of them spent their lunchtime working out in nearby gyms or playing squash. These days sweat, and not liquor, was the desirable fluid to drown in. He knew old-time newspapermen who would not believe him when he joined them in Hell, where he was sure he was going.

Then he saw young Ross Huxwood striding down between the desks. The boy had worked in the newsroom during his university vacation; Beckett had been instructed to take him under his wing and teach him the ropes. It had been a difficult time for both teacher and pupil. Ross Huxwood had been interested in nothing but keeping an eye on the clock and on Rosie Gilligan.

Beckett got up and stood in the doorway of his office. He saw Ross walk straight into Rosie Gilligan's office, closing the door behind him. Grace Ditcham, the senior crime reporter, swung round in her chair from her desk just outside Beckett's cubbyhole.

'Wonder Boy is back, looks like he's come home to Mother.'

'Mi-aow. Put your claws back in, Grace. How're you going on the murder?'

Grace Ditcham was in her mid-thirties, her prettiness fading from too much sun-baking; Beckett was always warning her against mela-nomas. She had dark blue eyes that appeared to have faded, perhaps from too much staring at what so-called civilized humans could do to each other. As a young reporter she had had a generous mouth, but now it had turned in as if in disapproval at what she had had to witness. But she had never turned nasty, though she could come close to it when asked for an opinion on Rosie Gilligan and the other women who wrote what she called 'fluff'.

She ran a hand through her sun-bleached hair and gestured at the blank screen of her VDT. 'I've had bugger-all to write about the last two days. I talked on the phone this morning to Scobie Malone and you'd have thought we'd never met, he was so unforthcoming.'

'Unforthcoming? You going to use that? I'd run a blue pencil through that one if I were still a sub-editor.' He glanced down the room again towards Rosie Gilligan's office. 'Hullo, looks like Mother's giving him the rounds of the kitchen.'

Most of the newsroom was giving its attention to the silent but demonstrative argument behind the glass wall of the fashion editor's room. Then Alexandra got up from her desk and went in to join the argument, closing the door behind her.

'Enter Big Sister,' said Grace Ditcham. 'She looks after him as if he shouldn't be allowed out on his own.'

'Maybe he shouldn't be,' said Beckett.

The silent argument went on in the tiny office at the end of the

203

newsroom. Some of the reporters grew tired of watching it and went back to their work; unlike their television opposition, who are satisfied with pictures, newspapermen like to hear the words. Beckett wondered what the words were in Rosie's office.

Then her door opened and Ross marched out and down between the desks and out of the newsroom; he was bursting with temper and his face, to Beckett, seemed a shade of apricot. A moment later Alexandra came out and went back to her desk; she looked unperturbed and seemingly oblivious of the stares of the others in the big room. But when one of the girls went across to her, Alexandra brusquely waved her away.

'Do you want me to go down there and find out what it was all about?' asked Grace Ditcham.

'Do you think she'd tell you? Just wait, we'll find out soon enough.'

He went back into his cubbyhole, sat down and waited. Gossip was as much part of the fashion trade as needle and thread; it was endemic and he knew Rosie Gilligan had caught the disease. Within five minutes she was at his door.

'I come in?'

'Sure. You don't mind if Grace joins us?' He had seen Ditcham rise from her desk. 'This has something to do with the Huxwoods, right? Grace is covering it for us.'

Rosie did not look pleased at the suggestion, but she nodded. 'I don't think this should be written about. Not yet.'

'What?' Grace had come into the tiny office, hoisting herself to sit on Beckett's desk. She was a small trim woman and her feet did not come near the floor. Rosie had dropped into the only chair besides Beckett's own. 'I don't like embargos.'

'I think Upstairs would embargo this one, at least for now.' Rosie tossed the mane of hair. She looked frustrated: she had just been presented with news that she couldn't run on the fashion pages: 'The Huxwood kids have inherited all Harry's share of the holding company. They've got the money and the voting clout.'

Beckett and Grace looked at each other. Then Grace said, 'Looks like the geeks shall inherit the earth after all.'

'They're going to throw away the inheritance,' said Rosie. 'Ross wants to sell everything. Lock, stock and barrel, as they say.'

'And do what with his share of the loot?' asked Beckett.

'Run off with me.' She said it without a blush. 'Though maybe it wouldn't be a bad idea. Older women can teach younger men how to handle their money. It's happened before.'

'The success rate isn't good,' said Grace. 'Older women can go through a guy's money just as fast as a young one.'

'The will's been read?' said Beckett before war could break out.

'Not officially, I gather. There was some sort of family meeting this morning at which sides were drawn, for and against. At the moment it's five-all, with Michael the banker still to make up his mind.'

'So the sale is still up in the air?' said Grace. 'If Michael the banker comes down against the sale, what happens?'

'The kids don't get the loot. They'll just go on drawing their dividends, plus their share of Harry's dividends, divided six ways.'

'Not enough to entice an older woman to go into business with a younger man?' Beckett smiled at her to take the edge off it.

'You're my favourite sonofabitch, Ossie. You have a knack of boiling everything down to the essential.'

'It's the old sub-editor in me.'

'Okay,' said Grace, 'that establishes you two are platonic lovers. But where does it leave the rest of us? Do we call a staff meeting and go and see Derek?'

'I'll have a word with him.' Beckett leaned his chair back against the wall; his head rested against the only decoration in the office. A narrow strip of yellow paper carried a message in large black letters: *Speak out, hide not thy thoughts.* 'The big tragedy here is that the bloody sale is overshadowing Harry's murder. I don't think Harry would have had enough irony in him to appreciate that.'

The two women, each of whom knew men backwards, forwards and sideways, nodded: for the moment they forgot their differences. Rosie said mournfully, 'I don't want to leave the paper. But if it's sold . . .'

'I've only been here a year,' said Grace, then shrugged. 'It's grown on me.' She slid off Beckett's desk. 'What did Alex have to say? Is she for or against the sale?'

'I don't know. Alex doesn't confide in me.'

'Why do you keep her as your assistant then?'

'Because her father insists that I do. And she does the job better than anyone I've had before. So we put up with each other. And she can control Ross.'

Why did you ever get involved with him? But Beckett knew better than to ask a woman such a question. 'Okay, leave it with me. Like I said, I'll have a word with Derek.'

'The natives are getting restless,' said Grace. 'There's got to be a staff meeting within the next coupla days.'

'Derek may talk to me. Sometimes there are certain advantages to being the Old Inhabitant.'

Rosie stood up, then nodded at the strip of yellow paper behind Beckett's head. 'Speak out, hide not thy thoughts. Good advice. Who wrote that?'

'Homer.'

'Homer Simpson?'

'Yes, while he was writing *The Iliad.*'

4

When Malone got back to Homicide John Kagal was waiting for him. He looked a little crumpled; or anyway, less immaculate than usual. 'I've been up in the ceiling of the Harods' house.'

'You find anything?'

Kagal shook his head. 'No gun. Neither at the Harods' or at his girl friend's flat — she wasn't too happy about giving up her lunch-hour to come back to Stanmore with us.'

'What about the BMW?'

'Nothing. We gave it a good going-over, without tearing it to pieces.'

'Dwayne will be relieved to hear that.'

Then as Kagal went back into the main room Malone's phone rang. It was Don Cheshire, from Fingerprints. 'Scobie? Sorry I've been so long with those prints on that note to Jack Aldwych. We're up to our eyeballs in work, you got no idea —'

Give Cheshire five minutes and he'd take twenty. 'Go on, Don.'

'There were two sets of prints on it. One, I guess, were Aldwych's son. The other were Jack's — I checked our records on him.'

'Only two?' Malone couldn't keep the disappointment from his voice.

'I'm coming to that. There was a third set. I went through all the sets our guys brought in from the Huxwood house – all the family, the servants, all them. The third set of dabs match.'

'Match whose?'

'I'm looking at 'em right now. Cordelia Huxwood's.'

Chapter Ten

1

'You go in to the *Chronicle*,' said Malone, 'and pick up Derek. Tell him what's happened after you get him into your car, don't let him get on to his wife. I'll meet you out at their house.'

'Did you ever suspect she might be the one who hired Dwayne?' said Clements.

'No, she wasn't on my list. Or yes, she was, but right at the bottom of it.'

'You think Derek put her up to it?'

'I dunno. Let's wait and see, till we get the two of them together.' He looked at his watch. 'If Derek says he has to stay for the four o'clock editorial conference, tell him to forget it.'

They went down to their respective cars and went in opposite directions. The peak hour traffic had begun and Malone, never a patient man in a car, no matter how patient he might be in other circumstances, wished he had commandeered a police vehicle and had someone drive him out to Vaucluse, siren going and red and blue lights flashing. Stopped at traffic lights, he looked at people in other cars and, as often in the past, ever since he had come to Homicide, wondered what black thoughts, what guilt lay behind the eyes waiting for the green light.

Out past Rose Bay the traffic thinned; out here lived the executives who did not leave their offices till six or after. He swung down the slope towards the harbour and a few minutes later pulled up outside the iron gates of La Malmaison. They were closed and he had to get out of the car and tell someone in the Big House who he was and whom he wanted to see.

'Leave the gates open. My colleague will be here soon with Mr Derek.'

208

'Lady Huxwood insists that the gates always be closed.' It was Krilich, the butler.

The gates closed behind him as he drove down the main driveway. Quental's Bentley (or was it Linden's?) and a top-of-the-range BMW were parked at the front door of the Big House. He skirted them and swung into the side drive that led to Little House One. As he got out of his car Dan Darling came up across the lawn from the sea-wall. He was carrying a large bucket and a spray-gun.

'Bloody bugs, they make a meal of the gardenias. How're things going?'

'You mean the murder? We're getting there, an inch at a time.'

'Just like growing flowers. An inch at a time, then all of a sudden – whoosh, you've got blooms.'

'Yeah, it happens sometimes like that in a murder investigation. Whoosh, and you've got your man. Or woman, as the case may be,' remembering two recent cases. 'Dwayne around today?'

'He was here, but he always knocks off at four, right on the dot. He's got an in-built clock, I tell him.'

'How's he been?'

Darling shrugged. 'I dunno, like he's got something on his mind. He's a good worker from eight till four, but come four o'clock and he'll knock off with a bush half-pruned. Kids his age are all the same.'

Malone wasn't going to get caught on either side of the generation gap; he had enough of that at home. 'Is Mrs Huxwood in? Mr Derek's wife?'

'I saw her a coupla minutes ago. Some of the women aren't taking it too well, the murder. I think the possible sale is on their minds, too – the big meeting, so I hear, is Monday. It'll be a big wrench, the family selling out. If they do.'

'How do you feel about it, Dan?'

'Sick. This country doesn't have too many institutions, not like older countries. I hate to see the ones we've got go down the drain. Some of our newspapers, the *Chronicle* is one of 'em, they're older than most of our other so-called institutions. I'll hate it if it happens, if they sell.' He held up his maimed hand and grinned the dry, cracked smile. 'Part of me is somewhere there in the *Chronicle*.'

Ten minutes later Clements' car came down the driveway. Before it came to a stop Derek Huxwood was out of it and, with just a nod to Malone, hurried towards the front door. He fumbled with his key, pushed open the door and, whether intentionally or not, would have slammed it in Malone's face. But the latter had followed him and put a foot against the door, just like a television reporter. He pushed it open and waited for Clements.

'He doesn't believe she did it,' Clements said. 'He's either a bloody good actor or he hadn't a clue what she was up to.'

They went into the entrance hall, a smaller version of the large hall in the Big House. There was no curving staircase, no stage for grand gestures of dismissal; the stairs leading to the upper floor were at the back of the hall. The two detectives heard raised voices coming from a side room and they followed the sound.

'You know why they're here?' Derek was almost shouting. 'Some bullshit about a threatening note!'

'Not bullshit, Derek,' said Malone in the doorway. 'Excuse me, Cordelia.'

The room was almost too exquisitely furnished to be called a living room; Malone couldn't imagine a family lolling about in it, *living* in it, as his kids did in the similar room at Randwick. He had remarked the surroundings in the Big House and since then Lisa had commented on them; everything had been expensive but somehow austere; like Lady Huxwood herself, Lisa had said. But this room was rich in its drapes, its carpet, the tables and chairs and couches; everything in it was meant to be admired, not lived amongst. Whether the taste was Cordelia's or her decorator's, no money had been spared in indulging it.

Cordelia sat in a chair of silk stripes, knees together under her tan skirt, hands together on her knees; she looked up at her husband and the two detectives in the doorway as if all three were intruders. She said nothing, just stared at the three men, then turned her head and looked out the windows that fronted on to the wide lawn and the view of the harbour.

Malone and Clements, uninvited, sat down. Derek stood a moment, as if adrift in his own house, then he dropped into a third chair. Outside on the lawn half a dozen mynahs argued in a loud chatter with a seagull that walked amongst them with disdain, occasionally pecking at a mynah that got too close, as if to remind them who was the native here.

210

'Why did you send the note, Cordelia?' Malone sat back in his chair, not wanting to be threatening at this stage. She was wearing glasses this afternoon and she looked older than when he had last seen her.

She did not turn her head. Derek opened his mouth, then shut it again; he made a despairing gesture, then glanced at Malone and shook his head. At last Cordelia turned back, blinked as if surprised to find these strangers in her exquisite room. Clements, seated on a small brocaded settee with thin curved legs, looked like an ox waiting to be gift-wrapped.

'How did you know?' Her voice was thin but steady.

'Your fingerprints were on it. They took all your fingerprints last Tuesday morning—'

'Christ—' Derek's voice was hoarse. 'We were all suspects as early as that? Is that what you mean?'

Why not? 'We always do it, Derek. So that we can eventually identify the stranger's prints we find at the scene of a crime.'

'Did you find any? A stranger's?'

'No ... You weren't careful enough, Cordelia. Going to all that trouble to cut out letters and paste them into a message and then leaving your prints on the paper. You didn't help yourself by using type from the *Chronicle*. You were too loyal to the paper.'

'I was defending it,' she said.

'Why did you do it?'

'I thought I was helping you,' she told her husband; then turned back to Malone. 'It will break Derek's heart if we have to sell — I couldn't bear to see that. I knew Jack Aldwych — Jack Junior, is that what they call him? — I knew he was in the bidding. I thought if I scared him off, the others, Beatrice Supple and the London crowd, would back off—'

'Jesus!' Derek flopped back in his chair, a matching one to Cordelia's; the silk stripes were like bars that he had only just managed to escape. 'World War Three wouldn't make that lot back off.'

'Didn't you think the shots at Jack Junior were enough warning?' said Clements.

Cordelia frowned. She picked up a porcelain figurine from the low marble-topped table in front of her and absently stroked it. 'The shots? I had nothing to do with those.'

211

'You didn't hire —' Malone held back his tongue. 'You didn't hire someone to shoot at Aldwych and his wife?'

'Oh, for Crissake, Scobie!'

'Relax, Derek. We have to ask these questions. Did you hire someone to shoot at them? A warning?'

'Of course not!' She put the figurine back on the table; it hit it with a thump, but didn't break. 'I had nothing to do with that! Good God, I'm not a *murderer*! All right, I read about the shooting and that was when I got the idea of the note, a sort of follow-up . . . But try to kill someone? I could never do that!'

'You could have hired someone to do it for you.'

'That's enough! You're going too far, Scobie!'

Derek reached for his wife's hand; it was a stretch and Malone waited for him to get down on his knees beside her. Which he did, sliding into a sitting position at her feet. She put her hand on his shoulder and Malone suddenly saw the incongruity of it: she was the protector. Perhaps, after all, there was truth to what she had told them.

'We often have to go too far,' said Clements quietly; he shifted his bulk on the fragile settee and it seemed to squeak in protest. 'We don't solve murders by being polite. It's your father's murder we're trying to clear up.'

There was silence, both inside and outside the room; the birds' clamour had stopped, the seagull had won out over the invaders.

'Yes. Yes, of course.' Derek all at once seemed to realize where he was, at his wife's feet. He got up awkwardly and sat back in his chair. 'But you really can't think that Cordelia had anything to do with his murder?'

'No,' said Malone, convinced now that Cordelia had been stupid but not murderous. 'But it was dangerous, what she did. For a number of reasons.' The two Huxwoods looked at him. 'Don't you know who Jack Junior's father is? He's *the* Jack Aldwych.'

Derek nodded. 'I knew who he was, but he's not involved, is he? Christ, think what the Murdoch papers and the Packer *60 Minutes* would make of that! Not to mention *Four Corners*.'

'You'd better face it — Jack Senior is involved, one way or another, in everything his son does. You could have had your head blown off,' he told Cordelia: *make her suffer a little, at least.* 'He's retired, so he says, but anyone foolish enough to threaten his son would bring him

212

out of retirement as soon as he'd learned who sent that note.'

He was threatening Cordelia; but she deserved it. She had complicated an already complicated case; she had wasted valuable police time. She was obviously frightened, suddenly appalled at her stupidity; she had put a foot inside a jungle to which she had no maps. 'I know who he is *now* – but I never thought. Does he know I sent it?'

'No.'

Derek said, 'Does he need to? Does anyone?'

Malone turned towards Clements; the big man was giving nothing away. 'I think we might ask Sergeant Clements what he thinks. He's the supervisor, the one who's had to waste his staff's time on this.'

'Thank you, Inspector,' said Clements, dry as drought dust. 'I can understand why you did what you did, Mrs Huxwood, but since I'm being asked to close my eyes to it, I think I can be frank. Okay?'

She nodded.

'I think you were bloody stupid and you've had us wasting time on a piece of paper we thought would lead us to whoever murdered your father-in-law.'

'Thank you, Sergeant. That's being frank enough.' She sounded as if she had never been spoken to like that in her life. Except, perhaps, by Lady Huxwood.

'So it all ends up here in this room?' said Derek.

Malone stood up. 'Not quite. You owe us, both of you. If you learn of anything that will help us, we'll want to know immediately. I don't care if it means pointing the finger at someone in the family, we'll want to know.'

Both the Huxwoods had stood up; Derek had taken Cordelia's hand again. They are vulnerable, thought Malone: which meant they would help.

'That's asking a lot, Scobie –'

'Like I said, Derek, you owe us. You also owe your father.'

He led the way out of the room, not bothering to say goodbye: he had had the last word. He did hear Clements murmur something, but he didn't look back. Outside the house Clements caught up with him. The big man did not look angry, but he was curt.

'Next time you're gunna leave me like a shag on a rock, gimme some warning.'

'I thought that was our technique. Switch the bowling.'

'I never played cricket, I played football. What you gave me was a hospital pass.'

'Righto, I'm sorry. But you put it more bluntly than I could have.'

'Bullshit.'

Malone knew that perhaps he had done the wrong thing, but before he could apologize he saw four people come out of the Big House and walk down across the lawns to the sea-wall. Half a dozen gulls, lords of sea and shore, the mynahs vanquished and vanished, moved aside reluctantly.

'Hello, another family conference?'

'Nigel and his missus.' Clements sounded less curt; nothing improved a cop's temper more than seeing more suspects present themselves. 'And Linden and her bloke. Shall we go and threaten them?'

Malone grinned. 'Up yours. But why not?'

The four by the sea-wall turned as the two detectives approached them. Nigel and the two women were wearing dark glasses, but Quental was not, though his eyes narrowed, not from the sun, as he saw the detectives.

'Oh dear,' said Nigel. 'Not more interrogation?'

'Not unless you have something new to tell us?' Malone felt he owed Nigel nothing but official politeness, which never has any value.

'Nothing,' said Nigel, but sounded like an actor who wished he had more lines.

All four of them were casually dressed, though Quental wore a woollen tie and a stockman's hat, which made him look like a well-dressed toadstool, every other inch a gentleman farmer. Malone liked none of them except, perhaps, Linden.

She said, 'I hope you're not going to bother my mother?'

'We weren't intending to. Where's Michael?' he asked Nigel and Brenda.

'Michael?' Nigel looked puzzled: a bit-part player was in demand? 'Why do you ask?'

'We understand he was the odd man out in the voting this morning.'

The four of them looked at each other, then Brenda nodded towards Little House One. 'Who told you that? Derek or Cordelia?'

'It doesn't matter.' The Huxwoods, it seemed, were doing their best to become a secret society; their business was theirs alone and nobody else's. 'Where's Michael?'

'He's at work, as far as we know,' said Nigel. 'When we saw him this morning he said he was on his way to his office. Kohn Brothers,' he added, though his tone suggested: *as if you don't know.*

Quental had said nothing, even standing a little apart: the outsider, not even married to the family. But he's the one, Malone thought, who needs money more than the others. Clements must have been thinking the same thing, because he said, 'Are Kohn Brothers your bankers, Mr Quental?'

'They are the investment bankers for all the family,' said Linden before Quental could reply. 'Our merchant bankers. My father insisted that we all deal through them.'

Clements nodded as if satisfied with that, but Malone, reading the big man from long experience, knew there had been something else behind his question.

'Well, take care,' he said. 'We'll be in touch again, I'm sure.'

'Inspector—' Brenda glanced at the other three before she looked back at Malone. 'Are we in any danger? I mean—'

Malone shrugged exaggeratedly, like a bad actor. 'Who knows? Like I said, take care.'

And again he left with the last word and Clements, recognizing an exit line, followed him. Without saying anything to each other they walked up to their cars, aware that they were being watched closely by the Huxwoods. At their cars Malone said, 'Why the question about Kohn Brothers being Quental's bankers?'

'Because I wanted to hear what he'd say, but Linden chopped him off. I checked—the Commonwealth handles all the Huxwood working accounts, but they raise their finance and get their advice from Kohns. Quental is in hock up to his dandruff to two other banks, Westpac here in Sydney and one over in Perth. They're pressuring him and I'll bet he's got sweat running outa every orifice. They're that far—' he held up his thumb and forefinger half an inch apart, '—from moving in on him and taking him for everything he's got. Or what Linden's got, because I'll bet it's her money that's in their stud.'

'Do you think they paid Dwayne?'

'They're on my list.'

'What about Nigel and Brenda?'

215

Clements chewed his lip. 'I dunno. I don't think Nigel could organize a church raffle, let alone a hit job. He's all piss and wind – but very cultured. But no, I'm not pointing the finger at him.'

'What about Brenda?'

'You'd know her better than I would – you're Irish. You're not all leprechauns, the IRA knows how to organize itself. Or did.'

Malone shook his head. 'Not Brenda. She's as phony as a political promise –' He had been listening to them all week, the flights of fancy that always materialized when an election was due; like every voter in the State he would be glad when tomorrow was over. 'But I don't think she'd go out and hire someone like Dwayne. How would she know where to find him?' Then he looked at Clements and said, 'You and I are slipping, mate. Jack Aldwych told me that this afternoon.'

In any police investigation the accumulation of detail is the first priority. In the file room at Homicide there were cartons of detail, enough running-sheets to paper the whole of the fourth floor. Yet the very mass of particulars could sometimes result in the obvious being overlooked. It had happened to Malone before and it would happen again.

'Who amongst all the Huxwoods was up in Queensland in the past three months?'

2

That night Lisa and Malone took the children to see *West Side Story*. The tickets had cost him sixty-seven dollars and fifty cents, *each*, a sum that in his fiscal appreciation amounted to an arm and a leg. He sat paralysed in the fifth row, wondering if he should call up the Fraud squad. Then the overture began, the curtain went up and he saw Claire, Maureen and Tom lean forward, excitement and expectation shining in their faces; suddenly the pain, like childbirth, was worthwhile. Lisa, feeling his pain, pressed his hand and smiled.

Halfway through the second act his pager beeped. Behind him a man snarled, 'Oh, Christ, not another mobile! Ignore it!'

'I'm a doctor,' said the inspector. 'It's an emergency.'

'Oh sorry –'

Malone slid out of his seat and crept up the aisle. He went out into the foyer, found the manager's office and asked to use the phone.

'I've got some bad news, Inspector,' said the duty officer at Waverley. 'Our fellers just rang in. They've lost the suspect Harod.'

Malone went out into the foyer, stood there, totally unaware of his surroundings. The theatre had been a neglected barn for years, but some months ago it had been virtually rebuilt to its old baroque style and grandeur; for all the notice Malone took of the foyer he could have been standing in a bus shelter. Then he decided that the disappearance of Dwayne Harod was Steve Lozelle's problem; at least till tomorrow morning. He went back into the theatre, groped his way back into his seat.

'Emergency over?' growled the man behind him.

'He died,' said Malone and Maureen, sitting beside him, punched him on the thigh.

3

Next morning Malone was at Waverley police station at seven o'clock. He had called Clements and the latter arrived a few minutes later. The task detail gathered in the incident room and, while Malone remained silent, were taken to task by Superintendent Lozelle, who did not enjoy being called out so early in the day, especially on a Saturday.

'How did you lose him?' he demanded.

'We followed him out to Marrickville, sir. He parked his car in a side street and went up into Marrickville Road and let himself into a shop, a delicatessen —'

Lozelle looked at Malone, who said, 'His uncle's. Did he have a key?'

'Evidently, sir.' The young officer was redheaded and freckled; he looked too young to be a police officer. At the moment he also looked as if he would have given anything to be something else, an airline pilot or a plumber or even a down-and-out at the Matthew Talbot hostel. 'I'd got out and followed him, while Constable Brubeck remained in the car. He didn't put the lights on in the shop, so I guessed he was using a torch. I waited fifteen minutes, our instructions were we weren't to intercept him —'

'Did he know you were trailing him?' Malone asked.

'I think so. He'd sometimes wait at traffic lights for us – he's a real smartarse . . . Well, I decided I better see what was going on. I went into the shop, the door was still unlocked –'

'That wasn't too smart of him,' said Lozelle.

'I dunno, sir. We got the feeling he was just giving us the finger – you know, catch me if you can.'

He looked at Malone for confirmation and the latter nodded. 'That's our Dwayne. What then?'

'He'd shot through. There was a back door and he'd gone out that way and over the fence of the house behind the shop. I switched on the lights and had a look around. Nothing much had been disturbed, but it looked as if he'd swiped some food. Some boxes of pasta had been pulled down from a top shelf. I got up there and found the box there on the table, the Thirty-twos. The box had been opened and some of them were missing. Three.'

'One for Sir Harry and two at the Aldwyches,' said Malone.

Clements said, 'We shoulda got a warrant to search the shop. That was where he hid the gun.'

'Too late now. Did he come back to his car?'

'No, sir. Looks like he just abandoned it. We got Marrickville to come down and impound it. I'm sorry, sir,' he said to both Lozelle and Malone. 'We didn't fall down on the job. The bugger was just too smart for us.'

Lozelle looked at Malone. 'You know him better than us.'

'Constable Ambrose is right, he's smart, no argument. Cunning as the proverbial. Well, now all we have to do is see he doesn't get to hit someone else.'

'Anyone in particular?'

'Any one of half a dozen.'

'And you want all of them secured?' Lozelle looked as if he had been asked to send a detail to clean up the Bosnian war. 'What'm I going to use to keep my command going? Girl Guides?'

Malone grinned, appreciating the area commander's problem. 'I can give you five officers, but they can't work around the clock. We'll only need one at a time with each of the married couples. We've already got someone covering Michael, one of the grandkids. That leaves five other grandkids.'

218

'Poor little rich buggers,' someone murmured, but the two senior men in the room ignored the comment.

'What about Lady Huxwood?' said Clements.

The subject abruptly became delicate. Malone waited till Lozelle had dismissed all his staff but his two senior sergeants. One of them closed the door of the incident room, then Lozelle said, 'Bill Zanuch has been on to me again about her. She's not to be *harassed*, that was the word he used.'

'Who's harassing her?' Senior-sergeant Chris Gallup was in his late thirties, tall and bony, with large awkward hands and a way of moving from one leg to the other as if he had hip trouble. Malone had not worked with him before and he wondered how much the Waverley officer resented Homicide's intrusion. This was a big case, *big*, and it had happened on his turf.

'Jesus, we haven't been near her! You're the only ones who've talked to her,' he said to Malone and it sounded like an accusation.

'We haven't harassed her. But whatever AC Zanuch says, she's got to be protected, whether she likes it or not.'

'You want to tell him that?' Lozelle's grin barely moved his lips.

'I don't think we'll tell him anything, not till Lady Huxwood complains. If the surveillance is discreet, maybe she won't notice it.'

'You wanna bet?' said Clements. 'That old lady has her own satellite dish.'

'Well, we'll take the risk —'

'Hold on a minute,' said Lozelle. 'Do we name this kid now? Do we have a photo of him?'

'You mean we let the media know?' Malone nodded. 'Maybe his aunty and uncle have a photo of him. Who knows, it may help scare the shit out of whoever paid him . . . Our immediate concern is the grandson, Michael. If Dwayne knocks him off, the vote is back to even-stephen.'

'Then we have to see if someone else has to be knocked off,' said Clements. 'What we don't know, is who's paying him? Someone who wants to sell or someone who doesn't?'

'Who'd be rich?' said Lozelle, and the poor looked at him, waiting for him to smile. Which he did. 'Only joking. Okay, Scobie, you get your surveillance, round-the-clock. I'm looking forward more and more to my superannuation.'

'Then *you'll* be rich,' said Malone. 'Or so the social workers will tell you.'

The meeting broke up. Gallup waited till only he and Malone remained in the incident room. 'I hope you appreciate we're doing all the donkey-work on this case,' he said.

'I do appreciate it.'

'But we never get any credit.'

Malone had met this complaint before. 'Chris, that's the way the game's played. When the shit hits the fan, if it does, it won't be the donkeys who'll be sprayed. The credit and the shit go to superintendents and above. Ask Steve Lozelle.'

Gallup hesitated, then nodded, unconvinced, and went out. Malone knew how he felt: his own feelings were often the same.

He remained for a minute or two in the incident room. He looked at the flow-chart, at the maps and the graphs and the photo of Sir Harry, rich but dead in his bed. Then he looked at the list of names, the Huxwoods in one column, the staff, including Dwayne Harod, in another. The flow-chart, like all charts, had all the known facts. All that was missing was the answer.

When he got outside Clements was waiting for him. 'You want me today?'

'What were you planning on?'

'I was taking Romy to the footy. If she's pregnant, I want the baby to grow up ready to play league.'

'Even if it's a girl? Anyhow, Romy's German. Maybe he or she will want to play soccer . . . You can have the afternoon off, but right now get back to the office and organize our part of the surveillance. Get someone out to see Sophie Carpano and Mr and Mrs Harod, in case Dwayne turns up at either of their places. See if you can get a warrant to tap Sophie's phone.'

'Maybe we should put a tap on all the Huxwood phones.'

'We'd never get away with it.' Like most cops, Malone did not have much patience with the civil rights of suspects. 'Just do what you can.'

'Where are you going?'

'At the moment the chief target has gotta be Michael. I'm going to find out where he is and have a word with him.' He consulted his notebook, then dialled Nigel Huxwood's number on his car phone. 'Mr Huxwood? I'm looking for Michael.'

220

'Why?'

'Mr Huxwood, you've played police officers on the screen.' He didn't have much patience with Nigel Huxwood, either. 'You know how we work.'

'I should've taken lessons from you, Inspector.' Nigel, Malone conceded, could be gracious when he wanted to be. 'I see your point. Michael has his own flat in Double Bay, but right now I think you'll find him out at the Rose Bay polling station. He's handing out how-to-vote cards for the election.'

'At the Coalition booth, I take it?'

'What makes you say that?'

'No offence, but he looks to me like a natural-born conservative.'

'Wrong. He's a Greenie.'

'A banker? You're kidding me.'

Nigel laughed. 'When this is all over, Inspector, you must come to dinner with us.'

Malone hung up. 'Well?' said Clements.

'I've just talked to a son who lost his father six days ago in a murder. He sounded like someone who never had a father.'

'Maybe he didn't. We dunno half of what went on in that family. Incidentally, Kate called me last night. There were two hits up in Queensland in the last four months, pro jobs they thought, both shot with a Thirty-two. A bookie and a drug dealer that someone wanted outa the way. Maybe we should ask Dwayne about them.'

'When we find him.'

Malone drove down to Rose Bay, stopped in its small shopping section. The shops here catered to the well-heeled who objected to the prices in Double Bay, two kilometres back along the road to the city. He had pulled up outside a shop selling Persian rugs that had fallen off the back of a camel. The bane of his life, a parking officer, appeared out of nowhere, their usual habitat. 'Move it, sir. You're in a No Parking zone.'

'I am about to vote for the Freedom for Motorists party.'

'That's your democratic privilege, sir,' said the officer, taking out his book. He was two metres tall, a Tongan, and this afternoon he would be out on a rugby field ploughing over opponents in what would laughingly be called a practice match. 'In the meantime, let me give you my vote –'

The game had gone on long enough; Malone showed his badge. 'Send the ticket to Homicide.'

The Tongan displayed a blinding flash of teeth: you had to have a sense of humour to survive amongst these Aussie bastards. 'Homicide? That's murder, isn't it? You win. But I've written down half your car number and we're not allowed to tear up tickets. Now I'll have to find another vehicle with a number like yours.'

'I'm sure you will. I'm looking for the polling station.'

'Going to arrest a politician?'

Malone humoured him, he was such a big bastard. 'Yes.'

The parking officer directed him to the polling station and Malone got back into his car and drove down a side street to the local State primary school. He got out, dodged the party workers ambushing him with how-to-vote cards, thrusting them at him like wedding invitations, and found Michael Huxwood, dressed appropriately in green slacks and green shirt, beside the Green table. Michael shoved a card at him, but Malone pushed it away.

'I have a word with you, Michael?'

The young man followed him, still clutching the sheaf of cards. They went into the school yard and across to an area where they were alone. This school, at least on the outside, looked well-kept: like the kids who attended it. Malone had seen worse, far worse.

He sat down on a bench, all at once weary. He had not slept well and he had been up since five-thirty. It struck him, too, that he was weary of the Huxwoods and their battles.

'Do you know we've had you under surveillance since yesterday afternoon?'

Michael frowned, then laughed. 'Me? Why? Am I some sort of suspect or something?'

'Well, yes, you're on our list – like everyone else in the family.' He was tired enough to be frank. 'But mainly, we're afraid you might become another victim. Like your grandfather.'

Michael looked around. 'Where? Here?'

'It could happen anywhere. I think that's our man over there.'

Malone had seen the young man in jeans, a blue-checked shirt and a black blouson detach himself from the crowd going in to vote and walk across to sit on one of the benches against a school building. The windows were up and from inside the building came the sound

222

of music and the faint thump-thump of feet: a dancing class was in progress. The plainsclothesman, if that was what he was, was tapping his feet to the beat of the music.

'This is just between you and us, Michael, at least till we release it to the media. We think the man who shot your grandfather is Dwayne Harod, the assistant-gardener out at La Malmaison. Do you know him?'

Michael shook his head. 'Why would I know him? I hardly ever go out there. I'll go out sometimes at night to have a drink or maybe dinner with my grandparents. Or I did –' He stopped, as if he only just now realized that one of his grandparents would no longer be there. Then he went on, 'No, La Malmaison, the Big House and the Little Houses, all that crap, it's not my cup of tea. Why would Dwayne or whatever his name is, have it in for me?'

'You're the odd man out in the voting, so I'm told. Someone paid him to kill Sir Harry. We think he's a professional hitman and if someone pays him again, he'll do you.'

'This is fucking incredible!' So far Michael did not look afraid, just puzzled and unbelieving. 'Why haven't you picked him up then?'

A cop hates being accused of incompetence or even a hint at it. 'We've got no evidence that would stand up in court. You may not believe it, but the police are more hamstrung by the law than those outside it. We've had him tailed, but –' this hurt '– last night he got away from us. That's why we're looking after you. If we didn't and he got to you, you wouldn't thank us.'

'Not if I were dead, I wouldn't.' His wry smile suddenly made him look more like his father. 'Okay, I get your point. Can I meet this guy who's keeping me company?'

Malone raised a beckoning finger to the young man still sitting on the bench and tapping his feet to the dancing class music. He stood up and came briskly towards them. He was short and square, with a thin, chin-receding face and a crop of fair curly hair above shorn sides. Crumbs, thought Malone, where are the tall, athletic, square-jawed cops like me?

'Constable Steinbeck, sir. I'm from Rose Bay, one of Sergeant Akers' men.'

Malone introduced him to Michael Huxwood and the two shook hands rather perfunctorily, like New South Wales and Queensland cricket captains. Malone wondered whether he should tell them they were both on the same side, but thought better of it.

'Do you know the suspect, Harod?'

'Yes, sir. I was at the Huxwood place last Tuesday morning and then again on Wednesday morning – I was in uniform then. I didn't interview him, though.'

'I want you and your relief, whoever they are, to stay with Mr Huxwood all the time. That okay, Michael? I want them, one at a time, to move in with you. It'll only be for a coupla days, we hope. Do you have a flatmate?'

'Yes. My girl friend –'

'I think it would be a good idea if she moved out.'

Michael did not look pleased, but he was sensible. 'I know all this is for real, but it's still . . . Okay, whatever you say. But who is supposed to have paid this guy?'

'We don't know that yet.'

Michael frowned again. 'For Crissakes – you don't think it's someone in the family, do you?'

'It could be.'

'Jesus!' He considered this a moment, then he said, 'What about someone outside the family?'

'You got any suggestions?'

'Well, yes – one. Do you know Jack Aldwych, the old man?'

'Slightly.' Malone was abruptly cautious.

'Well, we – I mean us at the bank – we know his son, Jack Junior I think they call him, we know he's linked with the English crowd in a buying consortium. I looked him up, him and his companies – due diligence, we call it –'

'We invented it,' said Malone. 'Us cops.'

'Oh?' Then Michael grinned and nodded. Constable Steinbeck looked pleased with himself, as if he had been there at the invention. 'Yeah, I guess you did. Anyway, looking up the son, I found out who his old man was. He was before my time, but he was the king-pin, *the* crime boss – it sounds melodramatic, but he was Mr Big. I suppose you know all that?'

'A little,' said Malone, trying not to sound sarcastic but not succeeding. 'You're suggesting he ordered the hit on your grandfather?'

'He's the obvious one, isn't he?'

'Put it the way you have, yes, I guess he is. We'll look into it. Did you do due diligence on the other member of the consortium, Mr Bentsen?'

Michael nodded. 'You don't miss much, do you? How'd you get on to him, there's been nothing in the papers?'

'Jack Aldwych told me.' He was tired and he couldn't resist it. 'In the meantime, don't trust anyone closer to home. *Anyone*, got it?'

Michael said nothing for a while, then he nodded again. 'Okay, but you're asking a lot. My father and my sister? My stepmother?'

'I know how you feel, Michael. But for a coupla days, till we pick up Dwayne Harod, we have to suspect *everyone*.'

'You're sure you're going to pick him up?'

'Oh, we'll get him all right. Incidentally, have you been up to Queensland lately?'

'I go up there once a month, we have a branch up there. Why?'

'Just checking . . . Look after Mr Huxwood, Constable. Take care, both of you.' He paused, listening. Inside the dancing class a scratchy record or tape was playing *Singin' in the Rain*. 'One of my favourite songs.'

'Mine, too, sir,' said Constable Steinbeck and Malone waited for him to break into a couple of Gene Kelly steps; he looked like a dancer.

Michael didn't appear to be listening to the music. He looked at the sheaf of cards in his hand as if he didn't understand why he was holding them. Malone said, 'How do you think the Greens will go?'

'Oh, we'll surprise everyone,' said Michael, recovering, and held out one of the cards. 'We shan't win government, we're not *that* optimistic, but you're going to be surprised how many concerned people will vote for us.'

'Do all the other bankers around town know you're the nigger in the woodpile?'

Michael grinned. 'Since we're being politically incorrect, no, I'm the nigger in the woodchips. That's what we're fighting, the spoiling of our forests.'

'Don't they make newsprint from woodchips? How did your grandfather feel about you being a Greenie?'

'He hated me for it – and so does my grandmother. But it takes all sorts to make a Huxwood. Neither of them ever really understood that.'

4

Late on Saturday afternoon Assistant Commissioner Zanuch had just come back to his Dover Heights home after voting (for the conservative Coalition, naturally), when his phone rang. Usually he never picked up the phone at home, for fear that it might be some media person; though, if the truth be told, media persons never ring police brass, whose eleventh commandment is No Comment. Mrs Zanuch, a stoic woman, or their three children, usually did phone duty. This afternoon, however, they were all out.

Zanuch picked up the phone and was instantly hit in the ear by, 'Bill? Your damned police are harassing me!'

'Phillipa, you mean they've been down to talk to you again?'

'No. I could handle that — I'd tell them to buzz off! No, they're spying on me!'

'Phillipa,' he said patiently; he had learned that society leaders required a lot of patience, 'they are not spying on you. It's protective surveillance —'

'Protective —?' Then she sounded as if she had gone off the boil; she was, despite being difficult, a sensible woman. 'What from? Who from?'

He hesitated. 'Phillipa —'

'Come on, dammit! Who from? I'm being protected from someone. Who?'

'We suspect that your under-gardener, Dwayne Harod, is the one who killed Harry.'

She said nothing for a long moment; her voice was matter-of-fact when she said, 'Why would he have done that?'

'We think he was hired by someone. We have reason to believe he is what we call a professional hitman, someone who —'

'I know what a hitman is, I read the papers! You have reason to believe . . . Sometimes, Bill, you police have a habit of talking as if you have a mouthful of phrases from some manual. What you mean is you have no proof.'

226

'If you put it that way —' Occasionally, but rarely, he wondered if the social climbing was worth it: you ran into too many yeti, usually female.

'How else should one put it?' Then, less abrasively, 'You really think he was hired by someone to commit the murder? Someone I know, someone in the family?'

He was not insensitive: he heard the sudden pain in her voice. 'We don't honestly know.'

There was a long silence, then a low anguished cry: 'What did we ever do to deserve this?'

But he knew the question was not meant for him.

Chapter Eleven

1

Sunday morning Malone went to Mass with the family, sat or knelt and, as usual, let his mind wander. What did God think of law and order as a policy? Both major parties in yesterday's election had campaigned on the law and order catch-cry, each promising more drastic punishment than the other for wrongdoers. If all the promises were kept the jails would be overflowing; since neither of the parties advocated capital punishment, even though some individual members might, there would be no natural culling by that method. Not as there was in other countries where, as Hans Vanderberg had been heard to say, they didn't pussyfootle with their pragmatism.

Labor, under the Dutchman, had won the election. They had a majority of only two seats, with five Independents holding the balance of power. Vanderberg did not like the situation, seeing all Independents as unhinged, political aberrations, but he would handle them.

Bevan Bigelow, in a three-minute speech conceding defeat, had used the expression 'at this point in time' five times; he had lost and he had looked lost; he had been sent into limbo, where there was no point to time, at least not for another four years. Hans Vanderberg, on the other hand, had relished his victory with all the appetite of an old pol who wouldn't have recognized mercy if it had been handed to him.

'Against all the odd ones, we upset the apple tarts,' he said, and not even his press secretary knew whether he was intentional or not in his mangled invention. For good measure, not only would he be Premier but he would be Police Minister, which he had been when previously in power, and Minister for Sport. He knew nothing of sport except kicking a man when he was down, but he knew who should be in charge of Sport with the Olympics looming up on the horizon of the century. He would be in his eighties by then, but still would be

228

capable of kicking the legs out from under a weight-lifter or anyone else with his mind elsewhere.

After Mass Malone drove in to Homicide. He remarked Lisa's look of disapproval, but she said nothing; she was a cop's wife and she knew he would not be going to the office unless it was necessary. 'I'll be home for lunch,' he said, trying not to make it sound like a concession. 'We'll drive over and visit your parents.'

'They're down in Melbourne,' she said in that voice that silently says, *I told you that only two nights ago.*

'Of course, I forgot.' Which he had. 'Well, if you can get the kids out of the way, I'll come home and we'll go to bed.'

'I'll look forward to that. I'll take a book to bed, just in case you forget.'

He kissed her. 'You should go into politics. You have the right sort of tongue for it.'

'You ain't heard nothing yet. See you in bed.'

At Homicide five officers were on duty; there had been three Saturday night homicides. 'One of them was a political murder,' Phil Truach told him. 'A guy shot his wife because she didn't vote the way he told her.'

'Labor or Coalition?'

There was some discussion about the return of The Dutchman as Police Minister, a prospect that gladdened none of them, then Malone went into his office to look at Saturday's sheets from the computer print-out.

Kate Arletti followed him. 'Russ has had me chasing up the Huxwoods who might've been up in Queensland in the past three or four months. Seems practically all of them have been up there.'

'Nothing about the Huxwoods is simple. Go on, spoil my weekend completely. Is there any word on Dwayne?'

'None so far.' She sat down rather stiffly and he wondered why. She was in casual clothes today, slacks and a shirt with all the buttons done up; she looked neat and efficient. And stiff. 'Mr Quental and Linden were up in Warwick in December looking at cattle – a coupla hours would have taken them on into Brisbane . . . Nigel and Brenda were up at Noosa in January – they own a flat there . . . Michael –'

'I know about Michael. What about Derek?' Though Derek had already been crossed off his mental list.

229

'He goes up there sometimes twice a month – Huxwood have half a dozen interests up there, a radio station, TV . . . Alexandra was up at Noosa – she was with Rosie Gilligan on a fashion shoot. Ross was there, too – staying with Rosie, I guess.'

'That leaves who? Colin and Camilla?'

'And Lady Huxwood. She and Sir Harry were in Brisbane in December – they were donating a painting to the Art Gallery there. There's one other –' She paused. 'I widened the net a bit.'

'Just to make it harder.'

She smiled, but even that seemed stiff. 'Jack Aldwych, Jack Junior, was in Brisbane in January. He's on the board of a coupla Queensland companies.'

'Where did Dwayne work in the canefields?'

'The Queensland police have come good there. Dwayne worked in the canefields, yes, but up around Ingham – that was six, seven months ago. His mother still lives in Ingham, living on her own.'

Malone pushed the sheets away from him. 'And we still haven't had a sight of him since Friday night?'

'No, sir.'

He studied her for a while, then said, 'What's biting you, Kate?'

She sat primly, as if for an examination; but he sensed he was the one being examined. 'Why has Russ put me on desk duty? Have I done something wrong?'

'Kate –' He abruptly realized that what he was about to say would sound like gender bias: 'Kate, last year I lost Peta Smith.' He held up a hand. 'No, hear me out. It's not that I think you, or any other girl, can't do an outside job as well as Russ and the fellers. But –'

She sat waiting, not helping him at all.

'My daughter Claire is studying law, but she wants to join the service when she graduates. I'm not going to stand in her way, if that's what she wants. But last year, when I saw Peta lying in Martin Place with two bullets in her back, I saw my daughter . . . It's nothing personal against you, Kate. Or you being a woman. It's just my own personal problem. I couldn't face the same thing happening to you as happened to Peta.'

She stood up, still stiff. 'I understand, sir,' she said and went out into the big room and down to her desk, where she sat down, facing away from him, and stared out the windows. He had not convinced

230

her, but there was nothing he could do about it. It was her life and hers to risk and, despite what she had said, she did not understand that he could never see it her way.

His phone rang: it was Jack Aldwych. 'Scobie? I got someone up in Brisbane to get Doodles Leyland to gimme a ring. He's just called, sounding like I've scared the shit outa him. He thought I was gunna lean on him for something he might of done years ago.'

'Jack, do you blame him? Don't you ever have feelings of guilt about something?'

Aldwych laughed. 'Never. Scobie, I'm a realist, not a moralist. I'm like you, like all cops. That's why cops and crims, old-timers like me, why we always understand each other.'

Malone was prepared to admit half the truth of that; but he would always carry the baggage of a moralist. 'What did Doodles have to say?'

'There was talk about three months ago that someone up in Brisbane was looking for someone to do a hit. They were said to be offering good money, more than the usual.'

'What's the usual, Jack? The cost of living is cheaper up there than down here in Sydney.'

Aldwych chuckled. 'The cost of killing, you mean. I dunno for sure. These days I hear you can get a job done for as low as five grand. Anywhere between that and twenty-five.'

'I think this kid would've asked for more than that. The stakes are higher in this case, Jack. Did they say who was asking for a hitman? Male or female?'

'Doodles didn't know, but he's gunna try and find out. Have you picked up the kid yet?'

'It'll be on the news tonight. We've lost him, Jack. He's out there somewhere with a gun. I'd keep your head down if I were you.'

2

Dwayne Harod was not panicking, but he knew he had done the wrong thing in going on the run. At the outset there had been a sort of juvenile excitement at evading the cops who were tailing him. It had been something like the feeling he'd had when he had run away from the cops in Marrickville; in those days they had been after him for ripping seats in trains, spraying graffiti on walls, dumb things like that. Now they were after him for something more serious and he felt he had been safer when he had been playing that cat-and-mouse game with the man Malone. And that had given him much more excitement, which, Christ knows, was about all he had gotten out of this fucking business so far.

There had been no excitement when he had actually put the bullet into Sir Harry's head; he had found that he could kill with no feeling at all. It had been only a small surprise to him that he had no regard for other people's lives, except, perhaps, his mother's. And he would never want to kill her.

The first murder had been accidental, but he had felt no pangs about it. One weekend he had gone down to Townsville from Ingham, where he had been working in the canefields. He had met a woman named Janine in a pub and had gone home with her for a one-night stand. Her husband had been away for the night and she had told him what a bastard her husband was, that she knew he was screwing other women, and she wanted him taught a lesson. She had read about the Bobbit case in America, seen it on TV, but she didn't think she could actually come at cutting off her husband's dick. She always got, you know, squeamish when she saw blood.

'You could shoot it off,' he had said.

'Geez, could you? Just the top, you know, the tip of it or the whole lot?'

'Whatever you want. I take off the whole lot, that's not gunna leave much for you to enjoy.'

They had giggled at the idea, made love a couple of more times, then he had gone down to Townsville again the next weekend, when the husband was home.

'It'll be dead easy for you,' she had said; she seemed unconcerned that her conjugal delights were about to be blown away. 'He won't fight, he's a real wimp.'

'Why'd you marry him then?'

She had shrugged, as if he had asked her why she had bought steak instead of sausages. But, he had told himself, he had never understood women.

She had gone to the pub, to be out of the way when it happened, and he had gone to the house, no feeling at all, walked in and bailed up the husband, telling him to take his trousers down. Then things had gone wrong. Instead of doing as he was told, as the wimp was expected to do, he had jumped Dwayne. There had been no alternative but to shoot him. Dwayne had done so, without fuss, and the husband had died instantly with a bullet through his heart and his penis intact. Dwayne's only surprise when it actually happened was that he felt nothing: no excitement, no panic, no guilt, nothing.

He had left the house and gone straight back to Ingham. He waited there a week till the woman was exonerated, till he was sure she had not dobbed him in. The murder was put down to an unknown intruder, someone the husband, 'a really brave guy' as his tearful wife described him, had disturbed while the house was being robbed. A month later Dwayne told his mother he was tired of working his guts out in the canefields and he was going south, to Brisbane or the Gold Coast, to make a living without so much sweat. His mother had cried and that had hurt him, but he had gone south anyway. He did his best not to think about the fact that he was the second man who had deserted his mother; Christ knew where his father, the shit from Kayseri, was. He promised himself he would write her every week and he did, almost. Once a month, maybe once every six weeks.

Despite his two years in the canefields, which had required not much more than strength and stamina, he was no slouch mentally, as he would tell anyone who queried his intelligence. While he had been at school, when he had bothered to attend, he had always come close to the top of his class, especially in maths. He had a brain that, when figures were thrown at it, could work quicker than a calculator; unlike most of the other kids at school, whose figures were in their fingers, his were in his head. A week after leaving Ingham he had a job with a starting-price bookmaker on the Gold Coast.

The bookie, a short round man with two-toned tan hair that matched his shoes and a voice like gravel rolling down a chute, worked from a ten-metre motor-cruiser that sidled up and down the canals behind the Gold Coast like a giant white shark inviting sucker-fish to string along. And there were suckers, in a different context. Punters in every second or third house along the canals, dialling a number they had been given, never knowing that the two mobile phones were on that white boat cruising past the bottom of the garden. A police boat would occasionally go past and Len, the bookie, would see them coming and go out on deck and wave to them. And some of the police, officers who had been on his payroll back in the days when the then Commissioner had believed that corruption was a public service, would limply wave back to him, sometimes running the boat into a canal bank as they day-dreamed of the good old days.

Dwayne had been working for the bookie for a month when the latter came to him and said he had a job for him.

'You're younger'n fitter'n me, son. We got a client who's beginning to think I'm running a dole office. He's reneged twice now on paying his debts, which ain't the way we play the game. I've tried reasoning with him, because that's the way I am, reasonable, but all he does is bullshit me. You got enough muscle to be a male stripper – I saw the wife eyeing you off the other day. I want you to go down to Coolangatta, that's where he hangs out, and have a word with him. Teach him a lesson, you know what I mean?'

Dwayne went down to Coolangatta, which he always thought of as the arse-end of the Gold Coast. He found the man and when the punter tried to bullshit him, he shot him. Len the bookie was horrified when he learned of the murder; he couldn't at first believe that Dwayne had so misunderstood him. He at once paid off Dwayne, gave him a bonus and wished him luck somewhere else, *anywhere* else. Dwayne was not upset by his dismissal; he did not want to spend the rest of his life on a river cruiser, taking each-way bets on horses as remote from him as the African quagga; he had never been on a racecourse and he could not understand the 'dead cert' philosophy of punters. He took a last look from the deck of the floating S.P. shop at the mansions along the canals and decided that one day he would come back and own one of them.

He discarded the gun that had already killed two people, a Twenty-two that he had used for shooting vermin in the canefields. He threw it into a canal, in front of a house that was advertised as first prize in an art union lottery. He then went and bought a ticket in the art union, giving his mother's address. From there he went and bought another gun, and this time a silencer, from a dealer who asked no questions and gave no answers. A week later, pulled over for speeding in a rented car, he was picked up and charged with being in possession. He pleaded not guilty, but was fined and bound over for twelve months.

234

He then got a job as a used car salesman, working on commission; almost every day he drove past the prize house. He had been working in that office, earning good money, when a man, who never gave his name, came to see him, said that Len the bookie had recommended him as a reliable man. He was short and thin and very neat, as if his wife had arranged him before allowing him out: indeed, that was what he was, an arranger. He wanted someone, a drug dealer, taken care of – 'You know what I mean?' This time Dwayne asked for specific instructions and got them: the drug dealer was to be 'hit'.

Dwayne went back to the gun dealer, asked this time for a gun that couldn't be traced and took delivery of a Browning Thirty-two. Then he took care of the hit, again with no feeling, and was paid ten thousand dollars. A month after that the man, neat and arranged as ever, came to see him again.

'The price has gone up,' said Dwayne, who had been studying the market. 'Twenty-five thousand.'

They were on the beachfront, with sunbathers on the sands below them cultivating melanomas. Behind them the high-rises stood waiting to block out the sun as it swung west. Two meter-maids strolled along, seemingly clad in thin sashes and nothing else; their buttocks swung like melons in an earth tremor and as they passed a meter it had palpitations and *Expired*. Dwayne looked at the car parked at the meter, a BMW, and decided he would have one of those one day.

'You'll price yourself outa the market, kid. Don't get greedy.'

'I'm not,' said Dwayne. 'I'm professional. Who do you want done this time?'

This time it was another S.P. bookie. Dwayne wondered, but didn't ask, if Len had decided to get rid of some of the competition. He was paid five thousand down, did the job neatly (the arranger would have been proud of him), then was paid the balance. Two weeks later the man came to see him again.

'It's a job down in Sydney this time. Different. I dunno who's to be done, all I know is the money'll be good, better than anything you've had so far.'

'How do you know that?'

'My commission tells me that.' A neat smile. 'Ten thousand down for you and the rest by arrangement. You do your own arranging, that's the way they want it.'

235

'Do I get to meet the client?'

'That's up to the client, but I wouldn't think so. Only dumb wives do that.' Dwayne thought of Janine, probably living it up on her husband's insurance and superannuation. 'I'll give you a phone number, a mobile.'

Dwayne rang the number and the client told him what was to be done. 'We want someone – eliminated? Is that what you do?'

'Call it anything you like. I just do it.'

'Okay, you come down to Sydney. There's a job to be advertised, you'll apply for it and you'll get it – we'll see to that. Once we've looked you over, then we'll tell you who is to be – eliminated.' The client seemed to be having some difficulty with the term.

'Why do I apply for the job? I don't hang around, not with what I do.'

'Things are happening – we have to see how they pan out.'

'What's the price?'

'Forty thousand? Payable on delivery.'

The client was still having difficulty with the proposition. He, or she (Dwayne couldn't tell from the voice; it was obviously disguised) was trying to sound matter-of-fact but was not quite bringing it off. 'I'll want some sorta deposit. It's just like buying a house, you know what I mean? Ten thousand down and I'll need wheels, I'm coming to Sydney. It's a big city.' Where the big money was. 'Lease me a BMW –'

'A BMW?' The voice went up; it could have been a woman's. Or a man with a high voice.

'Okay, not one of the big 'uns. A 318 convertible. Lease it in your name.'

The client laughed, a low chuckle; he or she suddenly seemed more at ease. 'You must think I'm dumb. Okay, you get a BMW. In your name.'

Dwayne had come to Sydney, collected the BMW, got the job; it had all been much easier than he had expected and for a day or two he wondered if he was being set up. He met Sophie Carpano, and everything had gone swimmingly. The sour taste in his Turkish Delight were his uncle and aunt, who welcomed him back with folded arms.

He had been at La Malmaison a week, still coming to terms with how the *real* rich lived, appreciating now what a real mansion was, when he learned who the client was and who the victim was to be. He also learned what lay behind the hit, how the riches were to be split.

Now, two days after he had eluded the police, he was in a phone-box in Blacktown in Sydney's western suburbs. Out here there were few, if any, mansions and if there were any riches they were hidden under the mattress. Most of the voters out here were battlers, people who had to count their money out of necessity, not out of greed; this was working class territory and the biggest mansion in town was the Blacktown Workers Club. It had hurt Dwayne, who had become a snob since coming south from Ingham, to retreat to territory where he was not conspicuous. The locals never gave him a second look.

'Look,' he was saying, 'I don't want no more shit. You owe me money —'

'I've told you — I don't have it. Not yet. Things went wrong — you killed the wrong one, it wasn't necessary —'

'I did the one you told me to. Don't blame me if things've been fucked up. You're still gunna get your share of the loot —'

'That's not certain, we shan't know till tomorrow. There's a board meeting, they'll decide if everything is going to be sold —'

'That's your problem, not mine. My problem is I'm in the shit with the police — they know I did the hit —'

'It was on the six o'clock news. Your photo — they want to question you —'

He suddenly felt queasy, a feeling he hadn't had since he was a kid; not since his mother had told him his father had gone away forever. He looked down at the canvas gym-bag he had bought yesterday morning at K-Mart; in it was the change of clothing he had bought at the same time. For the time being, and for Christ knew how long, it was all he owned. That and the Browning Thirty-two and the box of ammunition, wrapped in the towel he had stolen from the motel where he had stayed last night.

'You and me'd better meet —'

'No!'

'Listen, I need money —'

'I paid you ten thousand a month ago, all I had in cash —'

'Use your fucking head, willya! You think I carry cash like that around with me? It's in the fucking bank. I go to draw it out, I'm done —'

'Don't you have a card? Use the automatic teller –'

'Jesus, you're fucking dumb!' The trouble with the rich was they never had to use an automatic teller; you had to be poor to stand in front of a machine that made a noise like a sneer as it doled out your pittance. 'I can only draw eight hundred bucks a day from the machine – how far's that gunna fucking get me? I gotta get outa the country –' He had no idea where he would flee to; anywhere except fucking Turkey. 'You gotta have *some* money – you get dividends –'

'Only once a year, in September –'

'You better get yourself organized, you hear? I want a hundred thousand – you'll be able to afford it after tomorrow –'

'Only if the sale goes through.' The voice had steadied, had become cold.

'And if it doesn't?'

'Then there'll be nothing. I'm as broke as you are. More so. I don't have ten thousand or whatever in the bank.'

He stared out through the glass of the phone-box. On the other side of the street, under a street-lamp, some sort of deal was going on between four youths; money and something else were exchanged. A police car came cruising down the street and the four youths were suddenly gone, like smoke figures blown away by a wind that nobody else felt. Dwayne turned his face away from the two officers in the car, out of the corner of his eye saw it glide away into the darkness.

'Dwayne, you still there?'

'Yes,' he said. 'I want the money. A hundred thousand.'

There was silence; then: 'Get lost, Dwayne.'

He took his time; then: 'You're dead, Alexandra.'

3

She sat at her desk outside Rosie Gilligan's office, trembling with dread. She had known there might be danger when she had contacted the stranger to kill her grandfather; she had not expected that his gun might be turned on herself. She put her hands flat down in front of her, tried to steady them by pressing them into the desk. She stared at her VDT, at the message there: *Sportswear is fashion with attitude . . .*

She had no idea what was to follow that statement; three times a week she was expected to dream up phrases that had the resonance of toy balloons. She had no interest at all in fashion as a profession. Indeed, she hated it because it meant working with Rosie Gilligan, but her father had insisted she spend a year in the fashion pages — 'Rosie will teach you everything you need to know about a newspaper, not just fashion.' Well, all Rosie had taught her was how much one could hate her.

It was only during the past year that she had come to realize how much hatred she was capable of. First, there had been Rosie; then there had been her grandfather. Not till she had started work on the paper had she learned what a lecher he was; whispers about him circulated like flatulence; it had not taken her long to recognize that Rosie had been one of his girls, might still occasionally be one. Then, as rumours of a sell-off had surfaced, as she had talked with her cousins and they had all begun to see how their fortunes might be changed, she had started to take note of another side of her grandfather. He had only two interests, himself and the dynasty: dynasty not as family but as institution. He did not even care for Grandma.

That last recognition had shocked her; something had happened to change him in the past month. He had become withdrawn; he would just nod whenever she or Ross or Colin would speak to him at La Malmaison. Here at the newspaper he had virtually stopped visiting the newsroom, something that had been almost a daily ritual with him; she had asked her father what was wrong with the old man and Derek had told her he didn't know. It could, of course, be the efforts of the heirs or some of them, to force the sale of Huxwood.

Old Harry, as the grandchildren called him, had never had any favourites amongst them; she had been the one who had never got even remotely close to him. He had never done anything to encourage her to like him; she had never done anything to make him smile on her. It had taken her some time to realize that he rarely smiled on her father. Derek, the one who worked to keep the dynasty on a financial footing, was the least appreciated. It was as if Old Harry envied the rebellion of Nigel and Linden, the two bludgers, as her father called them, who took what Huxwood gave them and gave nothing back.

Two months ago, without any deliberation on her part, she had had a blazing row with her grandfather. She had been at home at La Malmaison, sitting on the sea-wall, reading the latest Margaret

Attwood and occasionally lifting her eyes to gaze abstractedly out at the Saturday afternoon yachts on the harbour. Then he had come striding down across the lawns and, without preamble, attacked her.

'You're the one who started this campaign to sell off everything!'

Perhaps she was, but she couldn't remember; the idea had floated up out of a swamp of idle discussion. There had been no scheduled discussion; that had come later. She put her bookmark carefully in place, closed the book.

'I don't think you should talk to me like that, Pa.'

'Don't tell me how I should talk to you!' She had never seen him like this before; he had always been so *controlled*. Cold, when it came to addressing her and her brothers. 'I tell you now, and you can tell the others, none of you get anything more than you do at present – not till I'm ready to give it to you!'

She dared to say, 'Does Grandma feel like that?'

'Leave her out of it!' He looked back towards the Big House and she had a sudden intuition that he had just come from a similar fierce row with her grandmother.

The argument had grown more heated; partly because she was bearing the brunt of what should have been spread amongst the others who favoured selling. Yet part of her mind had remained cold. He was not arguing only with her; she had just been the most readily available. Something had happened to him; he was arguing with the world, with his life. But she felt no pity for him. It came to her, though as no surprise, that she was as cold-blooded as she had always thought her grandmother was. She had no love for either of them; and now she had hatred for Old Harry.

'I wouldn't miss you if you all dropped dead!' he said and stalked stiff-legged back up to the Big House. She watched him go, then saw her grandmother, like a dark wraith, in one of the upper windows. She had never understood what bound the two old people and she never would. She re-opened her book and went back to Margaret Attwood.

Over the next two weeks, without any discussion with her brothers or her cousins, she had looked at her life ahead. Old Harry and Grandma might live another ten years; the family had a history of longevity. She could not wait that long.

On the fashion shoot at Noosa she had made up her mind, deliberately and without any stab of conscience or even a faint ache. The

240

Chronicle had been running a series on a well-known criminal, now in jail, who had turned informer; hitmen came and went through the series like sudden-death messenger boys. When the shoot was over she had taken two days off and gone down to the Gold Coast, where, another *Chronicle* story had told her, retired criminals could be found like nesting eagles amongst the high-rises. A *Chronicle* stringer had introduced her to one of them; she had told the stringer she wanted to test a rumour that there was criminal money in some of the boutiques along the Coast. The retired criminal, a large man in a large shirt that looked like a slice of tropical forest, was flattered at being interviewed by a pretty girl from a major daily, especially since she did not ask him about his previous record. Innocence cloaked him like a smelly miasma as he told her he had no knowledge of any dirty money in boutiques. Then he had introduced her to other retirees, all born-again honest men. The chain eventually led to the neat man, the arranger, who still had a few years to go before he could retire to honesty.

Now everything had fallen apart.

She looked down the big newsroom, still busy with news. In another hour the country edition would be put to bed; in two hours the city edition. The columnists had finished their pieces, were sitting back in their chairs or had congregated outside Ossie Beckett's office; as the reporters finished their stories, they too got up and went down to join the group. There had been a staff meeting this afternoon and rebellion was in the air; nobody wanted the *Chronicle* sold, least of all to buyers from Fleet Street. Stuff the lot of you, she thought. Tomorrow morning the decision would be made and she could not care less what happened to the staff. Nor to what happened to the *Chronicle*: newspapers soon would be like history books, read only by the retired. So stuff the staff, if they couldn't read the writing on the wall. The owners, and she was one of them, were all that counted.

Rosie Gilligan, tossing her mane at the men she passed, came down between the desks, paused by Alexandra's. 'Ossie and I have just been up to see your father. We were the staff delegation.'

'Only the two of you?' She didn't care if there had been a dozen or fifty of them.

'Shoemaker and Gates were there and Jerry Hipwell from downstairs.' Hipwell was the printers' union representative. 'If Derek has any say, there will be no sale. That should please you.'

'Why?' That was a mistake: she had kept her intentions to herself here in the office.

Rosie looked at her. 'You don't want to work for outsiders, do you?'

'I guess not.' She tried to cover her blunder: 'I'm worn out by all the bloody wrangling. And my grandfather's murder,' she added and managed not to sound piously grief-stricken.

'You hate my guts, Alex, and I'm not exactly in love with yours. But I've felt sorry for you this past week.'

Hatred of others, the text books at uni had told her, grew out of self-hatred. But her hate for Rosie and Old Harry and Grandma had no connection with what she felt for herself. Freud believed that mankind (and womankind? Why hadn't he mentioned that?) was inherently destructive; so she was one of the destructors. The thought neither pleased nor displeased her: she just accepted it. Rosie's attempt at some sort of reconciliation meant nothing.

'Thank you,' she said almost primly: like the little girl she had once been, a long time ago. She gestured at the meaningless phrase on the screen in front of her. 'Can this wait? I'll finish it tomorrow. I've got my period on top of everything else.' Which was a lie, but it was always a good lie.

'Do you have a boy friend, Alex?'

'Not at the moment.' There had been boys and, once, an older man; but none of them, not even the older man, had measured up to the future she saw for herself. She enjoyed sex, but never felt it meant any sort of commitment. In a much less indolent way, she sometimes felt she resembled her Aunt Linden.

Rosie scanned her critically. 'We're never going to get through to each other, are we?'

'No.' It was a pleasure to be honest.'

Rosie tossed the mane again; she had it down to a fine art, did it almost in slow-motion, as the models with the unbelievable hair did it in commercials. 'Like I said, I feel sorry for you. You'll never believe that, but I do.'

She went on into her cubbyhole. Alexandra sat a while, staring at the group at the far end of the room; none of them would have a vote at tomorrow's board meeting, but they were still the enemy, capable of influence. She was glad that that prick Michael would not come here to the newsroom and be influenced by the enemy and their arguments about loyalty.

She was about to leave her desk, had her jacket on and her handbag hanging from her shoulder, when she thought of Dwayne Harod lurking out there in the night.

She hesitated, then walked down the length of the room. Some of the group outside Beckett's office nodded to her, but no one spoke to her; the word must have got around that she would be voting for the sale. She nodded in reply, but that was all.

She came to the young man seated by the door, a handsome, well-dressed young man. 'You're the guy who's been shadowing me, right? Protecting me?'

'Yes.' He stood up. 'Detective Constable John Kagal.'

'Will you see me home, John?'

Chapter Twelve

1

Malone awoke despondent on Monday morning, feeling in his bones that another bad day lay ahead. He got up, put on his track suit and went for his usual walk down round Randwick racecourse. He heard the drumbeat of hoofs coming out of the morning gloom like a message from the coming day; he would not have been surprised if the Four Horsemen of the Apocalypse had galloped by. He passed a laughing woman trainer whose remarkable run of recent successes had put the misogynists of the racing game into a male tizz as they predicted the end of the world as it should properly be. He completed the circuit of the track, then climbed the low hill into the sun, going home, feeling no better.

He showered and dressed. He went to put on his police tie, then abruptly decided he needed something brighter. He chose a flowered pattern, a tie that Claire had given him for his birthday and which, up till now, he had worn only once and then at night.

'Well, look at him,' said Claire as he sat down to breakfast. 'You've decided to come out?'

'Great,' said Maureen. 'We'll buy him an ear-ring for Father's Day.'

'The gays in Oxford Street will blow him kisses,' said Tom.

'Shamrocks and pansies,' said Lisa. 'The Irish gays will love you.'

'Keep it up,' he said. 'You're talking me into taking it off.'

Malone tried to remember the conversation at the table in the house in Erskineville when he had been twelve, Tom's age. His father had talked of strife on the wharves, his mother had gossiped about the neighbours; any chat with sexual overtones would have been as remote as talk of cybernetics, a word not then invented. If his mother knew anything at all of homosexuality, she denied its existence. Con Malone would have known of it, but, if a queer had fallen off a wharf, wouldn't have thrown him a lifebelt. Another time, another country: the good old days?

'See this?' Lisa passed him the *Chronicle*.

It was a small item at the bottom of the front page: DECISION TODAY. *Board To Discuss Sale*. The main story was in the Business section, where it was discussed in strictly economic terms. If the staff felt they were being sold down the river, if one hundred and fifty years of history was being thrown out the window, the business editor was apparently unmoved. Malone suddenly felt he was witness to a second murder: the *Chronicle*, as he and five generations before him had known it, was about to be killed off. It would never be the same paper again if the sale went through.

He folded the paper and tossed it on to a nearby bench. 'I've got my own problems.'

'Who hasn't?' said his three kids and even Lisa nodded in agreement with them.

But at the front door, as he was leaving, she kissed him with more sympathy than usual. 'Don't let it get you down. Come home tonight and take me out to dinner. Just the two of us.'

He put his hand under her loose hair, stroked the back of her neck. 'You're good for me.'

'I wouldn't want it any other way,' she said.

He drove in to Homicide and hadn't been in his office ten minutes when his phone rang. It was Roger Ladbroke, The Dutchman's press officer and chief minder. 'I've been channelled down to you, Scobie. The Old Man asked me to get on to the Commissioner, he put me on to the Deputy Commissioner, he put me on to Assistant Commissioner Zanuch, he put me on to Chief Superintendent Random, he put me on to Superintendent Lozelle and he put me on to you.'

'Just a minute,' said Malone. 'I'll get Sergeant Clements.'

'Cut the bullshit, Scobie. It stops with you.'

Malone sighed. 'Righto, Roger, what is it? He's playing Police Minister already, is he?'

'He's never stopped playing it – but don't quote me, not till I've written my memoirs. He wants to know how close you are to an arrest in the Huxwood murder. Do you expect to pick up that guy was on the news last night? Or have you already got him?'

'No-o.'

'Do I detect a note of frustration? The Old Man wants something more upbeat than that. He's just won an upset election, you know.'

'We're investigating five other murders, Roger. We've nailed the killers in four of them. Isn't that upbeat enough for him?'

'If you want an honest answer – no. Last time we were in power, the *Chronicle* beat the shit out of us –'

'They were impartial in this election.'

'The Old Man doesn't recognize impartiality, he wouldn't know the meaning of it. He wants to stuff it up them. He'd like the killer to be someone in the family.'

Malone clamped his teeth in front of his tongue. He had never really understood the viciousness that one found in local politics, both Federal and State; the Prime Minister wore hand-tooled Italian hobnailed boots. He knew it happened in other countries, both democratic and totalitarian, but he had never had to deal with those animosities. The ones here at home were more than enough.

'I'll try to oblige him,' he said and hung up.

Clements said from the doorway, 'Don't tell me – Ladbroke from the Premier's office? Let's go out and pinch someone. *Anyone.*' He came into the room and slumped on the couch. 'We haven't had a sight of Dwayne since yesterday morning. A motel owner out on the Great Western highway, the other side of Blacktown, said he thought he recognized him from the TV story, said a guy looking like him stayed at the motel Saturday night. He had no car, just a bag. Said he'd just got off the train, gave an address in Nyngan. He registered as Kemal Brown.'

'Perfect.'

'What?'

'Kemal means ''perfect'' in Turkish. He just can't resist showing off.'

'We've got Blacktown and Penrith keeping an eye out for him and we've alerted the Blue Mountains area, just in case he heads west.'

Malone shook his head. 'I'll give you twenty to one he'll head back this way. I'll also give you twenty to one he's hanging around because he hasn't been paid yet. They always do.'

'For a non-betting man you're pretty rash.' But Clements nodded.

'You're right, though . . . I like your tie. Did it fall off the back of a Mardi Gras float?'

Then the phone rang again. It was Jack Aldwych this time. 'I've had another call from Doodles Leyland. He's told me about Big Bum Barwick – you remember him? He used to bring in the one-armed bandits before they were legal. When the pokies became legit he was already in the front door, he couldn't believe his luck. I don't think he's ever got over the shock of making so much money honestly.'

'Where is he, Jack?' Malone waved Clements back to the couch.

'Up on the Gold Coast, living the life of Riley. Doodles tells me he's got more white shoes than you'd find on a cruise ship. He also had some information.'

Malone waited.

'He said two or three months ago a girl came to interview him, said she was doing a story for the *Chronicle* on the rumour that he and a few others like him had money in boutiques. Big Bum, of course, said he was no longer interested in laundering money.' Aldwych chuckled. 'There's no hypocrite like an honest crim, is there?'

Malone waited again.

'The girl must of stroked him up the right way, he put her on to a coupla other guys. By the time she left the Gold Coast, he'd heard she'd seen five old crims – all retired, like me. Soaking up the sunshine, drawing the pension. One of them told Big Bum she said she wanted to interview a hitman.'

'As blunt as that?'

'Well, I dunno. One or two of the guys Doodles mentioned, you'd have to hit 'em between the eyes before they understood the question.'

'Big Bum told Doodles her name?'

'Of course, I wouldn't be on to you now if he hadn't. Alexandra Huxwood.'

The day suddenly grew brighter. Or did it? 'He's sure of it?'

'Certain of it.' There was silence for a moment, then Aldwych said, 'I don't envy you, Scobie. How do you tell her mother and father?'

'You get used to it, Jack.' That wasn't true; you never did. 'I'll leave you to thank Doodles. Maybe he won't want to know you've been talking to me.'

'I've already fixed him. I gave him a Mother's Day voucher for a brothel I used to own in Brisbane.'

Malone could feel his leg being pulled out of its socket; but he was grateful. 'Thanks, Jack. I'll be in touch.'

He hung up, got up and went to stand and stare out the window; then he looked down at Clements, still lounging patiently on the couch. 'Derek's daughter, Alexandra, is the one.'

'Shit!' Clements stood up, taking his time to raise his bulk. 'But we knew all along it had to be one of the family. I just hoped —'

'That it was one of the outsiders? Quental, maybe?'

Clements nodded, made an admission that must have hurt him: 'It just shows, prejudices get you nowhere. Okay, what do we do?'

Malone looked at his watch. 'None of the surveillance team has reported in that anyone's missing, so they should all be at the meeting at the *Chronicle*. Who's been shadowing Alexandra?'

'John Kagal was, but he was on night shift. He wouldn't be with her this morning. Probably one of the guys from Waverley.'

'Righto, start the ball rolling to get a court order to look at Alexandra's bank account, see if she drew out any large cash to give to Dwayne — she wouldn't have been stupid enough to give him a cheque. I'll take Kate with me and we'll bring her back here for questioning. We'll have her bank and account number for you.'

'Do we let anyone know?'

'Just Greg Random, but ask him to keep it to himself till we get her back here. Then we'll tell Steve Lozelle and —' he shook his head '— and Assistant Commissioner Zanuch.'

'You go in to the *Chronicle* to pinch her, someone there is gunna be on to it right away. They're *media*.'

'Her father'll just have to keep a lid on it.'

'How are you gunna tell him?'

'Reluctantly and with a fair amount of pain.'

2

Before the Huxwood Press board met in the boardroom with the Metropolitan consortium, there had been a meeting of the family in the chairman's office. They were all there, crowding the large room as it had never been in Sir Harry's day nor, Derek guessed, in the days of his predecessors. Derek was now chairman, but he had said

248

nothing when his mother had taken the chair behind the desk. He had
sat on the edge of the desk and looked at the family as they arranged
themselves around the room. He was capable of love, but he never
squeezed it dry; looking around this lot, he turned off the tap. Today
he was the *Chronicle*, nothing more: not son, not father, not brother,
not uncle.

'Well, in a few minutes Mum and I go in there —' he nodded at the
door that led to the boardroom '— and either sell the Press or tell the
buyers to pack up and go home. What's it to be? The voting still
the same as last time?'

Everyone, it seemed, was suddenly neutral; then Nigel said, 'Still
the same. Right, everyone?'

There were nods from the voters; only two hesitated. Derek said,
'Alex? Have you changed your mind?'

She said nothing and Ross, her brother, snapped, 'Come on, Alex,
for Crissake! Don't start having second thoughts!'

'Leave her alone,' said Colin, the other brother.

Camilla, her cousin, sitting beside her, pressed her arm. 'Come
along, Alex — you know what we want.'

'It's not too late, darling,' said Cordelia. 'Vote not to sell.'

'Listen to your mother,' said Sheila, her aunt. 'Think of the family.'

'Hear, hear,' said Ned Custer and looked badly in need of a
drink.

Alexandra looked up from her hands folded together in her lap.
Christ, thought Derek, she hasn't looked that young and vulnerable
since she was fourteen. 'What about Michael?' she said. 'How are
you going to vote?'

'That depends.' Michael was the eldest of all the grandchildren by
only two years, but he looked and sounded at least ten years older. If
the Press survives, Derek thought, he'll be chairman some day. 'I've
talked it over with Lester Kohn —' He addressed himself directly to
Derek. 'He's going to advise you, once you get in there, that the price
isn't high enough. If they'll offer fifteen dollars a share, I'll vote we
sell.'

'Greed,' said Lady Huxwood and the word dripped with contempt.

'You're living in the past, Grandma,' said Ross, suddenly excited.
'Fantastic, Michael!'

They all waited for the vitriolic burst of anger at this rude rebellion;

but none came. She just turned her head and looked away from them and Derek, who was closest to her, was the only one who heard the sigh that could have been a soft sob.

Then Alexandra said, 'I haven't changed my mind. I still vote that we sell.'

'Okay.' Derek wearily straightened up; he knew he had no fight left in him. 'We'll try them at fifteen dollars a share. If they don't come at it—?'

'They'll agree to it,' said Michael. 'They know the true value as well as we do. Better, maybe.'

Then Derek and Lady Huxwood had come into the boardroom where the other board members and the Metropolitan consortium had already assembled. Derek took his place at the head of the table; he could not help but wonder how much longer he would occupy this chair. His mother was seated on his immediate right; below her sat the eight other directors. There were two each from the two main shareholders, the big insurance companies, shedding their rivalry in the interests of mutual profit. There were two outside directors, both looking on this particular morning as if they would rather be elsewhere. There was a director from the staff superannuation fund and, at the bottom of the table, Lester Kohn, the corporation's banker, with the cast-iron look of a man who had been through a dozen takeovers. Behind them sat the support troops: lawyers and financial advisers, brief-cases at the ready. Ordinary shareholders, the sheep and the goats, as Clements, one of them, called them, were not represented.

Opposite them, with Beatrice Supple at their head on Derek's left, were the bidders and their advisers: the barbarians at the gate, as the phrase now had it. Still, the atmosphere was affable, if constrained; the knives and the bludgeons were not yet out in the open. Derek had not previously met Metropolitan's bankers and lawyers; all of them looked to be starched pillars of the City of London. Though, as the *Chronicle*'s London correspondent had reported more than once, the pillars of the City these days were as pockmarked as those of the Parthenon and not as revered.

'Before we go any further,' said Derek, 'we'd like to know what will happen to the *Chronicle*? It is only part of Huxwood, but it is our cornerstone and a major concern to my mother and me — and to all who work for it.' With a nod to the director from the superannuation

250

fund. 'Will its editorial policy be changed, will there be interference from London?'

'Not at all,' said Jack Aldwych junior and Charlie Bentsen nodded in agreement.

'We can't make any promises,' said Beatrice Supple and Derek all at once saw who she really was: Margaret Thatcher writ large, Boadicea riding an invisible chariot. 'No modern newspaper can lay down its policy for the years ahead. Circumstances change, a newspaper has to change with it.'

'You mean the paper could become a Fleet Street tabloid, Down Under edition?'

'Not at all.' Beatrice's tone was sharp. She was warming to the task ahead; or was the word 'colding'? 'We'll do our best not to antagonize the paper's current readers, but our policy will be left to our editors.'

'Who will be from Fleet Street?'

'Possibly.'

Derek looked down his side of the table. His mother shook her head sharply, but said nothing. The directors from the insurance companies sat expressionless, unmoving; editorial policy did not concern them, only profit. The two outside directors looked perturbed and one of them shook his head; he was also a director of the *Chronicle*'s newsprint suppliers. Lester Kohn just raised his eyebrows, but the man from the superannuation fund looked apoplectic.

'The British Empire still reigns?' said Derek. 'I thought it was finished – seems I was wrong ... All right, let us get on with the nitty-gritty. You are still offering –'

'Thirteen-fifty a share,' said Charlie Bentsen, who obviously was not going to play chariot-boy to Beatrice Supple. 'Fifty cents more than yesterday's market price. That should please you chaps?' He glanced at the four directors from the insurance companies, who were beginning to unbend, looking as if they had been offered free life policies.

'Not enough,' said Derek. 'I believe you have a new valuation, Lester?'

Lester Kohn took some papers from one of the advisers sitting behind him. 'This is the result of two weeks' solid work, seven days a week. It is probably the first time Huxwood has been examined as

251

thoroughly as this – we've given a new meaning to due diligence.'

'I always thought it was the buyers who did that,' said Jack Junior mildly.

'Perhaps it is a sign of how casually Huxwood has been run,' said Beatrice and looked across the table at the directors of the insurance companies, who nodded. There was no stricter due diligence than in examining an insurance claim.

'Not any more,' said Kohn. 'You'd be surprised how *un*-casual we have been. Fifteen dollars a share, not a cent less.'

'Ridiculous!' said Beatrice Supple.

Then the door behind Derek opened and Ned Custer came in and whispered in his ear. He frowned, looking at his brother-in-law in puzzlement, then he abruptly stood up.

'I'll have to ask for an adjournment, ten minutes or so. You'd better come with me,' he said to his mother. 'Something's happened in the family.'

3

'I'm sorry,' said Malone, 'but we're taking Alexandra in for questioning.'

'Questioning on what?' snapped Derek.

'Suspicion of conspiracy to murder.'

Lady Huxwood, who had been standing beside Derek, suddenly sat down; fortunately there was a chair right behind her, though one might have doubted that she knew it was there. Cordelia, her chair up close to Alexandra's, was awkwardly holding her daughter to her. The others in the room stood or sat in silence, then Camilla buried her face in her hands and began to weep.

'This is fucking ridiculous –'

'Shut up, Ross,' said his father. 'Is it true, Alex?'

'Of course it isn't!' Cordelia sounded on the verge of hysteria.

Linden stood up and a moment later Sheila followed her; they moved across to stand behind Cordelia, their hands on her shoulders. They were a tableau – but of what? Malone wondered. Of comfort, of defiance? He abruptly remarked the tension in the room, the antagonism scorching him and Kate Arletti. The family might have been

252

divided over the sale of Huxwood, but now they were united against the outsiders.

'I think you'd better come with us, Alexandra.' Kate made a move towards the tableau. 'Don't make trouble for yourself.'

'What evidence have you got?' said Nigel, and he sounded as if he were reading lines from a script, one that had just been thrown at him.

'Enough,' said Malone.

'I don't think she should go with you without a lawyer accompanying her.' Enrico Quental this morning wore a tie with tiny flags on it and a double-breasted navy blazer with six or eight buttons; Malone thought he looked like the admiral of a very small fleet, the Portuguese Navy, perhaps. Careful, he told himself: as Clements had said, prejudices got you nowhere. Quental had been one of his principal suspects and his suspicions had proved dead wrong.

'You can arrange for one to meet us at Homicide.'

Then Lady Huxwood spoke for the first time. 'Have you caught the man who actually killed my husband? Our under-gardener?'

'Not yet, Lady Huxwood.'

'So all this is just suspicion, nothing else?' But Derek sounded as if he had no faith in his argument. He kept looking at Alexandra but had made no effort to approach her.

'No,' said Malone. 'We have more than that.'

Cordelia was still holding her daughter, clutching her to her. 'You didn't do it, darling, did you? Please —'

Alexandra gently freed herself from her mother's arm, stood up and faced her grandmother, like a schoolgirl before her head-mistress. 'I'm sorry, Grandma. Really.'

The old woman stared at her, her face suddenly gaunter than it had ever looked, her eyes seemingly blind; it was impossible to tell whether she suffered for her granddaughter or hated her. The aunts and the uncles and the cousins did not move, as if they could not comprehend Alexandra's quiet implied confession of guilt.

Linden helped Cordelia to her feet. 'Sheila and I'll come with you —'

'So shall I,' said Lady Huxwood and got unsteadily to her feet. 'You did a terrible thing, Alexandra, but we'll help you. Go back in there, Derek —' She nodded towards the boardroom door. 'Tell them everything is postponed.'

253

'There's no need to postpone anything,' said Michael. 'Go back in there, Uncle, and tell them the sale is off. I'm voting against it, no matter what the price. That'll settle the issue.'

Then Kate Arletti's mobile rang. She stepped round the group and went into a corner. She spoke quietly, but Malone, watching her, saw her tense. Then she switched off the phone and came back into the middle of the room.

'Dwayne Harod is out at Malmaison, holed up in Little House One. He's taken the gardener, Dan Darling, hostage.'

4

'He's in Little House One,' said Clements, and the State Protection Group sergeant standing beside him looked disbelieving, as if he and his men had been called out to some children's party that had gone wrong.

'What happened?' asked Malone.

'The housekeeper called Waverley. She saw Dwayne first, then the gardener stumbled on the scene and Dwayne grabbed him and took him into the house.'

'Why didn't Dwayne grab the housekeeper as well?'

'Evidently he didn't see her. She'd been out shopping and came back . . . Oh-oh. Here comes the white shirt to take charge.'

Assistant Commissioner Zanuch had got out of a car at the top of the driveway and was coming down towards them; with him was Chief Superintendent Random. The SPG sergeant jumped to attention, but Malone and Clements just acknowledged their superior officers with a nod.

'You've got a siege situation here, Inspector?' said Zanuch.

'Yes, sir. We have twelve SPG men here – this is Sergeant Bass-ford.' The sergeant, a broken-nosed young man with close-cropped fair hair and bulky shoulders bursting out of his tactical vest, snatched his cap from under his arm and put it on, then clicked his heels. 'Superintendent Lozelle is down at the harbour end of the estate with half a dozen of his men.'

'Has he made any threats or demands, the – what's his name, Harod?'

'Not so far. But he will – Dwayne isn't the sort who can keep quiet for long.'

'I understand you've arrested the girl Alexandra for conspiracy?'

'Yes, sir.' How had he got the information so quickly? Kate would have had the girl back at Homicide no more than twenty minutes ago; nothing would have been put into the pipeline.

'Lady Huxwood rang me. You're sure you've got all you need to make the arrest stick? We don't want complications.' He made it sound as if they didn't want World War Three breaking out.

'We've got all we need, sir.'

Zanuch didn't say *good*; nor did Malone expect him to. 'All right, let's see how we are going to handle this situation. We don't want a fire-fight –' He looked at Sergeant Bassford.

'I'm hoping we don't have to fire a shot, sir.'

Zanuch nodded in appreciation, as if he were here to protect the Huxwood real estate. 'Can we get in touch with – Dwayne?'

Clements held up his mobile. 'I was just about to, sir. I have the Little House One number.'

Malone saw the SPG sergeant blink again, and he grinned. 'I'd deploy some of your men across the front lawn, in Little House Two.'

'You're having me on,' said Sergeant Bassford, then saw Zanuch's look of disapproval. 'Sorry, sir.'

As Clements dialled his phone, Greg Random drew Malone aside. They were on the eastern side of the Big House, beside the main rose garden. The last rose of summer was gone; Old Blush China was just a few faded petals on the dry earth. Malone hoped that it was not an omen for Dan Darling, the rose lover.

'You're sure the girl is involved, Scobie?'

'She may change her story when the lawyers get to her, but she as much as confessed to Lady Huxwood what she'd done. She's the one, Greg.'

'Okay, if you're satisfied, so am I. What about this kid Dwayne? Is he likely to go berserk?'

'I dunno. If he's wound up, seeing all the fellers around –' He waved an arm at the SPG men in their black caps and vests, their Remington twelve-gauge shotguns held at the ready.

Random nodded. 'I'll try and get them out of sight until –' He broke off as Clements gestured at Malone.

255

'Dwayne wants to speak to you, Scobie.'

Malone took the mobile from Clements. 'Yes, Dwayne?'

'I want you to come in here, I wanna talk to you.'

'Dwayne, why don't you come out? If you've got a gun, throw it out ahead of you and then come out with your hands up. Is Dan all right?'

'He's okay. I'm not coming out there, not till I've talked to you. What's this shit, all those guys running around with fucking shotguns?'

'You brought it on yourself, Dwayne —'

'Don't start fucking lecturing me!' He sounded very much on edge, his voice rising to a shout; Malone held the phone away from his ear. 'You come in here, I wanna talk to you!'

'Dwayne, I'm not going to lay my life on the line just because you want to talk to me — I have a wife and kids —'

'You'll be okay, I promise. Don't bring a gun with you, that's all — take your coat off so's I can see you're not carrying a gun —'

Malone looked at Zanuch and Random. 'He wants me to go in and talk to him.'

'No,' said Zanuch.

'I think I can trust him on this, sir. He sounds as if he'll break any moment. If I can get him to release the gardener —'

Zanuch looked at Random and the latter, after a moment's hesitation, nodded. 'It's worth the risk, if Scobie's willing to take it. Otherwise, Christ knows what'll happen.'

Malone slipped out of his jacket, undid his holster and handed it and his gun to Clements. 'Keep your men out of sight,' he told Bassford. 'No pot-shots at him, not while I'm in there.'

Clements patted his shoulder. 'Good luck, mate. Just don't be a hero.'

Malone felt anything but a hero. It was not the first time he had been in a situation like this, but you never got used to it; as on the other two occasions he wondered if a sense of duty was sometimes an act of stupidity. As he walked across the lawn towards Little House One, alone in the open but for a seagull searching for pickings in the grass, he thought of Lisa and the children, of what they would think of him if they were here to see him walking into a house where a nervous hitman with a gun waited to talk to him. Out of the corner of his eye he saw a television cameraman clamber over the sea-wall from the narrow beach. He pulled up sharply, waved the man away; it struck him later that the only reason he did it was that he did not want Lisa and the children to see him in this situation on the news tonight. Then he saw two of the SPG men appear behind the cameraman, wave their shotguns at him, say something that was obviously not friendly, and the cameraman ducked back, falling over the wall in his haste. Then Malone walked in the front door of Little House One.

'Dwayne?'

Dwayne and Dan Darling appeared at the head of the stairs that led up from the entrance hall; Dwayne was holding a gun to the head gardener's back. 'Come up here, Mr Malone.'

Malone mounted the stairs, taking his time; now he was in the house, his legs had suddenly become unsteady. 'You all right, Dan?'

'So far. I been trying to talk to Dwayne –'

'Shut up. This way, Inspector. The main bedroom – I can keep an eye on all those bastards with the shotguns. Why the fucking army?'

'What did you expect?'

The bedroom was as expensively furnished as the rooms down below; Derek and Cordelia slept as well as lived amidst luxury. Malone sat down, as much to settle his legs as to try and settle Dwayne. 'Nice place for a siege.'

The young Turk sat down to one side of a window that looked out across the lawns to the rest of the estate. Dan Darling stood a moment, as if not sure what he was supposed to do, then he sat down on a small bench with his back to Cordelia's dressing-table.

'You're in a no-win situation, Dwayne,' said Malone. 'What the hell did you expect to achieve, coming back here?'

Dwayne was fondling the Browning Thirty-two, but abstractedly; maybe he sees it as his comforter, Malone thought. 'I dunno. I was just so pissed off. I was gunna grab Alexandra – you know she's the one got me into this?'

Malone nodded. 'She's being charged right now.'

He was surprised. 'You cottoned on to her? You're better'n I thought. What are you charging her with?'

'Conspiracy to murder.'

'What'll she get? Jail, I mean.'

Malone shrugged. 'That's up to the judge. Life, probably. With

257

good behaviour she could be out in maybe 14 or 15 years.'

'She'll get less than that. She's rich – they always get off better'n us fucking poor. Right, Dan?'

'That's the way it goes, son. Even revolutions can't change it.' The head gardener appeared calm; if it was an act, it was a good one. He leaned back with his elbows on the dressing-table, knocked over a cut-glass perfume-spray. He looked over his shoulder at it, but didn't attempt to pick it up. Then Malone knew the calmness was an act, but still a good one.

'She hasn't paid me, you know. The bitch.'

'What did she offer you, Dwayne?' Malone wanted to keep him talking, that might quieten him.

'Forty grand. All I got was ten, then she reneged, said she'd run outa cash. The rich running outa fucking money – that's a joke. I was gunna grab her and hold her to ransom, you know? Get the family to pay me a hundred grand. Petty cash to them.'

'How did you expect to get away with it?'

A flock of Indian mynahs arrived in a tree outside, chattering in bird-argument. Dan Darling turned his head to look out the window, then grinned the dry grin at Malone. 'The foreigners again.'

'Meaning me?' said Dwayne, but didn't seem put out. 'The wog?'

'I was talking about the birds –' The gardener's reassurance was hurried; he was not so calm after all.

Dwayne nodded, but didn't seem really interested in Dan Darling. 'Mr Malone, what'll I get if I give myself up?'

'I told you, the judge decides that, not the police. The same as Alexandra, I guess.'

'Shit!' He shook his dark head. 'I'll be thirty-six, thirty-seven, if I get time off. All my best years down the gurgler.' The two older men looked at each other, but said nothing. 'What's in it for me if I turn – what do they call it? Queen's evidence? That right? State's evidence? You know what I mean.'

'I can't make any deals, Dwayne. I've got to be honest with you – I don't think they'll listen to you. You didn't come into this with your eyes shut – she didn't seduce you –'

'Seduce?' He smiled, his face relaxing for the first time. 'Christ, she's as cold as a witch's tit. She'd freeze your balls off.' The two

258

older men exchanged glances again. 'Well, like they say, it's all academic now, ain't it?'

'I'm afraid so,' said Malone. 'Give me the gun.'

'I walk outa here, they gunna blast me, the goons with the shotguns?'

'They're not goons, Dwayne, they don't blast people just to hear their guns go off. You'd be surprised how few shots they've had to make in a situation like this. They're here because nobody knew what you were going to do with Dan.'

Dwayne looked at the old man with the maimed hand. 'I wouldn't have hurt you, Dan. You can be a pain in the arse sometimes, but I got respect for you. I never see anyone love flowers, especially roses, like you do. All I ever did with nature was cut cane — it ain't the same.' He reversed his hold on the Browning, held it out butt first to Malone. 'It's all yours, Inspector. Now begins the hard part, right?'

Chapter Thirteen

1

Alexandra Huxwood and Dwayne Harod were charged and held without bail pending an appearance before a magistrate's hearing. Derek tried to have the appearance brought forward, but the system works at its own pace; or appears to. Derek, still suffering from shock, not thinking clearly or fairly, was convinced the delay was due to the new Labor government, milking the Huxwood scandal for all it could get out of it. The delay was not due to the government, but Hans Vanderberg, if not milking the situation, did nothing to temper the rumour and gossip. Some time in the future, when the Huxwood girl was behind bars, he would begin to stroke the *Chronicle*, now safe in Huxwood hands again. As with all politicians, the light on the hill was always the next election; he might need the paper to carry him towards it. As he told Roger Ladbroke, a bird in the bush needs a guiding hand. Ladbroke, like a good minder, agreed with him, though he wasn't sure what the Old Man meant.

Time slipped by, though once or twice the cogs caught and time stood still. On the day that a police officer called on Mrs Zubeyde Harod in the small weatherboard cottage in Ingham to tell her that her son had been charged with murder, a letter arrived from an art union office to tell her a ticket in her name had won a million-dollar home on the Gold Coast. On the other side of the world Oklahoma City exploded on to the map and the world's front pages and Americans suddenly had to recognize that terrorists could be homegrown. Eight thousand Rwandans died, but the story was becoming stale and nothing troubles editors more than a stale story. Serbs and Croatians were still fighting each other and the UN peace-keeping force, caught in the middle, wondered which peace it was that everyone kept talking about. The Russians still fought the Chechens, the Turks the Kurds, the

Islamic fundamentalists fought everyone. The world turned on its normal violent axis and nobody, except the dead, fell off.

'It's confirmed,' said Clements. 'Romy's pregnant, it's due in November.'

'Congratulations,' said Malone. 'That'll make Lisa's and the kids' year. In the meantime . . .'

Since the Huxwood homicide there had been twelve other murders. The rate was increasing, but since the election was now over the politicians were no longer beating the law-and-order drum.

'I've got everyone out,' said Clements, waving at the empty room. 'The file room is chockablock. I wonder what the file room in Detroit or Washington, D.C., looks like?'

Malone heard his phone ring and he went back into his office. It was Derek Huxwood. 'Scobie, this is short notice – would you care to come out and have lunch with us?'

'Last time I was out there for a meal –'

'Relax, Scobie – I'm not going to put any pressure on you. Cordelia and I have accepted what's happened – well, maybe not accepted it. Resigned to it. Losing a child – we're going to lose her, aren't we?'

'I'd say so.'

There was silence a moment, then Derek went on, 'We'd just like to see you, to thank you for the way you handled the whole thing.'

Malone did not want to accept the invitation, but it would be churlish not to. And he felt an immeasurable pity for Derek and his wife. 'Righto. Twelve-thirty okay?'

He hung up and Clements said, 'Huxwood? What does he want?'

'He wants to thank us.'

Clements bit his lip, then nodded. 'I've got a lot to learn about being a father.'

'It'll take most of your life. I'm still learning.'

He drove out to Vaucluse, found the gates open and Derek, in slacks and a sleeveless sweater, looking thinner than Malone remembered him, waiting for him at the bottom of the driveway.

'My mother wants us to have lunch with her. Is that all right with you?'

'Is she going to thank me, too?' Then in his own ears that sounded rude and abrupt. 'Sorry, I didn't mean that the way it sounded.'

'I don't know how she feels. She's changed . . . Come on, let's go in.'

Lunch was to be served not in the big dining-room, where Malone had first met the family, but in the garden room. A glass-topped table was set up by the bank of palms in their big brass-bound wooden tubs. Lady Huxwood and Cordelia were already at the table.

'You're late, Mr Malone.'

'Only five minutes, Lady Huxwood.' She might have changed, but not completely. 'It's the Irish in me. My mother told me that with an Irishman there are four times – Greenwich mean time, which he doesn't recognize, ordinary time, parish time and God's time.' He was talking more than usual, trying to find his niche in the atmosphere. He sat down. 'I apologize.'

Krilich, the butler, brought in the first course, a light soup. As he moved round the table he kept glancing at Malone, as if puzzling out why the police officer, the enemy, had been invited here. Malone gave him a smile, but got none in return.

The conversation at first was seemingly idle; but Malone was aware that it was more than that. The Huxwoods were as wary as he; more so. It struck him that perhaps expressing their thanks for whatever he was supposed to have done was going to be more difficult than they had anticipated. He knew that gratitude did not always come easily to some people and the Huxwoods, God knew, were in a more difficult situation than most.

It was Lady Huxwood who got to the point. 'Perhaps we should have invited Mr Zanuch here to accept our thanks, but Derek was quite right – Bill Zanuch had nothing to do with the way things worked out.'

'Careful, Mum. Bill is Scobie's boss.'

'I don't think Mr Malone is the sort who spends his time defending his boss. Am I right?'

'No comment,' said Malone with a grin.

Cordelia, in black sweater and black slacks (already in mourning?), reached across and put a hand on Malone's arm. The gesture surprised him, made him feel uncomfortable. 'Scobie, when you came into the room that day at the *Chronicle* and told us . . .' He felt the hand tighten on her arm. 'I wanted to jump at you, hit you . . .'

'I know. I've had it happen.'

'Well, the thing is,' said Derek, 'you never at any time tried to put the boot into us. We weren't always co-operative – I think we knew in our hearts that someone in the family was – was involved. We just never dreamed . . .'

'That it was Alexandra?' Malone tried to ease their re-awakened pain. 'Neither did we.'

'Who did you think it was?' said Lady Huxwood.

'No comment.'

For the first time Phillipa smiled. 'As I said before, Mr Malone, you would make a good opponent.'

Then the main course was served and as he cut into his salmon Malone said, 'Have you got a new under-gardener?'

'A Vietnamese,' said Derek. 'From up on the Chinese border. I think he grew poppies originally — you can guess why — but he's learning about roses. Mum and Dan are teaching him.'

'I started to teach him who the Empress Josephine was,' said Phillipa; she appeared to be relaxing by the moment. 'Then he told me the Vietnamese did not like the French. A very independent young man.'

'So was Dwayne,' said Derek, but so softly that only Malone heard him.

When lunch was finished Malone rose. 'I have to be getting back to the office —'

'More murders?' said Cordelia, then looked as if she had uttered a dirty word.

'Too many . . . I'd like to thank you. Yes, for lunch, but also for keeping the *Chronicle*, not selling it.'

'Something had to be saved,' said Lady Huxwood and the gauntness abruptly settled on her face again.

Derek escorted Malone out to his car. 'Thanks for that remark about the paper. It means a great deal to us.'

'How are Cordelia and your mother taking what your daughter did?'

'Badly. We just can't understand why — none of us. Cordelia cries herself to sleep every night. I think my mother does, too — but maybe that's because she misses Dad so much. She'd never let us know.'

'What about the others?'

Derek leaned on the car, looked down at the ground. He had aged in the past couple of months; perhaps it was the light, but the iron-grey hair seemed to have streaks of white in it. The quagmire of the family had taken its toll.

'Nigel and Brenda have gone back to England — Nigel always ran away. Sheila and Ned?' He shrugged. 'Sheila's sympathetic, but Ned is hitting the grog as much as before. Maybe more.'

'Linden and Quental?'

Derek looked up. 'Was Enrico ever on your list of suspects?'

'Yes. He had a lot to gain if some of the money came his way.'

'That's what they all thought. Even –' But he couldn't bring himself to condemn his daughter any further. 'Linden and Enrico have split up. She's been a milch cow all her life for hangers-on and bludgers. I think she's at last waking up to herself. Enrico's gone back to Portugal or Spain or maybe Majorca – somewhere where they can't chase him for bad debts. He can swap stories with Christopher Skase. Linden's still up on the property, but she'll sell it – raising bulls is not her thing. Not four-legged ones.' He smiled. 'I love my sister, but she has been a pain in the arse at times.'

'What about the kids?'

'All of them are in shock. We think modern-day kids are shockproof, but they're not. The one who's taking it best is Michael. Some day he'll take my place, he'll keep the – dynasty? – going. He has more balls than Nigel ever had.'

There was nothing more to say; the family had been accounted for. 'Take care, Derek. We should never have walked off the cricket field, right?'

Derek nodded. 'The good old days.'

2

Once outside the gates of La Malmaison, Malone pulled up and dialled his mobile. 'Darl? I've just been to lunch with the Huxwoods.'

'Lucky you.'

'Let's take the kids out to dinner tonight. Book a table for five at the Rockpool.'

'Are you out of your mind? It's sixty or seventy dollars a head –'

'Book it.'

He would tell her later, not here outside the gates of the Huxwood estate, why a happy family was cause for celebration.

Kirribilli
August 1994–May 1995